Best Rail Trails
ILLINOIS

Help Us Keep This Guide Up to Date

Every effort has been made by the author and editors to make this guide as accurate and useful as possible. However, many things can change after a guide is published—trails are rerouted, regulations change, facilities come under new management, etc.

We would love to hear from you concerning your experiences with this guide and how you feel it could be improved and kept up to date. While we may not be able to respond to all comments and suggestions, we'll take them to heart and we'll also make certain to share them with the author. Please send your comments and suggestions to the following address:

Globe Pequot Press
Reader Response/Editorial Department
P.O. Box 480
Guilford, CT 06437

Or you may e-mail us at:

editorial@GlobePequot.com

Thanks for your input, and happy travels.

Best Rail Trails
ILLINOIS

MORE THAN 40 RAIL TRAILS THROUGHOUT THE STATE

TED VILLAIRE

FALCONGUIDES

GUILFORD, CONNECTICUT
HELENA, MONTANA
AN IMPRINT OF GLOBE PEQUOT PRESS

To buy books in quantity for corporate use
or incentives, call **(800) 962-0973**
or e-mail **premiums@GlobePequot.com.**

FALCONGUIDES®

FalconGuides is an imprint of Globe Pequot Press.

Falcon, FalconGuides, and Outfit Your Mind are registered trademarks of Morris Book Publishing, LLC.

Project editor: David Legere
Layout artist: Maggie Peterson
Maps by Trailhead Graphics, Inc. © Morris Publishing, LLC

Interior photos by Ted Villaire unless otherwise noted.

Library of Congress Cataloging-in-Publication Data
Villaire, ted, 1969–
  Best rail trails illinois : more than 40 rail trails throughout the state / Ted Villaire.
    p. cm.
  ISBN 978-0-7627-4691-0
  1. Rail-trails—Illinois—Guidebooks 2. Illinois—Guidebooks. I. Title.
  GV191.42.I3V54 2010
796.509773—dc22   2010015096

Printed in the United States of America

10 9 8 7 6 5 4 3 2 1

CONTENTS

CENTRAL ILLINOIS

SOUTHERN ILLINOIS

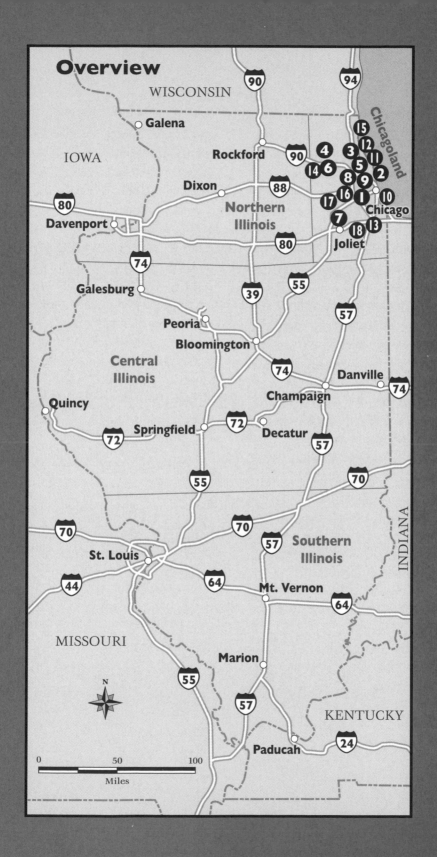

ACKNOWLEDGMENTS

Illinoisans are fortunate to have many people in state and local governments who see the value in creating recreation trails within easy reach. My gratitude goes to the local and state agencies that maintain these trails, often on a shoestring budget. We're fortunate also to have organizations such as the League of Illinois Bicyclists, the Illinois Trails Conservancy, and a host of local advocacy organizations that work to create, protect, and maintain rail trails throughout the state. Thanks to all the friends, acquaintances, and strangers who shared with me a wealth of information about rail trails within the state. Pursuing a long project such as this guide would have been so much more difficult without the unflagging encouragement from a spectacular group of family members and friends. I'm particularly grateful to friends who accompanied me while exploring these trails, including Tim Merello, whose crackerjack plant identification skills helped me appreciate and share with readers more of the natural beauty along the way. Special thanks goes to my sister, Ann, one of my favorite companions for exploring trails.

FOREWORD

Living in the small village of Capron, Illinois, I have the great fortune of having an excellent rail trail practically at my front door. When I am stressed by the demands of life, I often get on my bicycle and ride the Long Prairie Trail. Along this trail, I see colorful flowers, singing birds, and wild animals. It's a place where I can relax, get some exercise, and escape the clamor of telephones, televisions, and auto traffic. Creating and preserving places like this for people throughout the state is my goal as president and director of the Illinois Trails Conservancy.

While I use the Long Prairie Trail mainly to relax and escape, other people seek out rail trails for a host of reasons. Families, for example, often head out to multiuse trails because they provide a safe place for kids to get fresh air and exercise. Runners and cyclists love the uninterrupted flow of the trail. Anyone who feels recharged by exploring the natural world will revel in the landscape, plants and trees, and wildlife along a rail trail. People trying to lose a few pounds by introducing a regular walking regimen can use rail trails to meet their goals.

Whether you're looking for peace and solitude, adventure and exploration, or a good workout, this guidebook will point you to the best trails in the state. Ted Villaire spent many months exploring the full bounty of Illinois rail trails in order to create this essential resource. I imagine you can get a pretty good overall impression of the state by visiting all the trails in this book.

As you use this book to explore Illinois rail trails, consider this advice: Don't take these trails for granted. If you want to ensure the continued existence and upkeep of your local rail trails, please help out. The success of a rail trail depends upon citizen participation. Here are just a few ways you can lend a hand to guarantee the future of these trails.

- Write a letter or send an e-mail to your city, county, or state elected official in favor of pro rail trail legislation.

- Contact your local Web and print publications, offering praise for a local trail. Describe why you, your family, and your friends value this treasure.

- Attend a local hearing to express support for a local rail trail project.

- Volunteer to plant flowers, trees, and grasses along a local rail trail or help with a cleanup project on a trail.

- Help out with fund-raising campaigns, special events, newsletter publishing, and other activities to promote a trail.

- Most importantly, get out and use the trails: Take your kids and your friends. Lead a group of scouts, or organize an outing for seniors.

While exploring Illinois's rail trails, keep in mind that these trails offer much more than a destination; they offer the opportunity to enjoy the sights, smells, sounds, and experiences along the way. Go slow and I guarantee you'll enjoy the experience.

Bev Moore
President and Acting Director, Illinois Trails Conservancy

INTRODUCTION

It all started in the mind of a Chicago-area woman. In 1963 the late natural-ist May Theilgaard Watts kicked off the national rail trails movement when she wrote a letter to the *Chicago Tribune* proposing that the abandoned rail line near her suburban Chicago home be converted to a long trail. "We are human beings," she wrote in the letter. "We are able to walk upright on two feet. We need a footpath. Right now there is a chance for Chicago and its suburbs to have a footpath, a long one."

Her idea caught on, and eventually that rail line became the Illinois Prairie Path, the centerpiece of Chicagoland rail trails. Soon rail trail proj-ects were under way all over the country. Illinoisans can take pride in their state's role in helping to inspire the creation of more than 1,500 trails throughout the nation.

Thanks to Watts and many others who have volunteered their time and effort over the years, Illinois claims more than 600 miles of existing rail trails and nearly 150 miles of trails currently in development. These trails allow you to explore some of the state's most beautiful settings. We have 80 miles of rail trails along the shore of the Mississippi River that run through charming river towns and nationally protected wetlands. In southern Illinois the Tunnel Hill Trail extends for nearly 50 miles through the bottomland woods of the Cache River Wetlands and the rugged ter-rain at Shawnee National Forest. Ambitious trail users can cross nearly the entire northern part of the state by hopping from the Old Plank Road Trail to the I&M Canal Trail to the Hennepin Canal Trail.

Illinois rail trails are not confined to the state's rural terrain and scenic natural areas. Trails in the central Illinois cities of Bloomington, Decatur, Springfield, and East Peoria introduce you to local neighborhoods, city parks, industrial areas, and downtown districts. You'll get introduced to plenty of local history, too. In many cases, you'll have the opportunity to combine your trip with visits to museums, restaurants, and shops. This is especially true in the metropolitan areas of St. Louis and Chicago, the two largest networks of rail trails in the state.

The What and Why of Rail Trails

Rail trails are the perfect answer to the question of what to do with innumerable miles of abandoned railway throughout the nation. Rail trails provide answers to other more pressing questions, too, such as: How do you encourage more people to exercise and spend time outdoors? How do you foster alternative modes of transportation? How do you preserve the rich history that developed alongside thousands of miles of national railroads? How do you connect communities and make them more walkable?

Rail trails offer exercise and relaxation, offer scenery and tranquility, and more and more serve as a place for social engagement. South of Chicago, the pleasant little town of Frankfort holds a farmers' market each weekend during the summer along the Old Plank Road Trail. Trail users stop in at the market for their lunch and then sit down to enjoy live music on the adjoining village green. Spontaneous conversations are unavoidable. Healthful locally produced food is de rigueur. Some trail users have taken full advantage of this alliance and make weekly trips along the trail specifically for visiting the farmers' market.

Whether you're cycling, walking, running, in-line skating, cross-country skiing, riding a horse, or using a wheelchair, rail trails offer a peaceful setting to pursue these activities. Sure, users must negotiate cross streets with traffic, but generally multiuse paths provide welcome relief from tailpipe emissions, noise, and the hazards of traffic. This is why parents find rail trails an especially attractive option for getting outdoors with kids.

In urban areas, multiuse trails have started taking the next evolutionary step: They have become routes for transportation as well as recreation. With the awareness of climate change growing and the cost of operating an automobile climbing, the appeal of rail trails as a transportation option only grows stonger. The transportation role played by rail trails will only increase in years to come.

Illinois Railroads

It's fitting that the state considered the nation's railroad hub should contain an impressive collection of rail trails. Following Texas, Illinois hosts the most miles of railway in the country. Efficient movement of coal, grain, lumber, and passengers enabled Illinois to become the agricultural, manufacturing, and cultural center of the Midwest. In 1939 thirty-three interstate railroads ran into multiple Chicago train stations. The stations themselves often were magnificent structures that celebrated the ascendancy of the railroad.

The Illinois railroad boom began in 1850 when the Illinois Central Railroad received 2.5 million acres as a federal land grant to build what would be the longest railroad in the world at that time. Between 1851 and 1856, as many as 10,000 workers at a time were engaged in building the railroad. Initially the 700-mile Illinois Central Railroad ran down the length of the state, but eventually it expanded, laying down thousands of miles of track in other states.

The Illinois Central Railroad had a profound effect on the direction and pace of development of central Illinois. In the 1850s, when the middle of the state possessed a meager population, the railroad laid out towns every 10 miles along the train route. Within these towns, main streets often led to the train depots. Typically the north–south streets were numbered and east–west streets were named after trees. And of course the railroad company named the town—typically for company bigwigs. By 1884 the Illinois Central Railroad had named thirty-two Illinois towns.

In coming years, dozens of railroad lines sprang up in every corner of the state. Some were just a few miles long; some branched out over North America. Railroads were the primary means of long-distance transport for almost a century. Then in the mid-twentieth century, when the automobile became affordable for the average family and trucks started transporting more goods, the railroads lost ground and many lines were abandoned.

USING THIS GUIDE

Trail Selection

My hope was to include the best rail trails in the state and offer generous variety in terms of length, location, and scenery. By and large I think I succeeded with this project. Unfortunately, for the sake of space some trails didn't make the cut. Usually a trail was left out because it was less than 4 to 5 miles, but in some cases there was an abundance of trails in the area and some picking and choosing had to occur.

It's true: Not all the trails described in this guide follow the routes of former rail lines. While the vast majority of the trails presented here are genuine rail trails, some of the trails also follow the routes of canals, levees, and highways. In all these cases the trail adheres to the spirit of a rail trail by serving as a linear multiuse pathway.

Each trail covered in this guide is open year-round. When enough snow hits the ground, many people strap on their snowshoes and cross-

A stretch of the Lowell Parkway Trail runs along the wooded banks of the Rock River.

country skies to explore these trails. Trail users should be aware of other types of trail users throughout the year but especially during winter, when some of these trails are open to snowmobiling.

Trail Surface

Illinois rail trails generally possess two types of trail surface. Urban trails most often have a smooth, asphalt surface; the suburban and rural trails tend to be surfaced with finely crushed gravel. The surprisingly flat and smooth surface of crushed gravel is great for bicyclists, walkers, runners, horseback riders, and wheelchair users. It's inadequate, however, for in-line skaters and skateboarders. On those rare occasions when the trail surface gets rough, such issues will be noted in the trail specifications so that you can plan accordingly. Even though road bikes with skinny tires work fine on a crushed gravel surface, you'll likely have a better experience using beefier tires that absorb bumps and grip the surface better.

Mileage and Maps

While exploring each of the trails described in this guide, I used a Global Positioning System (GPS) device to continuously track the route via satellite. After completing each trail, I loaded the GPS routes to a mapping software program and then marked mileage with the software. Maps for this guide are based on the maps I created with the mapping software. I have found this procedure to be fairly accurate in determining the route and the mileage for trails. Unfortunately, it doesn't mean our numbers will match up precisely. If you're a cyclist using a bike odometer, keep in mind that these have to be calibrated carefully; just changing to a larger tire can make a noticeable difference.

While GPS devices are generally more accurate, they too can lead you astray. If you do any backtracking or pursue a side trip and forget to subtract this distance from the total mileage covered, that will throw off the mileage reading.

On-street Sections

A number of rail trails described in this guide include short on-street sections. In almost every case, the on-street sections follow quiet roads and bike-route signs clearly point the way. Given that a bit of redundant information never hurts in route-finding, I've added directions and mileage for the on-street sections below the route descriptions.

UTM Coordinates

Readers who use either a handheld or car-mounted GPS unit can punch in the Universal Transverse Mercator (UTM) coordinates for each trailhead and have the GPS lead the way. The UTM coordinates are to be used with North American Datum of 1927 (NAD 27) datum rather than WGS83 or WGS84. Along with the UTM coordinates, the zone is also given. All coordinates were generated using mapping software rather than "in the field" readings.

The Illinois Prairie Path was one of the first rail trails in the nation.

Rules of the Trail

One of the beauties of rail trails is that they are built to accommodate a variety of users. This great triumph of rail trails highlights a small drawback. With all these different trail users, opportunities abound for everyone to get confused about issues of right-of-way and trail etiquette. Knowing the following rules will help ensure an enjoyable experience for all trail users:

- Cyclists and skaters yield to walkers.

- Cyclists, skaters, and walkers yield to equestrians.

- Keep to the right except when passing. This is especially important on trails that have a steady stream of users.

- Move off the trail when stopped. This is for your own safety as well as that of others.

- Call out when passing. It's better not to surprise your fellow trail users. Also, if they know you're approaching, they won't unexpectedly move in front of you or move into you as you're passing.

- Keep a close eye on young children when cyclists, skaters, and equestrians are near.

- Keep dogs on a short leash, and clean up after them.

- Approach road crossings with care.

- Respect the rights of property owners along the trail.

Legend

Local Roads	———————————
State Roads	——⑦——
US Highway	——(55)——
Interstate	——(80)——
Main Route	– – – – – – – –
Other Trail	- - - - - - - - - -
State Line	—·—·—·—·—·—
Rivers/Creek	———————————
Ocean/Lake/Pond	▭
Park	▭
Camping	⛺
Information	**I**
Parking	**P**
Point of Interest	■
Rentals	**R**
Restrooms	🚻
Start/End	◄ START END ►
Town	○

Key to Activities Icons

🦆	Bird-watching	🚲	Mountain Biking
⛺	Camping		Paddlesports
	Cross-country Skiing		Road Bicycling
🐟	Fishing	🏃	Running
🏛	Historic Sites	🏊	Swimming
🐎	Horseback Riding	🚶	Walking/Day Hiking
	In-line Skating	🦌	Wildlife Viewing

Best Rail Trails
ILLINOIS

CHICAGOLAND

Chicago-area residents are fortunate to live within the most extensive system of rail trails in the state. Spend some time on these rail trails and you'll see places that you never knew existed. You'll be introduced to countless towns and suburbs and dozens of parks containing woods, prairie, rivers, and lakes. Chicagoland rail trails provide a perfect escape from the cheek-to-jowl living that occurs within a metro area of nearly nine million people. Some Chicagoans I know regularly pack up their cycling panniers and let local rail trails lead the way on vacations to places like Milwaukee, Starved Rock State Park, and Lake Geneva, Wisconsin.

The centerpiece of Chicago's rail trail system is the Illinois Prairie Path, one of the first rail trails in the nation. Located in the western suburbs, the Prairie Path consists of a main stem and several branches and spurs that run through countless towns, parks, and residential neighborhoods. Each branch connects with the Fox River Trail, another great local rail trail. The Fox River Trail traces the wooded banks of the Fox River for 30 miles between Aurora and Algonquin and runs through a number of urban riverfront areas with parkland, gardens, walkways, and pleasant shopping areas. Taken together, the Prairie Path and the Fox River Trail are favorite destinations for local rail trailers because they allow a number of various-size trail loops.

The prize for the most historically interesting Chicago-area rail trail goes to the I&M Canal Trail. The 60-mile-long segment of the canal trail that runs from Joliet to LaSalle has locks, aqueducts, and locktenders' houses that allow visitors to learn much about nineteenth-century canal transportation. In addition to the human history, the natural beauty along the canal can be breathtaking. Near Channahon, for example, the trail follows a thin sliver of land bordered by the Des Plaines River on one side and the canal on the other.

While recreation and exercise are the focus of most trail users, more and more people also use the trails for transportation and commuting. For much of the year, weekday mornings bring a steady stream of bike commuters to the Lakefront Path in Chicago. The same scene occurs along local rail trails that run next to any school, whether it's a college or an elementary school. With a growing network of trails and more opportunities for combining modes of transportation on a single trip, rail trails will only become more of a draw for the transportation minded.

The suburban train system often can be used to access trails in the Chicago area. In a number of cases, Metra train stations are located right on or within several blocks of the trail. In recent years Metra has allowed passengers to board the trains with bikes during nonpeak hours. (See www.metrarail.com for more information.)

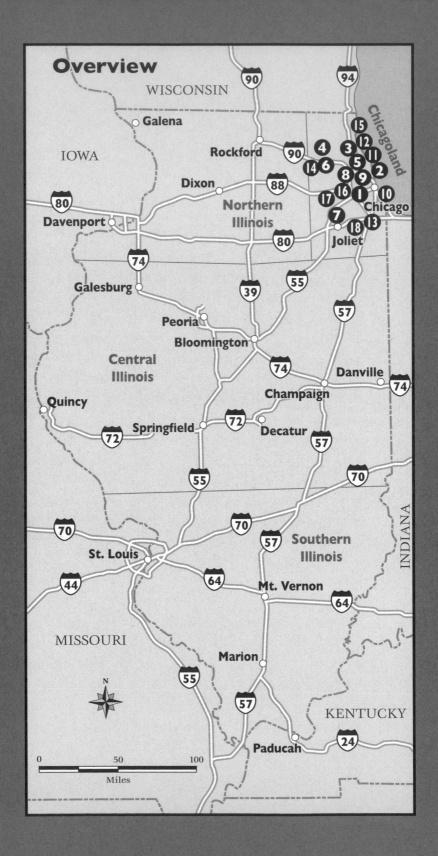

Top Rail Trails

1 CENTENNIAL AND I&M CANAL TRAILS

This route is jammed with scenic vistas and fascinating local history. While tracing the route of the Des Plaines River, the Chicago Sanitary and Ship Canal, and the I&M Canal, you'll pass two museums, several parks, and a couple of historic sites. Much of the northern half of the route offers a surprisingly remote feel as it cuts through many acres of wetlands and bottomland woods.

Activities:

Start: Columbia Woods Forest Preserve, located along the Des Plaines River in Cook County

Length: 20.1 miles one-way

Surface: Paved for the first 9.2 miles in Cook County; crushed gravel surface for the remaining 10.9 miles in Will County

Wheelchair access: The trail is wheelchair accessible, but the 3.0-mile section upon entering Will County has a gravel surface that is rough in places.

Difficulty: The length of this trail gives it an easy-to-medium level of difficulty.

Restrooms: There are public restrooms and water at Columbia Woods Forest Preserve, the Isle a la Cache Museum (0.3 mile off the trail), and the I&M Canal Museum and Visitor Center (Lockport).

Maps: USGS Joliet, Romeoville, and Sag Bridge; *DeLorme: Illinois Atlas and Gazetteer:* Pages 28 and 29; Chicagoland Bicycle Map, Active Transportation Alliance, www.activetrans.org

Hazards: Watch for trucks while traveling along the on-street section of the route.

Access and parking: From I-55 head south on US 12/20. Turn right onto IL 171 (Archer Avenue). Turn right again onto Willow Springs Road. Turn left into Columbia Woods Forest Preserve after crossing the Chicago Ship and Sanitary Canal and the Des Plaines River. In the forest preserve, stay left to reach the trailhead. UTM coordinates: 16T, 426593 E, 4620585 N

To reach the parking area on Kingery Highway (IL 83), head south on Kingery Highway from I-55. After crossing the Des Plaines River, park in the small lot on the right.

To park at the Schneiders Passage parking area on 135th Street, head south on Weber Road from I-55. Turn left onto 135th Street. Look for the parking area on the left after crossing the Des Plaines River.

To park in Lockport, head south on Weber Road from I-55. Turn left onto Renwick Road. In Lockport turn left onto State Street and then left again onto Eighth Street. Park in the lot on the right next to the Gaylord Building.

Transportation: The trail can be accessed by taking Metra trains to Willow Springs, Lemont, Lockport, and Joliet. In Lockport the Heritage Corridor Metra train stops mere yards from the trail.

Rentals: The Wheel Thing, 15 South La Grange Rd., La Grange; (708) 352-3822

Contact: Canal Corridor Association, 201 West 10th St., Lockport 60441; (815) 588-1100; www.canalcor.org

Cook County Forest Preserve District, 536 North Harlem Ave., River Forest 60305; (800) 870-3666; www.fpdcc.com

Will County Forest Preserve District, 17540 West Laraway Rd., Joliet 60433; (815) 727-8700; www.fpdwc.org

NOTE: In future years, the Cook County Forest Preserve District expects to extend the Centennial Trail several miles north to Lyons.

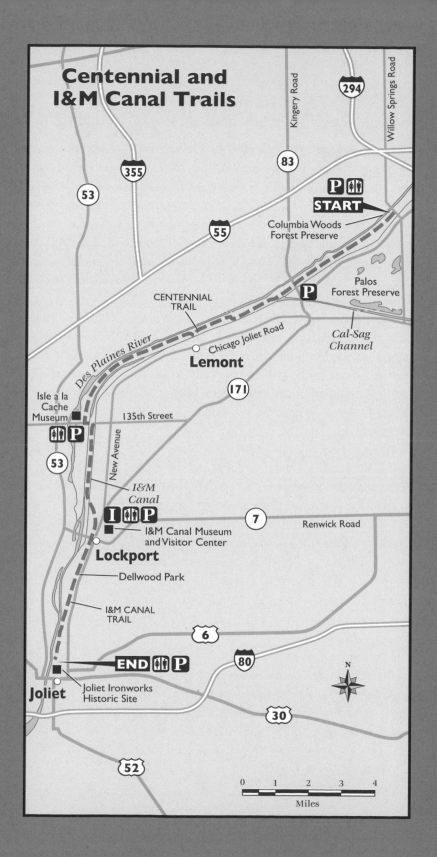

Centennial and I&M Canal Trails

Kingery Road

294

Willow Springs Road

83

355

53

P 🚻
START

Columbia Woods
Forest Preserve

55

P

Palos
Forest Preserve

CENTENNIAL
TRAIL

Des Plaines River

Chicago Joliet Road

Lemont

171

*Cal-Sag
Channel*

Isle a la
Cache
Museum

🚻 P

135th Street

53

New Avenue

*I&M
Canal*

I 🚻 P

7

Renwick Road

Lockport

I&M Canal Museum
and Visitor Center

Dellwood Park

I&M CANAL
TRAIL

6

80

N

END 🚻 P

Joliet

Joliet Ironworks
Historic Site

30

52

0   1   2   3   4
Miles

||||||||||||||||||||||||||||||||||||||||||||||||||||||||||||||||||||||||||||||||||

Heading south from Columbia Woods, the first section of this trail follows a thin sliver of land between the Des Plaines River and the Chicago Sanitary and Ship Canal. As the trail traces the top of a small bluff, the Des Plaines River appears on the right, fringed by moisture-loving trees such as box elder, maple, and cottonwood. Amid the dense bottom-land woods along the trail, you'll see piles of limestone excavated from the digging of the canal. Finished in 1900, the Sanitary and Ship Canal reversed the flow of the Chicago River in order to flush waste away from Chicago toward the Mississippi.

Soon the Des Plaines River meanders away from the trail and is replaced by a remarkably quiet stretch of open grassland. A bit farther south, the first bridge you pass under, IL 83 (Kingery Road), offers an opportunity for an extended side trip. A trail over the bridge leads to a section of the I&M Canal Trail on the opposite side of the Sanitary and Ship Canal. The path is 8.6 miles long and contains two connected loops that run beside the former shipping canal.

After the bridge, a small lighthouse-looking structure marks the con-fluence of the Sanitary and Ship Canal and the Calumet Sag Canal. Barges and tugboats chug along the Cal-Sag Canal on their way to and from Calu-met Harbor, the largest industrial port on Lake Michigan.

The next stretch of trail runs through wetland, bottomland woods, and patches of savanna before meeting up with a heavily industrial area crowded with barge offloading facilities. Near the town of Lemont, the Centennial Trail shares its route with Canal Bank Road. (Despite all the industrial facilities and piers along this route, the road is fairly quiet.) One offloading area contains mountains of salt; another is piled high with land-scaping mulch.

As you pass under I-355 and enter Will County, the pavement ends and the trail surface becomes a slightly rough combination of dirt and gravel. Bicyclists shouldn't have a problem on this section of trail unless riding on the skinniest of tires. The next 3.0 miles follow a raised embank-ment through wet bottomland woods at the edge of the Des Plaines River. The Centennial Trail ends with a crossing of a 300-foot-long historic swing bridge that once spanned the Sanitary and Ship Canal, nearby on 135th Street. The bridge, still with its pilothouse up top for controlling the bridge's movement, was transferred to this spot in 1990.

At the end of the Centennial Trail, you may enjoy a quick trip to the Isle a la Cache Museum, which focuses on local Native American culture and early European explorers and trappers in the area. The museum contains a birch bark canoe, an example of American Indian lodging used in the area, and items that were commonly traded between the Europeans and Indians. A handful of pleasant picnicking spots overlooking islands within the Des Plaines River backwater sit behind the museum. To reach the museum from the parking area at the end of the Centennial Trail, go several hundred yards to the right on 135th Street.

As you make your way alongside the I&M Canal Trail from the 135th Street Bridge for a few miles south to Lockport, you'll pass an enormous coal-fired power plant and then cut through an open area that once was the site of a massive oil refinery. This trail is one of three different seg-

This historic swing bridge was moved to this location at the south end of the Centennial Trail in 1990.

ments of the I&M Canal Trail in the Chicago region. Earlier when you passed IL 83 on the Centennial Trail, you had the option to take a side trip to visit the northernmost section of the I&M Canal Trail. Southwest of Joliet is a segment of the I&M Canal Trail that runs for 61.9 miles to LaSalle. The trail you're on now is a 7.6-mile segment of the I&M Canal Trail that runs between 135th Street and Joliet.

Once you arrive in Lockport, be sure to check out some of the historic attractions that are remnants from the days when the town hosted the headquarters for the I&M Canal. One of these is the Gaylord Building, which served as a warehouse for materials used in building the canal. The building now contains a museum focusing on the history of the canal, a visitor center, and an upscale restaurant.

In the museum you'll learn that the canal was built to provide the final shipping link between the East Coast of the United States and the Gulf of Mexico. From Chicago the canal angled southwest, running halfway across the state, first beside the Des Plaines River and then beside the Illinois River to where the Illinois was deep enough for boat traffic. After it was finished in 1848, the 96-mile-long canal catapulted Chicago into its position as the largest and most efficient grain market in the world.

Another historic structure alongside the path in Lockport is the Norton Building, which was used for grain storage and as a grocery store. Today the Norton Building houses a state-run art gallery that focuses on past and present Illinois artists. South of Lockport you'll find the first of many locks canal boats would encounter after leaving Chicago.

Getting closer to Joliet, a spur trail heads left into Dellwood Park, followed by a section of trail that zigzags back and forth across the canal as it passes a jumble of bridges, railroad tracks, and another lock. This is also where you'll see the castlelike guard tower for the Joliet Prison, built with locally quarried limestone in 1858 and codesigned by the same architect who designed Chicago's famous Water Tower. During its heyday, the prison was the largest and most state-of-the-art facility in the nation. Numerous films, including *The Blues Brothers*, have used the prison as a movie set. Since it's the most famous attraction in Joliet, the city recently built a small park outside the prison and is considering opening up the building for visitors.

The final stretch of the trail takes you through the Joliet Ironworks Historic Site, which provides a snapshot of how a large-scale iron-making operation worked more than one hundred years ago. In the nineteenth century, Joliet was known as the City of Steel and Stone. The stone was quarried from the nearby banks of the Des Plaines River, while the steel was produced here at the ironworks. Through interpretive signs posted among the crumbling ruins, you can trace the practice of iron making from raw materials to the casting bed. Constructed in the 1870s, the Joliet Ironworks employed some 2,000 workers when production reached its peak at the turn of the twentieth century. Much of the steel made in Joliet was used in the production of barbed wire and train rail.

Major Milepoints:

6.2   Keep straight to begin a 1.1-mile-long on-street section of the route that follows Canal Bank Road.

7.3   Pick up the trail again on the right.

Local Information:

- Chicago Southland Convention and Visitors Bureau, 2304 173rd St., Lansing 60438; (708) 895-8200 or (888) 895-8233; www.visitchicago southland.com

- Joliet Visitors Bureau, 30 North Bluff St., Joliet 60435; (815) 723-9045; www.visitjoliet.org

Local Events/Attractions:

- Joliet Area Historical Museum, 204 North Ottawa St., Joliet; (815) 723-5201; www.jolietmuseum.org. The museum offers a thorough introduction to the history of the Joliet area.

- Joliet-area rail trails; www.oprt.org/maps/westcon.html#iandm. Three other long rail trails can be accessed in Joliet. Check the Web site for route advice and on-street connections.

- Lockport Gallery, 201 West 10th St., Lockport; (815) 838-7400; www .museum.state.il.us/ismsites/lockport. The gallery, located in a historic building alongside the trail, features Illinois artists.

- I&M Canal Visitor Center and Museum, 200 West Eighth St., Lockport; (815) 838-9400; www.canalcor.org/gaylord. Located alongside the trail in the historic Gaylord Building, a National Trust Historic Site.

Restaurants

- Merichka's, 604 Theodore St., Crest Hill; (815) 723-9371; www.merichkas.com. Serving up American food since 1933; try the poor boy sandwich.

- Public Landing Restaurant, 200 West Eighth St., Lockport; (815) 838-6500; www.publiclandingrestaurant.com. Fish, seafood, and steak; sandwiches served at lunch. Located next door to the Gaylord Building.

2 CHICAGO LAKEFRONT PATH

The list of things to see and do along Chicago's Lakefront Path will make your head spin: two dozen beaches, three golf courses, two skate parks, Soldier Field Stadium, Buckingham Fountain, a handful of world-class museums, and a free public zoo. And don't forget the stellar views of the downtown skyline against the big mysterious lake.

Activities:

Start: South Shore Cultural Center, at the corner of 71st Street and South Shore Drive

Length: 17.7 miles one-way

Surface: Asphalt

Wheelchair access: The entire trail is wheelchair accessible, but be aware that the north half of this trail gets extremely crowded at peak times during the summer.

Difficulty: Expect a medium level of difficulty due to length, crowds, and exposure to sun and wind.

Restrooms: There are public restrooms at the South Shore Cultural Center, 47th Street, 31st Street Beach, along Chicago Harbor near the Chicago Yacht Club, the North Avenue Beach House, and Foster Avenue Beach House. Water fountains appear frequently along the trail.

Maps: USGS Chicago Loop and Jackson Park; *DeLorme: Illinois Atlas and Gazetteer:* Page 29; Chicago Lakefront Trail Map, Chicago Park District, www.chicagoparkdistrict.com/resources/beaches

Hazards: The north half of the path is swamped with people on summer evenings and weekends. Be patient: Bicycle travel can be very slow at these times. Stay on the right side of the path, and always be alert to those in front of you when passing. If you stop, step off the path. During heavy wind, water from the lake may splash onto the trail in places.

Access and parking: Exit I-94 at 71st Street and head east. Getting close to the lake, enter the South Shore Cultural Center on the left. Park in the lot on the west side of the building. Return to the main entrance and turn right, following the trail (it looks like a wide sidewalk at this point) north on the east side of South Shore Drive. UTM coordinates: 16T, 453025 E, 4624009 N

To park at Promontory Point, exit Lake Shore Drive at 57th Street. Turn right immediately onto Everett Avenue. Turn right onto 56th Street and then left onto South Shore Drive. Park to the right on 55th Street. Take the tunnel under Lake Shore to reach the Lakefront Path.

To park at 31st Street Beach, take Lakeshore Drive to the 31st Street exit. Turn east onto 31st Street and follow the driveway to the parking lot on the right. Alternatively, if you're approaching via I-90/I-94, exit onto 31st Street and head east toward the lake.

To park at the Adler Planetarium, go east on McFetridge Drive from Lake Shore Drive. Park in the free lot at 12th Street Beach.

To park at the North Avenue Beach House, exit Lake Shore Drive at North Avenue and go east.

To park at Montrose Harbor, exit Lake Shore Drive at Montrose Avenue and head east.

To park at the north end of the trail at Foster Avenue Beach, exit Lake Shore Drive at Foster Avenue and head east.

Transportation: The South Shore station on the Metra Electric Line is practically across the street from the South Shore Cultural Center, where the route begins. The Bryn Mawr station on the Red Line "L" train is just a few blocks west of the northern terminus of the Lakefront Path. There are dozens of other options for using public transportation to access the path. Visit www.rtachicago.com for a nifty online public transportation trip planner.

Rentals: Bike Chicago, 1600 North Lake Shore Dr., Chicago; (773) 327-2706; www.bikechicago.com; located in the North Avenue Beach House

Lakeshore Bike, 3650 North Recreation Dr., Chicago; (847) 742-6776; www.lakeshorebike.com; located next to the path at the Waveland Tennis Courts; seasonal

Contact: Chicago Park District, 541 North Fairbanks Court, Chicago 60611; (312) 742-7529; www.chicagoparkdistrict.com/resources/beaches

||||||||||||||||||||||||||||||||||||||||||||||||||||||||||||||||||||||||||||||||||||||

Before starting your journey northward, poke your head inside the grand South Shore Cultural Center, a landmark on Chicago's south side that was saved from demolition by local residents. Built in 1907 as a swanky country club, membership reached its peak in the 1950s. The country club continued to exclude African Americans into the 1970s, even when the surrounding neighborhoods were becoming heavily settled by African Americans. The country club is no more, but the golf course and the beach remain. There's a restaurant inside the center and a small nature sanctuary in back of the building.

Heading north from the center alongside Lake Shore Drive takes you by the 63rd Street Beach House, an attractive structure featuring open-air balconies and grand porticos. As you get farther into Jackson Park, you'll see remnants of one of the most important events in Chicago history: an enormous fair called the World's Columbian Exposition of 1893. A glance down Hayes Drive reveals a shining gold statue called *The Republic,* a replica of a much larger statue built for the exposition. The Museum of Science and Industry, visible along the path at 57th Street, is one of the only buildings remaining from the event.

After passing the museum and the 57th Street Beach house, take the path to the right as it loops around Promontory Point, perhaps the best slice of open parkland in the city. The park occupies a small piece of land jutting into the lake and offers plenty of benches and big rocks from which to enjoy the city skyline, about 9 miles north.

As the journey north continues, a few small hills come and go, as do beaches and the occasional bridge allowing access over Lake Shore Drive. Open parkland prevails, but the main spectacle is the big blue lake. Seasoned lake watchers will testify to this body of water's frequently changing appearance. On some days, factors such as atmosphere, sunlight, and water temperature conspire to give the water a dazzling blue glow.

With all the lovely scenery, what more could anyone want? How about the world's largest convention hall? Even better, how about a dreadfully ugly convention center that looks like a giant black metal box dropped from the sky? The effort to soften the mammoth horizontal presence of McCormick Place by installing a waterfall that magically tumbles from its interior along the edge of the trail only brings to mind the depressing atmosphere of a suburban mall. Thankfully the small bird sanctuary that occupies a fenced-in prairie south of the building helps humanize the place. Ditto the nearby flower garden and several small sculptures that are part of a memorial to Chicago firefighters and paramedics who died in the line of duty.

McCormick Place is situated at the mouth of Burnham Harbor, opposite Northerly Island. Built in 1925, Northerly Island was conceived by Daniel Burnham, an architect and urban planner known for helping plan the Columbian Exposition and for his Plan of Chicago, a comprehensive design for the city. Northerly Island was to be the first of a five-island chain of parks heading south, but the Great Depression came and the other four islands were never built. Some years later the city turned the island into a little peninsula by building a roadway to it. A private airport that oper-

The view of the Chicago skyline from behind the North Avenue Beach House.

ated on Northerly Island for fifty-five years was shut down in 2003. The city plans to build a lakeshore nature park on the property.

As you pass Burnham Harbor, Soldier Field appears on the left. Built in 1922, the stadium received a controversial face-lift in 2003 when a glass-and-steel top section was added to the existing neoclassic structure. Just north of the Chicago Bears' home turf is the Field Museum, one of the world's best natural history museums. This enormous marble structure, also designed by Burnham, houses a vast collection of exhibits on anthropology, zoology, botany, and geology. The main floor lobby contains the skeleton of the largest and most complete T. rex ever found.

Continuing ahead through the museum campus, the trail gains a bit of elevation and then drops down to a tunnel under Solidarity Drive, which leads out to Adler Planetarium and Northerly Island. As the trail circles the rear of the John G. Shedd Aquarium, paneled glass walls offer a glimpse of the oceanarium—the world's largest indoor saltwater pool and home to a family of beluga whales and a handful of performing dolphins.

As you pass another big harbor on the right featuring acres of moored boats, the revered Buckingham Fountain appears in the midsection of Grant Park on the left (during water displays, the center jet shoots water 150 feet straight up). Passing the Chicago Yacht Club, continue alongside the shoreline as it bends right and runs alongside more tied-up boats and a large passenger ship. Stay left along the lower level of Lake Shore Drive as the path crosses the Chicago River and the Ogden Slip.

After crossing the bridge, the opportunity to experience Illinois's biggest tourist attraction beckons (or repels, as the case may be). Navy Pier, 2 blocks to the right, offers oodles of obnoxious tourist-oriented shops and an array of mediocre, overpriced restaurants. Mixed in among the huge crowds and the piles of crud are some appealing elements, however, such as the Chicago Children's Museum, a 3-D IMAX theater, and the Chicago Shakespeare Theatre. There's also an open-air concert venue, a museum of stained-glass windows, and a monster Ferris wheel. A half dozen tour boats in a range of sizes offer water tours from the pier's south side. If you happen to pass Navy Pier during a less busy time, it can be an enjoyable spot for an open-air stroll out into the lake.

North of Navy Pier and east of the path is Milton Lee Olive Park, a pleasant little patch of green space with benches, water fountains, and great views. For the next 2.7 miles the greenery goes on hiatus as the path is squeezed—sometimes uncomfortably—between Lake Shore Drive and the lake. After the shoreline curves left you'll encounter Oak Street Beach, often a hotbed of activity during the summer, whether that's jugglers, BMX trick riders, or in-line skaters whizzing through a slalom course. Watch the action while dining at a small seasonal restaurant.

The crowds and the people-watching opportunities continue to grow at North Avenue Beach and Fullerton Avenue. During summer, North Avenue Beach sprouts an impossible number of beach volleyball courts. The North Avenue Beach House, topped off with a rooftop cafe, was built to look like a big ocean liner parked in the sand. Continuing north, the path skirts the Fullerton Pavilion, a Prairie-style structure built in the early twentieth century as a "fresh air sanitarium" to promote health among the infirm. Now the building is home to a snack counter and a summer theater that's been staging plays for fifty years.

Within Belmont Harbor you'll likely see boat owners tending to their yachts and sailboats (typically with a drink in hand). A small fenced-off bird sanctuary appears on the right, followed by the English Gothic–style park field house with a clock tower overlooking a public golf course. The real avian action happens during spring and fall migrations at Montrose Nature Sanctuary, a lightly wooded area on a small hill at the eastern tip of the jetty that forms Montrose Harbor. (Heading toward the lake on the north side of the harbor, bear left as the harbor curves right. Look for signs across the park road.) Montrose Beach appeals to many because it's a great big swath of sand and water and because, unlike many other Chicago beaches, it's located a comfortable distance away from Lake Shore Drive's six lanes of heavy traffic. From Montrose Harbor it's a short jaunt through grassy parkland to the end of the trail at Hollywood Beach.

Local Information
- Chicago Convention and Tourism Bureau, 2301 South Lake Shore Dr., Chicago 60616; (312) 567-8500; www.choosechicago.com

Local Events/Attractions
- The Field Museum, 1400 South Lake Shore Dr., Chicago; (312) 922-9410; www.fieldmuseum.org

- John G. Shedd Aquarium, 1200 South Lake Shore Dr., Chicago; (312) 939-2438; www.sheddaquarium.org

- Museum of Science and Industry, 5700 South Lake Shore Dr., Chicago; (773) 684-1414; www.msichicago.org. The museum contains an OMNIMAX theater and a working coal mine.

- Navy Pier, 600 East Grand Ave., Chicago; (800) 595-PIER (7437); www.navypier.com. Ride the Ferris wheel, but avoid the restaurants.

Restaurants
- Marina Cafe, 6401 South Coast Guard Dr., Chicago; (773) 947-0400. Midprice Creole- and Caribbean-influenced menu; small bar upstairs. Located right on the Lakeshore Path in Jackson Park. Open in the summer only.

- Oak Street Beachstro, 1001 North Lake Shore Dr., Chicago; (312) 915-4100; www.oakstreetbeachstro.com. Good selection of sandwiches and salads. Seasonally located where Oak Street Beach meets the Lakefront Path.

- Parrot Cage Restaurant, 7059 South Shore Dr., Chicago; (773) 602-5333; http://kennedyking.ccc.edu/washburne/parrot_cage. Operated by the Washburne Culinary Institute in the South Shore Cultural Center.

Accommodations
- The Benedictine Bed and Breakfast, 3111 South Aberdeen St., Chicago; (773) 927-7424; www.chicagomonk.org. The B&B is run by a Catholic monastery in the Bridgeport neighborhood on Chicago's south side.

- J. Ira and Nicki Harris Family Hostel, 24 East Congress Parkway, Chicago; (312) 360-0300; www.hichicago.org. A huge, clean, and affordable hostel located downtown; dorm-style rooms and a limited number of private rooms.

3 DES PLAINES RIVER TRAIL

If you like riparian landscapes, you'll love the Des Plaines River Trail as it winds alongside tree-laden riverbanks, through dense bottom-land woods, alongside ponds, and over footbridges. Quiet oak savannas and many acres of tallgrass prairie thick with goldenrod, asters, and big bluestem prairie grass decorate the trail borders. Spanning nearly the entire length of Lake County, the trail gives visitors an extended encounter with this attractive river and the surrounding—mostly wet—landscape.

Activities:

Start: Half Day Forest Preserve in southeast Lake County near Vernon Hills

Length: 24.8 miles one-way

Surface: Crushed gravel

Wheelchair access: Both the trail and the parking areas are wheelchair accessible.

Difficulty: The length and the gentle roll of the landscape create a medium level of difficulty.

Restrooms: There are public restrooms and water at Half Day, Old School, and Independence Grove Forest Preserves; You can also find restrooms at Growe Park, north of Wadsworth Road; and the north trailhead at Russell Road.

Maps: USGS Libertyville, Wadsworth, and Wheeling. *DeLorme: Illinois Atlas and Gazetteer:* Pages 20 and 21. Map boards are located along the trail; paper maps are sometimes available at the boards or visit www.lcfpd.org/docs/map_22079.pdf.

Hazards: There are many trail junctions along the way, but the plentiful trail signs make navigation easy. Thanks to careful planning, the trail runs under most of the busy roads. Occasionally, the rising river swallows up these underpasses. The county posts signs during flooding, in which case you cross the road at street level instead.

Access and parking: Several miles north of where I-294 and I-94 converge, exit I-94 at Half Day Road and head west. At IL 21 (Milwaukee Avenue) turn right. The entrance is on the right. UTM coordinates: 16T, 422931 E, 4673708 N

To reach the IL 60 parking area, exit I-94 at IL 60 and head west. Park on the left just across the river.

To park at Old School Forest Preserve, exit I-94 at IL 176 and head west. Turn left onto St. Mary's Road. The entrance to the preserve is on the left.

To access the trail from Independence Grove Forest Preserve, exit I-94 at IL 137 and drive west. The preserve is on the right.

To reach the Kilbourn Road parking area, exit I-94 at IL 132 and drive east. Turn left onto Kilbourn Road; the parking area is on the left.

To reach the Wadsworth Road parking area from the south, exit I-94 at IL 132 and drive east. Turn left onto IL 21 (Milwaukee Avenue). Turn left again onto US 41 and then right onto Wadsworth Road. Parking is on the right.

To park at Van Patten Woods Forest Preserve, exit I-94 at IL 173 and drive east; the entrance is on the left.

To park at the Russell Road parking area, exit I-94 at Russell Road and head east. The parking area is on the right.

Transportation: The Milwaukee District/North Metra Line stops in Libertyville less than 1 mile from the Des Plaines River Trail. The route from the train station to the trail runs along quiet streets and has paths and sidewalks along the way. Just north of where the train crosses IL 21, turn right onto Appley Avenue and then left onto Oak Spring Road. The trail crosses the road after you pass Minear Lake on the left.

Rentals: Smart Cycling, 2300 Lehigh Ave., Suite 100, Glenview; (847) 998-0200

Contact: Lake County Forest Preserves, 2000 North Milwaukee Ave., Libertyville 60048; (847) 367-6640; www.lcfpd.org

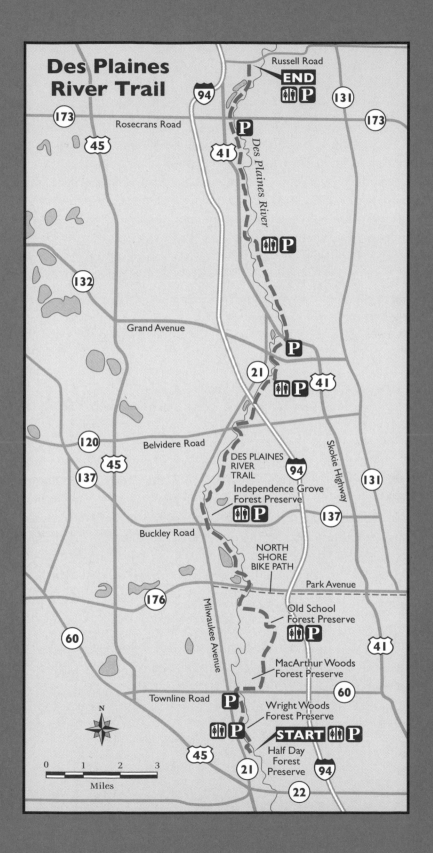

|||||||||||||||||||||||||||||||||||||||||||||||||||||||||||||||||||||||||||||||||||||||||

Given all the development in the area surrounding the Des Plaines River, it may come as a surprise to see how much nature lines the river. Indeed, the many forest preserves that accompany the Des Plaines River in Lake and Cook Counties serve as the longest greenway in the Chicago region. In Lake County no fewer than ten forest preserves lie along a continuous path within the Des Plaines River Valley as it runs from Vernon Hills to the Wisconsin border. (To the south in Cook County, the Des Plaines River Trail runs for about another 20 miles or so—although not continuously.)

In addition to the many benefits these greenways provide for humans, ecologists will attest to the advantages of long, extended natural areas for local plants and animals too. Plants and animals tend to be healthier when they are not cut off from one another and are part of a larger gene pool. Animals also are more likely to thrive if they have room to move around and don't have to cross busy roads regularly.

As you start heading north along the trail from Half Day Forest Preserve, you'll immediately encounter one of many footbridges along the trail. This footbridge sits in an especially attractive setting: Half Day Forest Preserve is on one side and Wright Woods Forest Preserve on the other. Across the bridge, spur trails spin off in various directions through the dense bottomlands of Wright Woods. Before the trail takes you beneath IL 60, you'll cross two more footbridges and pass through bottomland woods alongside the river and stretches of prairie that butt against a sprinkling of light industry on the left.

The next stretch of trail threads its way through two attractive forest preserves. The first preserve, MacArthur Woods, offers a mix of savanna and woodland. Among the hickories, maples, and oaks, look for birds such as brown creepers, red-shouldered hawks, and pileated woodpeckers. The next forest preserve, Old School, takes you through a great expanse of prairie decorated with goldenrod, heath and sky-blue asters, and big bluestem prairie grass.

The prairie at Old School Forest Preserve gradually slopes down in the direction you're traveling—toward the Des Plaines River. Even though development exists on both sides of the pathway, it's off in the distance and you don't feel cramped. Getting closer to the river, the path curls to the right and passes a housing development and thick bottomland woods and then brushes against a pond before heading under IL 176 and the North Shore Bike Path. (The North Shore Bike Path shadows IL 176 for 7.5 miles between Mundelein to the west and Lake Bluff to the east. In Lake Bluff you can connect with the Robert McClory Trail.)

Continuing north, the trail winds through groves of maple, hickory, and oak before cutting through marshland that hosts a scattering of ponds. After you cross Oak Spring Road, a small lake appears over the embankment on the left. Like many of the lakes and ponds along the river, this lake—called Minear Lake—was created by a former gravel mining operation. Up ahead, a sign points up the bluff to Adler Park, which contains picnicking areas and a Frisbee golf course. At Independence Grove Forest Preserve, the trail mounts a hill that allows an expansive view of the 1,110-acre preserve and the 6 miles of trails that wrap around the 115-acre lake (also a former gravel pit).

North of Independence Grove, the trail winds through prairie, savanna, and woodland and then weaves through a power line right-of-way before passing under IL 120. For the next 3.5 miles, between encounters with five busy roads, the trail runs intermittently alongside the river and through bottomland woods. Just before the Washington Street underpass, the roller coasters at Six Flags Great America Amusement Park appear above the trees to the west.

For those intrigued with floodplain forests and wet prairies, the next 4.0 miles after US 41 offer a special treat. First the trail mounts a raised bed and cuts through an area with dozens of little ponds surrounded by dense stands of elm, hickory, and maple trees. Beyond this very wet woodland, the trail skirts the edge of a pleasant expanse of water fringed by willows and cottonwood. The body of water seems to be a lake but is actually one of the pools of the river. After the pool, the trail swings left into open grassy wetlands, where you'll see groves of enormous oaks, a string of ponds to the left, and large spreads of cattails and wet prairie. The trail winds through more stunning wetlands, open prairie, and groves of oak after crossing Wadsworth Road. Traffic sounds come from US 41, which parallels the trail.

Before reaching the end of the trail, you'll encounter Sterling Lake—a former gravel pit that is now an attractive lake fringed by grassland and savanna. North of Sterling Lake the path runs through more prairie and savanna before hitting the Russell Road parking area at end of the trail.

Local Information
• Lake County Convention and Visitors Bureau, 5465 West Grand Ave., Suite 100, Gurnee 60031; (847) 662-2700; www.lakecounty.org

Local Events/Attractions
• Lake County Discovery Museum, 27277 Forest Preserve Dr., Wauconda; (847) 968-3400; www.lcfpd.org/discovery_museum. Nifty exhibits focusing on local history. Museum contains the largest postcard collection in the world.

• Offshore, 701 North Milwaukee Ave., # 348, Vernon Hills; (847) 362-4880; www.offshore-chicago.com. Paddling shop located close to the Des Plaines River; rentals available. Put in and take out at one of the many canoe launches on this stretch of river.

Restaurants
• Flatlanders Restaurant and Brewery, 200 Village Green, Lincolnshire; (847) 821-1234; www.flatlanders.com. Good food; several regular and seasonal beers brewed on-site. Located about 1 mile south of the trailhead.

Accommodations
• Illinois Beach State Park, Zion; (847) 662-4811; http://dnr.state.il.us/lands/landmgt/parks/r2/ilbeach.htm. The park has many campsites a stone's throw from Lake Michigan. Follow Wadsworth Road east to the lake.

4 FOX RIVER TRAIL

Located only 30 miles west of downtown Chicago, the Fox River Trail has plenty of great things going for it. As this pathway hugs the Fox River between Aurora and Algonquin, it passes numerous community parks and forest preserves. In Elgin the Fox River Trolley Museum sits alongside the trail. In Geneva the 300-acre Fabyan Forest Preserve contains a restored Dutch windmill. Also alongside the trail at Fabyan are a pristine Japanese garden and the Villa Museum, designed by Frank Lloyd Wright. Some of the towns the trail passes through—such as Elgin, Geneva, and Batavia—contain attractive urban riverfront areas with flower and sculpture gardens, pedestrian bridges, and scenic walkways.

Activities:

Start: In Algonquin, which is located in southeast McHenry County

Length: 32.8 miles one-way

Surface: Asphalt

Wheelchair access: The trail is wheelchair accessible.

Difficulty: The trail is flat and shaded for most of the route. Difficulty level increases in a few spots where you must climb river bluffs.

Restrooms: There are public restrooms at the Algonquin Road trail access (water), Fox River Shores Forest Preserve (water), East Dundee Depot (water) Trout Park, Tekakwitha Woods Forest Preserve, Island Park in Geneva (water), and Les McCullough Park.

Maps: USGS Aurora North, Crystal Lake, Elgin, and Geneva; *DeLorme: Illinois Atlas and Gazetteer*: Pages 20 and 28; Kane & Northern Kendall Counties Bicycle Map; Kane County Division of Transportation, www.co.kane.il.us/dot/com/publications

Hazards: Watch carefully for bike route signs while following brief on-street sections in St. Charles. Watch for traffic in the handful of places where the trail crosses busy streets. Sections of this trail are closed periodically for construction. Signs usually direct trail users along detours. Check with the Kane County Forest Preserve District for the latest construction news (see contact information below).

Access and parking: From I-90 west of the Fox River, head north on IL 31 toward Algonquin. In Algonquin turn left onto Algonquin Road. Turn right onto Meyer Drive and then left into the Algonquin Road Trail Access parking area. UTM coordinates: 16T, 392651 E, 4669502 N

NOTE: During winter, when this trailhead parking area is closed, use one of the other parking areas listed below. As the trail runs through a string of small towns, there is nearly always free on-street parking next to the trail.

To park at Fox River Shores Forest Preserve, head north on IL 25 from East Dundee. Turn left onto Lake Marian Road and then right on Williams Road.

To park in South Elgin, head south on IL 31 from Elgin. Turn left onto State Street and then right onto Water Street. Park and catch the trail as it runs through the riverside park.

To park at the Fabyan Forest Preserve, head south on IL 25 from Geneva. The parking area is just after the windmill on the right.

To park near the south end of the trail at River Street Park in Aurora, head south on IL 31 from I-88. At Park Avenue turn left, and then turn right onto River Street. The park and the trail are on the left.

Transportation: Metra trains bring you close to the trail in Elgin, Geneva, and Aurora. In Elgin the Milwaukee District West Metra line stops across the river from the trail. In Geneva, the Union Pacific West Metra line stops about 0.5 mile from the trail. From the station, go north on Third Street and then turn right on South Street. The BNSF Railway Metra line stops in Aurora across IL 25 from the trail.

Rentals: The Bicycle Garage, 11 Jackson St., East Dundee; (847) 428-2600; located across the street from the trail

Contact: Kane County Forest Preserve District, 719 South Batavia Ave. G, Geneva 60134; (630) 232-5980; www.kaneforest.com

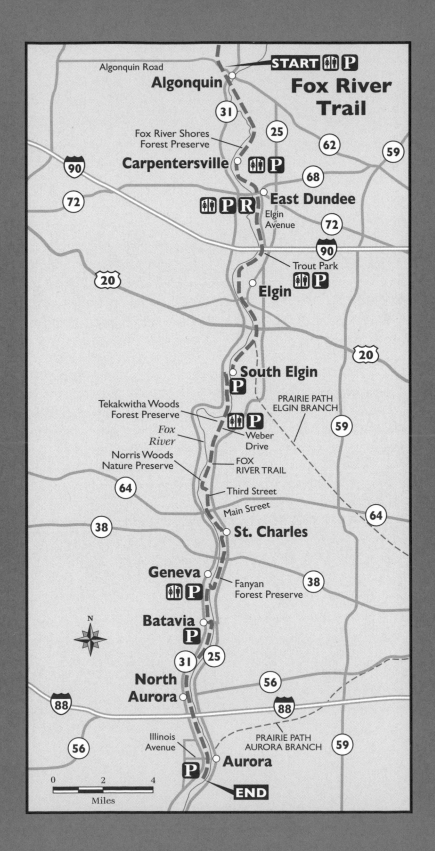

|||||||||||||||||||||||||||||||||||||||||||||||||||||||||||||||||||||||||||||||||||||

The Fox River Path promises an enjoyable excursion for people who like to explore. There are towns of varying size; many scenic natural areas; and a host of parks, museums, and options for dining and shopping. The many towns along the way contain an assortment of restaurants, ice-cream parlors, coffee shops, and watering holes. If you're keen on a longer trip, the trail allows you to hook up with a handful of other Chicagoland recreation trails. Heading north, for example, connects you with the Prairie Trail, which runs all the way to the Wisconsin border. The gamblers among us will be happy to know that the Fox River Path might be the only long multi-use path in the nation with two riverboat casinos located steps from the trail.

On the first mile of the trail, you'll make a dramatic crossing of the Fox River on a pedestrian bridge before entering a residential area, where you'll pass many dozens of wooded backyards. Before reaching Fox River Shores Forest Preserve (where you'll find a collection of perfect picnicking spots on the shore of the river), the trail meets up with a wide spot in the river where kingfishers and great blue herons loiter on the deadfall in the river.

It may be difficult to get through East Dundee without stopping at one of the coffee shops along the trail, a bakery that makes pies and cook-ies, or the Dairy Queen that's several feet from the edge of the trail. You'll also pass a former train depot with picnic tables at which you can sit to admire the handsome historic architecture on the surrounding streets.

On the way into Elgin, the trail runs through a long wooded stretch parallel to Elgin Avenue. Along the way is a remarkable brick house built to resemble a small tower. You'll also encounter Trout Park, which contains a rich display of spring wildflowers, and a pedestrian bridge that crosses the Fox River.

Elgin's river walk is an enjoyable stretch. Amid the plantings of flowers and trees, bridges reach out to islands in the Fox River. If you have kids along, they'll be thrilled with the imaginative sculptures and playground equip-ment at Festival Park, located just upstream from Elgin's riverboat casino.

After passing the Elgin Spur of the Prairie Path, the trail runs through the arched opening of a stone train bridge. From there you'll take a rollercoaster ride up and down a series of river bluffs. After crossing the river in South Elgin, the trail runs through a couple of riverside parks and then sweeps past a collection of old trolley cars on display at the Fox River Trolley Museum.

Just before making the biggest climb on the route at Tekakwitha Woods, the trail mounts a pedestrian bridge that meets a couple of islands as it crosses the Fox River. More wooded islands are visible as you look downstream. After the long steep climb up the river bluff, you'll leave the shore of the river and share the route for 1.0 mile along Weber Drive. (Weber Drive has some traffic, but it moves slowly.) Returning to the shore of the river, the quiet savanna and woodland at Norris Woods Nature Preserve offers refuge at the foot of a small river bluff. As you pass through St. Charles, you'll embark on another 1.0-mile-long stretch of on-street travel.

A host of scenic spots crop up south of Geneva. The trail traverses Island Park before arriving at the Dutch windmill, built in 1914. After the windmill, cross the river to visit the serene Fabyan Japanese Garden—a carefully landscaped environment with ponds, walkways, and a small

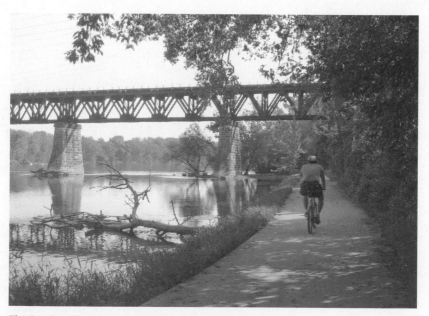

The Fox River Trail hugs the riverbank for long stretches.

arched bridge—located in the Fabyan Forest Preserve. The park also contains the Frank Lloyd Wright–designed Villa Museum, which showcases the history of the park and the family that once owned it.

In Batavia the trail runs by an old train depot that now serves as a local history museum. A collection of outdoor sculpture appears within Batavia's pleasant downtown riverside park. The final section of the path between Batavia and Aurora cuts through a wooded riparian terrain sprinkled with homes set back from the trail and the river. Brilliant views come and go as the path traces the top edge of a small bluff above the river. Aurora welcomes you with open grassy areas and a riverside park. After passing a fish ladder within the river, the trail ends at the back door of the Hollywood Casino.

Major Milepoints

19.8 Turn right on Third Avenue to begin a 1.2-mile-long on-street section of the route in St. Charles.

20.2 Turn right on North Avenue.

20.6 Turn left on Second Avenue.

20.8 Turn right on State Avenue.

20.9 Turn left on First Avenue and cross IL 64.

21.0 Return to the Fox River Trail.

Local Information

• Aurora Area Convention and Visitors Bureau, 43 West Galena Blvd., Aurora 60506; (630) 897-5581; www.enjoyaurora.com

• Elgin Area Convention and Visitors Bureau, 77 Riverside Dr., Elgin 60120; (847) 695-7540; www.northernfoxrivervalley.com

• St. Charles Convention and Visitors Bureau, 311 North Second St., Suite 100, St. Charles 60174; (800) 777-4373; www.visitstcharles.com

Local Events/Attractions

• The Depot Museum, 155 Houston St., Batavia; (630) 406-5274; www .bataviahistoricalsociety.org. The museum, which sits alongside the trail, chronicles the local history of Batavia.

• Fox River Trolley Museum, 361 South LaFox St., South Elgin; (847) 697-4676; www.foxtrolley.org. Old trolleys on display. The museum operates a trolley along a 4.0-mile section of track that parallels the Fox River Trail.

Restaurants

• Batavia Creamery, 4 North Island Ave., Batavia; (630) 482-3729; www.bataviacreamery.com. Great selection of premium ice creams. Located on the trail.

• The Mill Race Inn, 4 East State St., Geneva; (630) 232-2030; www.themillraceinn.com. Outdoor seating at a great riverside setting.

• Sage Bistro, 1 West Illinois St., St. Charles; (630) 444-3555; www.sagebistro.net. Riverside dining.

Accommodations

• The Mansion Bed and Breakfast, 305 Oregon Ave., West Dundee; (847) 426-7777; www.themansionbedandbreakfast.com. Turn-of-the-twentieth-century iron-ore baron's estate; affordable rates.

• Oscar Swan Country Inn Bed and Breakfast, 1800 West State St., Geneva; (630) 232-0173; www.oscarswan.com. English country manor with 8 guest rooms.

5 GREAT WESTERN TRAIL—DUPAGE COUNTY

As the Great Western Trail makes a straight shot west from Villa Park, it cuts through residential areas and brushes against community parks and forest preserves. Expect to see woods, prairie, and wetlands, particularly on the second half of the route where houses and trail users grow sparse. Consider short side trips to Churchill Woods Forest Preserve at the halfway point and Kline Creek Farm near the end of the trail.

Activities:

Start: The Villa Park Museum in Villa Park, located about 20 miles west of downtown Chicago

Length: 11.7 miles one-way, with options for short side trips

Surface: Crushed gravel

Wheelchair access: The trail is wheelchair accessible.

Difficulty: The trail is mostly easy; some sections leave you fully exposed to the elements.

Restrooms: There are public restrooms and water at the Villa Park Museum, Lombard Commons Park, Churchill Woods Forest Preserve (restrooms about 0.5 mile off the GWT), and Kline Creek Farm (about 0.25 mile off the GWT).

Maps: USGS Elmhurst, Lombard, and West Chicago; *DeLorme: Illinois Atlas and Gazetteer:* Page 28; Chicagoland Bicycle Map, Active Transportation Alliance, www.activetrans.org

Hazards: Use caution while crossing a few busy roads along the way.

Access and parking: To reach the Villa Park Museum, head west on St. Charles Road from I-290. In Villa Park turn left onto Villa Avenue. Park in the lot at the museum on the right. The museum is located on the main stem of the Illinois Prairie Path. Catch the Great Western Trail by heading west on the Prairie Path and then following signs north 1 block via Myrtle Avenue. UTM coordinates: 16T, 420174 E, 4637375 N

The best place to start the trail from the west end is the Timber Ridge Forest Preserve parking area on Prince Crossing Road. From I-355 head west on IL 64 and turn left onto Prince Crossing Road. The parking area is on the left; the trail is 20 yards south of the parking area.

Transportation: The Villa Park station on the Union Pacific West Line is just 0.5 mile away from the trailhead. From the station, head south on Ardmore Avenue. Look for the trail crossing after passing south of St. Charles Road.

Rentals: Prairie Path Cycles, 27 W 181 Geneva Rd., Winfield; (630) 690-9749; http://prairiepathcycles.com; located fairly close to the trail

Contacts: DuPage County Division of Transportation, Jack T. Knuepfer Administration Building, 421 North County Farm Rd., Wheaton 60187; (630) 682-7318

Many people use this section of the Great Western Trail (GWT) as an alternative to the Illinois Prairie Path, which runs parallel to the GWT for its full distance. While the two trails hit some similar terrain, they also possess important differences. The GWT tends to go through fewer residential areas and as a result is less used than the Prairie Path. In this case, fewer trail users also mean fewer trailside amenities such as restrooms, drinking fountains, and benches. The GWT intersects the Prairie Path's Main Stem at the beginning of this route and intersects the Prairie Path's Elgin Branch at the end of the route.

There are two sections of the Great Western Trail. This eastern section of the trail, which runs across the northern section of DuPage County, does not directly connect with the western section of the Great Western Trail, which starts in Kane County near St. Charles and runs west to Sycamore.

As you start the trail westward, the first few miles pass a couple of parks that are mixed in with residential backyards. In Lombard a trail leading into Westmore Woods Park branches right. This paved path hugs the shore of a small pond while taking a short trip to a grassy community park. Also in Lombard is a sprawling park called Lombard Commons,

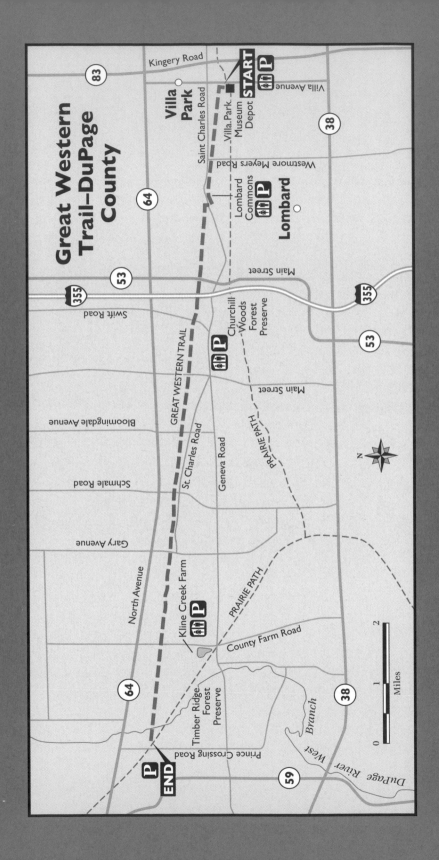

Great Western Trail–DuPage County

which contains more open grassy areas, a public pool, and multiple sports fields. (At the park, watch carefully for signs as they direct you across the railroad tracks and across St. Charles Road and back to the trail's right-of-way.) Heading west from Lombard, more residential backyards appear as the path traces the top of a 10- to 15-foot railroad embankment.

After crossing I-355 at 4.2 miles, take the crushed gravel trail that branches left alongside Swift Road for a side trip to Churchill Woods Forest Preserve. On the left, a hiking trail winds through the second largest prairie in DuPage County. Prairie flowers such as asters, bottle gentian, and prairie sundrops decorate this grassland during spring and fall. Continue ahead on the main trail for a winding wooded route through Churchill Woods. At St. Charles Road go left and head through the underpass. On the other side of St. Charles Road, continue ahead on the trail to a scenic picnic area alongside a series of islands within the East Branch of the DuPage River.

Back on the GWT, the path begins to do that magical thing that rail trails tend to do. The landscape surrounding the trail dips and rises, but thanks to surface grading for the railroad right-of-way, the trail remains extremely level.

Not far ahead, just after the path cuts straight through the middle of a gravel and concrete operation, you'll see a tiny old cemetery on the right. If the chain-link fence didn't prevent access, you would see that the gravestones date back to the 1850s, many with German names on them.

At County Farm Road you'll have the opportunity to visit a local landmark—the Kline Creek Farm. Kline Creek Farm is a county-operated

The Great Western Trail offers scenic vistas within Timber Ridge Forest Preserve in DuPage County.

living-history farm that demonstrates local farm life in the 1890s. Along with chickens, cows, sheep, and horses, there are several barns, an icehouse, a windmill water pump, and a farmhouse containing decor and furnishings of a DuPage County Victorian-era farm.

The final section of the GWT trail takes you on a very gentle downhill through rolling savanna and prairie in the Timber Ridge Forest Preserve. Wetlands with patches of open water and sedge grasses show up near the crossing of the West Branch of the DuPage River. The trail ends as it intersects the Elgin Branch of the Prairie Path.

Local Information

* Chicago Convention and Tourism Bureau, 2301 South Lake Shore Dr., Chicago 60616; (312) 567-8500; www.choosechicago.com

* DuPage Convention and Visitors Bureau, 915 Harger Rd., Suite 240, Oak Brook 60523; (800) 232-0502; www.discoverdupage.com

Local Events/Attractions

* Kline Creek Farm, 1 mile south of North Avenue (IL 64); (630) 876-5900; www.dupageforest.com/page.aspx?id=228. Living-history farm with education programs and a visitor center.

* Villa Park Museum, 220 South Villa Ave., Villa Park; (630) 941-0223; www.vphistoricalsociety.com. The museum contains exhibits relating to the town and the railroad line; serves as the starting point for this route.

Restaurants

* Augustinos Rock and Roll Deli, 246 South Schmale Rd., Carol Stream; (630) 665-5585 www.augustinos.com. Burgers, pasta, pizza, and submarine sandwiches in a 1950s-style diner with outdoor seating. Located right on the path.

* Pad Thai Etc. Restaurant, 563 West Liberty Dr., Wheaton; (630) 653-5337. Basic Thai offerings.

Accommodations

* Lynfred Bed and Breakfast, 15 South Roselle Rd., Roselle; (630) 529-9463; www.lynfredwinery.com. Luxurious and pricey; also a winery.

6 GREAT WESTERN TRAIL— KANE AND DEKALB COUNTIES

Setting out toward Sycamore from St. Charles, the first half of the path presents you with attractive woodland intermingled with acres of bright and shiny housing developments. A rural landscape takes over on the second half of the path as it slices through wide-open agricultural land alongside IL 64.

Activities:

Start: LeRoy Oaks Forest Preserve northwest of St. Charles

Length: 17.1 miles one-way

Surface: Crushed gravel with a short stretch of asphalt

Wheelchair access: The trail is wheelchair accessible.

Difficulty: The length of the trail and its lack of amenities may offer a challenge to some trail users.

Restrooms: There are public restrooms at the LeRoy Oaks' Great Western Trail parking area (water), Campton Township Community Center (portable toilets), and Sycamore Community Park (just south of the Airport Road trailhead; water).

Maps: USGS Elburn, Geneva, Maple Park, and Sycamore; *DeLorme: Illinois Atlas and Gazetteer:* Pages 27 and 28; Kane & Northern Kendall Counties Bicycle Map, Kane County Division of Transportation, www.co.kane.il.us/dot/com/publications

Hazards: The trail crosses only a few busy streets; use caution while crossing these.

Access and parking: From I-355 go west toward St. Charles on IL 64. After passing through St. Charles, turn right onto Randall Road and then left onto Dean Street. The Great Western Trail parking area is on the left, across the road from the main entrance to the LeRoy Oaks Forest Preserve. UTM coordinates: 16T, 388277 E, 4641642 N

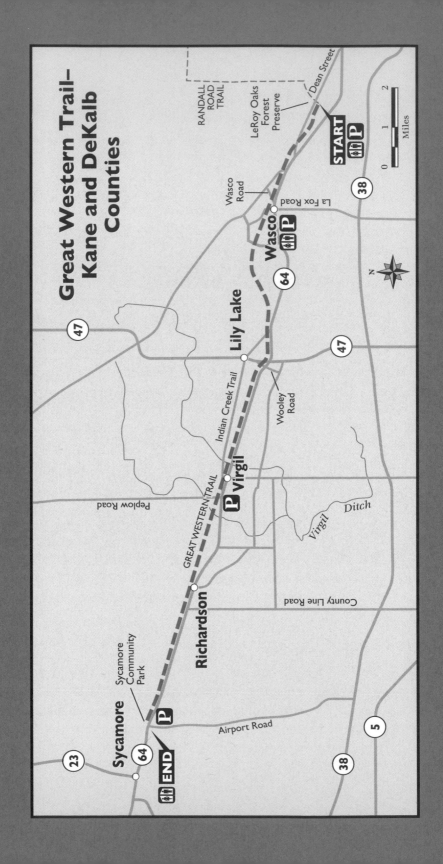

Most of the road crossings west of IL 47 have room for at least one car to park. Additional parking is available at the following areas:

To park at the Campton Township Community Center in Wasco, head west from St. Charles on IL 64. In Wasco turn right onto LaFox Road. Park in the lot on the left.

To park at the west end of the trail in Sycamore, take I-88 to DeKalb and exit north onto Peace Road. Follow Peace Road all the way to IL 64 and turn right. After passing through Sycamore, turn left onto Old State Road. The parking area is immediately on the right.

Transportation: The Union Pacific West Metra line stops in Geneva about 5 miles southeast of the trailhead.

Rentals: The Bike Rack, 2930 Campton Hills Dr., St. Charles; (630) 584-6588; located close to the trailhead

Contacts: Dekalb County Forest Preserve, 110 East Sycamore St., Sycamore 60178; (815) 895-7191; www.dekalbcounty.org/Forest/forest_preserve.html

Kane County Forest Preserve, Building G, 719 Batavia Ave., Geneva 60134; (630) 232-5980

First established in 1885 as a regional railroad between St. Paul, Minnesota, and the Iowa-Minnesota state line, the Chicago Great Western Railroad eventually linked Chicago, Minneapolis, Omaha, and Kansas City. The route—nicknamed the Corn Belt Route because it toured the most productive agricultural land within the Midwest—was mostly abandoned in 1968 when the railroad was merged with the Chicago and North Western Railway. Fortunately, long sections of the railroad in Illinois, Iowa, and Minnesota have been transformed into rail trails, including two sections in northern Illinois. In addition to the section described here, an 11.5-mile section of the railroad between Villa Park and West Chicago has been developed as a rail trail.

Starting in LeRoy Oaks Forest Preserve, the trail launches you into a large prairie fringed by woods and wetlands. After a sharp turn to the right, you'll arrive on the railroad right-of-way and then pass above Peck Road on an arched metal bridge. Initially, new housing developments peek through the woods now and then. As the developments multiply, you'll have little doubt that local homebuilders have done a brisk business in the past decade. Shortly after crossing another arched bridge over Hidden Oaks Road, the trail pulls alongside IL 64. As the trail follows IL 64, the woodland along the trail grows thin, reducing the shade but increasing the views. Briefly the trail plunges through one of those human-made ravines designed to make the railroad run level.

With all the development in the area, it's no surprise that traffic is more than a trickle on many local streets. Fortunately trail users hop over the busier roads on the handsome metal bridges, many with a graceful arch.

After passing through Wasco, the trail, which becomes asphalt for a stretch, temporarily breaks away from IL 64. Woodlands intermittently appear alongside the trail, as do marsh grasses and small ponds. Ferson Creek winds between the trail and the foot of the small bluffs rising on the right. Before the trail crosses IL 47 on an old train bridge, another small creek connects Ferson Creek with the wetlands on the left.

After crossing IL 47, the remaining 9.5 miles of the trail closely parallels IL 64. This is where housing developments subside and agricultural land begins to dominate the scenery. Vegetation tends to be sparse as the path runs about 30 feet north of the highway; occasional stands of trees interrupt the shrubs and prairie grasses. The lack of dense greenery allows long views from atop the 12-foot-high railroad embankment.

Before and after you bisect the hamlet of Virgil, the trail crosses arms of Virgil Ditch. In the little gathering of houses called Richardson, Friday and Saturday nights bring the roar of car engines at the Sycamore Speedway, located a few hundred feet north of the trail. The shaded picnic table at the end of the trail offers a place to take a breather before returning to the trail's starting point.

Those with energy to burn may consider a couple of tempting side trips. At the end of the trail, go 0.25 mile south on Airport Road to the entrance of Sycamore Community Park on the right. At the end of the 1.0-mile-long trail through the park, cyclists have the opportunity to follow an on-street bike route through Sycamore and into DeKalb.

Another side trip can be explored at the beginning of the Great Western Trail in St. Charles. Follow the trail north through LeRoy Oaks Forest Preserve and then continue north along Randall Road for a 7.0-mile connection to the Fox River Path outside Elgin.

Local Information

- St. Charles Convention and Visitors Bureau, 311 North Second St., Suite 100, St. Charles 60174; (800) 777-4373; www.visitstcharles.com

- Sycamore Chamber of Commerce, 407 West State St., Suite 10, Sycamore 60178; (815) 895-3456; www.sycamorechamber.com

Local Events/Attractions

- Midwest Museum of Natural History,425 West State St. (IL 64), Sycamore; (815) 895-9777; www.mmnh.org. Many animal specimens on display in exhibits focusing on different geographical areas.

- Sycamore Speedway, 50W086 Highway 64, Maple Park; (815) 895-5454; www.sycamorespeedway.com. Stock car and drag racing on Friday and Saturday nights since 1960.

The western trailhead for the Great Western Trail in DeKalb County.

Restaurants

- Cup of Joy Cafe, 40W450 Highway 64, St. Charles; (630) 377-9569. Located 1 block off the trail in Wasco.

- Niko's Lodge Bar and Grill, 41W379 Highway 64, Wasco; (630) 443-8000; http://nikoslodge.com. Chicken, salads, and sandwiches in lodge setting; a stone's throw from the trail.

- Sage Bistro, 1 West Illinois St., St. Charles; (630) 444-3555; www.sagebistro.net. Riverside dining.

Accommodations

- Oscar Swan Country Inn Bed and Breakfast, 1800 West State St., Geneva; (630) 232-0173; www.oscarswan.com. English country manor with 8 guest rooms.

7 I&M CANAL TRAIL

In 1848 the Illinois and Michigan Canal provided the final shipping link between the East Coast of the United States and the Gulf of Mexico. From Chicago the canal angled southwest, running beside the Des Plaines and Illinois Rivers halfway across the state. Thanks to the 96-mile-long canal, Chicago quickly became the largest and most efficient grain market in the world. The canal towpath, originally used by mules for pulling boats through the canal, has been transformed into a 61.9-mile crushed gravel path running from the outskirts of Joliet to the town of La Salle. From end to end, the route wanders through a variety of landscapes: dense woods, marshes, prairies, riverbanks, agricultural land, and small towns.

Activities:

Start: Southwest of Joliet at the Brandon Road trail parking area

Length: 61.9 miles one-way

Surface: Crushed gravel

Wheelchair access: The trail is wheelchair accessible.

Difficulty: The length of this trail may present a challenge even for well-prepared athletes. While amenities exist along the way, some sections are very remote.

Restrooms: There are public restrooms at Rock Run Forest Preserve (water), Channahon State Park (water), McKinley Woods Forest Preserve (water), the Aux Sable Aqueduct, Gebhard Woods State Park (water), the gas station/convenience store next to the trailhead in Seneca, beside the trail in Marseilles (portable toilet), the riverside park in Ottawa, Utica (take pedestrian bridge on right after crossing IL 178; water), and the La Salle parking area (water).

Maps: USGS Channahon, Elwood, La Salle, Marseilles, Minooka, Morris, Ottawa, Seneca, Starved Rock; *DeLorme: Illinois Atlas and Gazetteer:* Pages

34–36; Illinois Bicycle Map, Region 3, Illinois Department of Transportation, www.dot.state.il.us/bikemap/state.html

Hazards: The trail crosses a handful of busy roads. Use caution while crossing these. Small sections of the trail are occasionally closed due to erosion.

Access and parking: From I-55 head east on I-88. Go south on Raynor Road (exit 131). Continue ahead as Raynor Road swings to the right and turns into Meadow Avenue. Turn left onto Brandon Road. The parking area is on the right. UTM coordinates: 16T, 407662 E, 4595096 N

To park at Rock Run Forest Preserve, head south on Empress Road from I-80. The forest preserve is on the right.

To park at Channahon State Park, exit west on US 6 from I-55. In Channahon turn left onto Canal Street. The entrance to the park is on the right.

To reach the Aux Sable Aqueduct parking area, take I-55 south to exit 248 and head southwest on US 6. Turn left onto Tabler Road and then right onto Cemetery Road.

To park at Gebhard Woods State Park, head south from I-80 into Morris on IL 47. Turn right onto Jefferson Street, which soon becomes Freemont Street. Turn left onto Ottawa Street; the entrance to the park is on the left.

To park in Seneca, head south on US 6 from I-80. Turn left onto IL 170. Look for the trailhead on the right.

To park in Marseilles, head south from I-80 on 24th Road. Look for on-street parking as you cross over the trail while following Main Street.

To access the trail in Ottawa, head south on Il 23/71 from I-80. Turn left onto Superior Street. Before reaching the Fox River, park in the lot on the left.

To access the trail from the Buffalo Rock parking area, head south from I-80 on IL 23. Turn right onto US 6 and then left onto Boyce Memorial Drive. Veer left onto Ottawa Avenue, which soon becomes Dee Bennett Road.

To park in Utica, head south on IL 178 from I-80. In Utica keep straight ahead on Division Street as IL 178 turns left. Park in the lot straight ahead, and catch the trail on the other side of the pedestrian bridge.

To park at the west end of the trail in La Salle, exit south onto St. Vincents Avenue from I-80. Keep straight ahead as St. Vincents Avenue becomes Joliet Street. Look for the entrance to the parking area on the right.

Transportation: The Heritage Corridor and the Rock Island District Metra train lines both end in Joliet. The trailhead is several miles from the train station.

Rentals: Mix's Trading Post, 602 Clark St., Utica; (815) 667-4120

Contact: Canal Corridor Association, 201 West 10th St., Lockport 60441; (815) 588-1100; www.canalcor.org

I&M State Canal Trail, P.O. Box 272, Morris 60450; (815) 942-0796; http://dnr.state.il.us/lands/landmgt/parks/i&m/main.htm

Joliet to Seneca

Heading west from the Brandon Road parking area, wetlands rule much of the landscape. There are algae-covered ponds littered with deadfall, huge expanses of cattails, and swaying stands of 15-foot-tall sedge grasses. Water-loving birds such as red-winged blackbirds, green night herons, and kingfishers seem unfazed by the sounds of heavy industry nearby on US 6.

Before reaching Channahon, short spur trails head left into Rock Run Forest Preserve and Channahon Community Park. Both parks are less than 0.25 mile off the I&M Canal Trail, and each has a picnic areas, restrooms, and water. At Rock Run a short hiking trail leads to the shore of Rock Run Creek. After passing under I-55, the path runs through attractive bottom-land terrain alongside the canal's open water.

The diminutive Channahon State Park contains a tenting campground, a picnic area, a former canal lock, and one of only two locktender's houses remaining along the canal. Locktenders had to be available day or night to keep the boat traffic moving. They opened the gate for the canal boat to enter the 12- by 100-foot lock, closed the gate, and then filled or drained the lock to raise or lower the boat. Fifteen locks were needed along the canal for 141 feet of elevation change between Chicago and the Illinois River.

After the path crosses the DuPage River and passes two more locks, you'll embark on one of the best stretches on the eastern side of the I&M Canal Trail. For most of the next 5.5 miles, the trail occupies a 15-foot-wide strip of land between two bodies of water: The 20- to 30-foot-wide canal

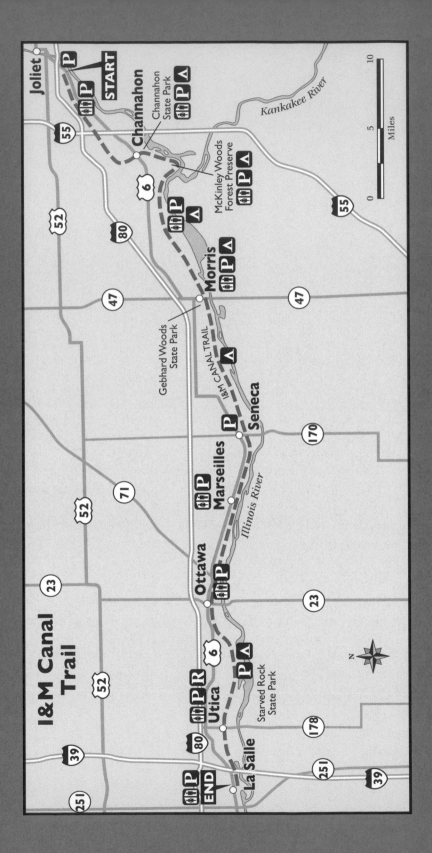

is on the right; the broad and mighty Des Plaines River is on the left. The surrounding landscape is wooded and hilly with bluffs and patches of farmland. With good weather, expect to see plenty of pleasure boats on the Des Plaines. Barges may come lumbering by, too, some as long as 2 city blocks. At McKinley Woods a pedestrian bridge over the canal leads to a picnic area, a small campground, and the hiking trails that lead through the park's rugged terrain.

The bluffs continue beyond McKinley Woods all the way to the Dresden Lock and Dam. Near the dam is the only mule barn left standing along the canal. (Mule barns once were situated every 10 to 15 miles so that the mules and horses could eat and rest before their next haul.) Another locktender's house appears along the path at Aux Sable Creek. This is also where you'll find a small camping area and an aqueduct where the canal is directed over the 40-foot-wide creek. (The I&M Canal Museum and Visitor Center in Lockport contains a scale model of the Aux Sable Aqueduct and locktender's house as it looked when the canal was in use.)

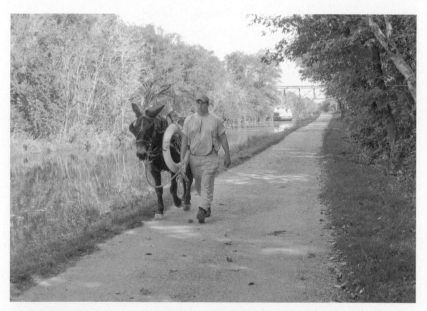

A young man dressed in period attire shows how mules once pulled the boats through the I&M Canal.

Before passing downtown Morris you'll likely see some anglers and boaters in a riverside park. Morris's surprisingly vibrant main strip runs straight north from a pedestrian bridge that spans the canal. Across the street from the bridge sits the Grundy County Historical Society.

After the aqueduct over Nettle Creek at Gebhard Woods State Park, the canal dries up and bottomland woods and sedge grasses take over. You'll see a small stream that trickles under the trail toward the Illinois River. Beyond the stream you'll duck under the curving wooden supports of a new bridge for Old Stage Road. Dense stands of bottomland woods occasionally open up to reveal big sprawling wetlands sprinkled with downed trees and muskrat lodges.

Seneca contains the only grain elevator that still stands along the I&M Canal. Built in 1861 and placed on the National Register of Historic Places in 1997, the 80-foot structure is a reminder of the cargo that weighed down most canal boats as they were hauled up and down the canal.

Seneca to La Salle

Leaving Seneca, the path follows a dirt road for a mile or so through farm fields. Once you've regained the trail, you'll catch glimpses of the Illinois River beyond the field on the left. In a residential area within the town of Marseilles, the trail passes a former lock beside the trail.

A dramatic crossing of the Fox River marks your arrival in Ottawa. Alongside the pedestrian bridge that takes you over the river is an enormous aqueduct that shuttled canal boats 50 feet above the Fox River. The riverside park on the west bank of the Fox River serves as a perfect picnicking spot. If you're in the mood for exploring, a few blocks south of the trail in Ottawa (on IL 71) is Washington Square, which hosted the first of the series of U.S. Senate debates between Abraham Lincoln and Stephen Douglas.

The remaining 15.0 miles of trail from Ottawa to LaSalle offer many scenic stretches of river bluffs, wetlands, and open water. Exposed sandstone appears now and then on the 80-foot-high bluffs to the right. In some places the exposed rock is the result of dynamite used to clear the route for a railroad line that runs at the foot of the bluff.

For those with the time and inclination to explore the area, Buffalo Rock State Park is well worth a brief detour. At the Buffalo Rock parking area, you can cross Dee Bennett Road to visit this park perched on a bluff above the Illinois River. Buffalo Rock State Park is a reclaimed strip mine that contains five enormous earthen mounds depicting creatures commonly found near the river.

Entering Utica, the trail shares the route with a quiet country road.

At the parking area near the end of the trail in La Salle, you'll come upon a full-size replica of a canal boat that traveled the canal more than 150 years ago. The wooden boat is long and narrow, with an open-air deck on the second level. During an hour-long boat ride, tour guides dressed from the era provide narration. At the end of the trail, about 1.0 mile beyond the parking area in La Salle, you can see the canal's confluence with the Illinois River off to the left.

Local Information

- Grundy County Chamber of Commerce, 909 North Liberty St., Morris 60450; (815) 942-0113; http://grundychamber.com

- Joliet Visitors Bureau, 30 North Bluff St., Joliet 60435; (815) 723-9045; www.visitjoliet.org

- Ottawa Visitors Center, 100 West Lafayette St., Ottawa 61350, (888) 688-2924; www.experienceottawa.com

- Will County Forest Preserve District, 17540 West Laraway Rd., Joliet 60433; (815) 727-8700; www.fpdwc.org

Local Events/Attractions

- Hegeler Carus Mansion, 1307 Seventh St., La Salle; (815) 224-6543; www.hegelercarus.org. Huge mansion from 1874 occupies an entire city block; tours provided.

- Joliet Area Historical Museum, 204 North Ottawa St., Joliet; (815) 723-5201; www.jolietmuseum.org. The museum offers a thorough introduction to local history.

- Joliet-area rail trails; www.oprt.org/maps/westcon.html#iandm. Three other long rail trails can be accessed in Joliet. Check the Web site for route advice and on-street connections.

- Illinois Waterway Visitors Center, Route 1, Dee Bennett Road, Ottawa; (815) 667-4054. Observation decks allow you to watch the boats using the locks.

- Lock 16 Visitor Center, 754 First St., La Salle; (866) 610-7678; www .lasalleboat.org. The visitor center, located several blocks from the trail, contains exhibits, a cafe, and a gift shop. Buy tickets for La Salle Canal boat rides.

- Starved Rock State Park, at IL 178 and IL 71, Utica; (815) 667-4726; http://dnr.state.il.us/lands/landmgt/parks/i&m/east/starve/park.htm. Visit the canyons and bluffs at one of the state's best (and most popular) state parks.

Restaurants

- Nodding Onion Restaurant, 522 Clark St., Utica; (815) 667-4990; http://thenoddingonion.com. Located a few blocks south of the trail; a great spot for lunch.

- Tracy's Row House, 728 Columbus St., Ottawa; (815) 434-3171; http:// tracysrowhouse.net. A nice atmosphere and good food in downtown Ottawa.

- Triple J Ice Cream, 110 East Canal Ave., Ottawa; (815) 434-8888. Located on the trail.

Accommodations

- I&M Canal camping. From the east, tent camping is offered at Channahon State Park, McKinley Woods Forest Preserve, the Aux Sable Aqueduct, and three hike-in sites along the trail between the Aux Sable Aqueduct and Seneca. There's also camping at Gebhard Woods State Park and three hike-in sites on the trail west of the Buffalo Rock parking area.

- Starved Rock Lodge and Conference Center, P.O. Box 570, Utica 61373; (800) 868-7625; www.starvedrocklodge.com. Guest rooms, cabins, and campground at the state park, located at IL 178 and IL 71.

8 ILLINOIS PRAIRIE PATH— AURORA AND ELGIN BRANCHES

These two connected branches of the Illinois Prairie Path take you through a suburban landscape that is largely residential, sometimes industrial, and often feels more remote than it actually is. As the route cuts through a number of forest preserves, the dense trailside greenery falls away, and majestic views of wetlands and prairie open up in front of you. At roughly the route's halfway mark, budget some time for checking out the shops and restaurants in Wheaton.

Activities:

Start: Veterans Memorial Island Park, just north of Aurora

Length: 27.2 miles one-way

Surface: Asphalt for the first mile or so; crushed gravel surface the rest of the way

Wheelchair access: The trail is wheelchair accessible.

Difficulty: The trail offers a medium level of difficulty due to the length.

Restrooms: There are public restrooms and water at Veterans Memorial Island Park, in front of the Warrenville city offices, the junction with the Prairie Path Main Stem in Wheaton (water only), and the Army Trail Road parking area.

Maps: USGS Aurora North, Elgin, Geneva, Naperville, and West Chicago; *DeLorme: Illinois Atlas and Gazetteer:* Pages 20 and 28; Chicagoland Bicycle Map, Active Transportation Alliance, www.activetrans.org

Hazards: The trail crosses a few busy streets; use caution while crossing these. Be mindful of other trail users, particularly on the busier sections of this trail.

Access and parking: From I-88 north of Aurora, head south on IL 31 (Lincoln Street). Turn left at Illinois Avenue. Park at Veterans Memorial Island

Park on the right. From the island, catch the trail by heading to the east shore of the Fox River and following the path left. UTM coordinates: 16T, 391214 E, 4624868 N

To park at the Eola Road parking area, head south from I-88 on IL 59. Turn right onto Diehl Road and then left onto Eola Road. Park on the right.

To park at the Winfield Road parking area, head north from I-88 on Winfield Road. Parking is on the left.

Wheaton contains many side streets where you can park at no cost near the trail. To park on Lincoln Avenue, go north on Main Street from Roosevelt Road. Turn left on Lincoln Avenue and look for parking as you get near the trail.

To park at the corner of County Farm and Geneva Roads, head west from I-355 on IL 64. Turn left onto County Farm Road. Park at the northwest corner of the intersection with Geneva Road.

To park at the Army Trail Road parking area, head south on IL 59 from I-90. Turn right onto Army Trail Road.

To park at the Raymond Street parking area, located at the north end of the route, head south on IL 59 from I-90. Turn right onto US 20 (Lake Street) and then left onto Raymond Street. Park on the right.

Transportation: The Aurora stop on the BNSF Metra line is across the street from south end of the trail in Aurora. The Wheaton stop on the Union Pacific West Metra line is a couple blocks east of the trail. In Elgin, the National Street station on the Milwaukee District West line is less than a mile north of the north end of the trail.

Rentals: Midwest Cyclery; 117 Front St., Wheaton; (630) 668-2424; www .midwestcyclery.com; located next to the Prairie Path Main Stem

Contact: DuPage County Division of Transportation, Jack T. Knuepfer Administration Building, 421 North County Farm Rd., Wheaton 60187; (630) 682-7318

Illinois Department of Natural Resources, One Natural Resources Way, Springfield 62702; (312) 917-2070; www.dnr.state.il.us

Illinois Prairie Path, P.O. Box 1086, Wheaton 60187; (630) 752-0120; www.ipp.org

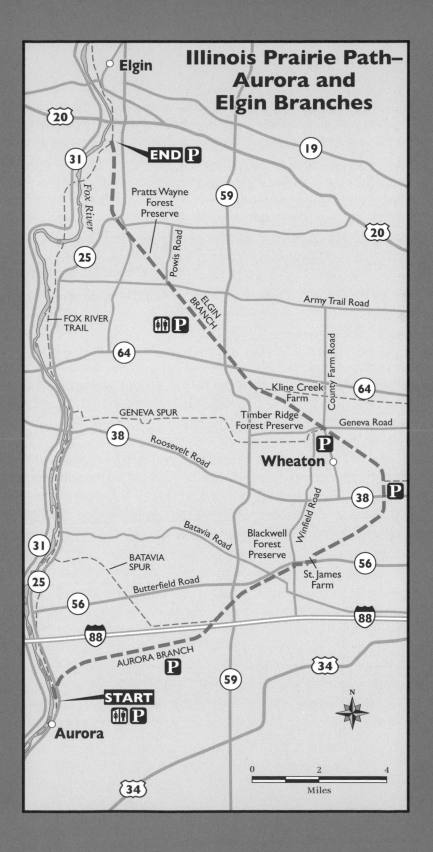

‖‖‖

In future years the area where this route starts will look much different. The city of Aurora is developing an ambitious riverside park that will contain a large outdoor performance venue, a wetland area where Indian Creek enters the Fox River, and a graceful curving bridge that connects to an island in the river and the opposite shore. The park will occupy the riverbank between Veterans Memorial Island Park and downtown Aurora. With or without the new park, downtown Aurora deserves a visit either at the beginning or the end of your trip.

The Fox River accompanies this route for just a brief moment as the path heads away from downtown Aurora and then climbs the wooded river bluff. At the top of the bluff, cross IL 25 (Aurora Avenue) and then catch the trail as it runs left off Hankes Avenue.

As you proceed, the greenery alongside the trail toggles between dense stands of trees and thick shrubbery. New residential developments proliferate, and this is where the trail shares a right-of-way with multiple power lines that crackle and hum overhead. After you cross Farnsworth Avenue, the shrubbery disappears briefly and a big grassy wetland opens on the left.

After this prairie-wetland oasis, you're quickly brought back to a heavily developed suburban reality as you pass an electrical substation and an office park and mount a pedestrian bridge over a busy highway. If you have kids along, they'll likely want to blow some money at Odyssey Fun World, an amped-up arcade with rides, games, and laser tag. (Look for the back parking area on the right after passing under I-88.)

In Warrenville the trail shoots across the West Branch of the DuPage River and then enters an attractive slice of Blackwell Forest Preserve. While accompanying Butterfield Road, you'll pass the St. James Farm, once a private estate but now owned by the DuPage County Forest Preserve District. The farm's brick barns, arena, and trails focus on equestrian activities.

The route toward downtown Wheaton offers densely wooded terrain, well-kept backyards, and crossings of low-traffic roads for the most part. You may also notice that this stretch of trail is well used by local residents. Proof of this path's popularity is demonstrated by homeowners posting HOUSE FOR SALE signs along the path.

After passing the main stem of the Prairie Path in Wheaton and following a long pedestrian bridge over multiple railroad tracks, the path curves left as it reaches a bench overlooking a wetland called Lincoln Marsh. At the corner of Geneva and County Farm Roads, a spur trail on the right leads to Kline Creek Farm, another farm operated by the county park system. Continuing ahead, the landscape grows wooded, lush, and dense. Again the path crosses the West Branch of the DuPage River. Near where the Great Western Trail intersects the Prairie Path on the right, you'll encounter wetlands with ponds and stands of cattails. Patches of wetland continue—intermixed with residential developments and industrial areas—as the trail shoots straight northwest.

Soon you'll arrive at Pratts Wayne Forest Preserve, a generous-size natural area that contains prairies, sprawling wetlands, and a collection of fishing ponds. As you enter the forest preserve, thick woods and a dense, leafy canopy turn the trail into a shadowy tunnel. The wooden railings and the wide treeless swath of marshland and wet prairie mark the spot where Norton Creek passes under the trail. Soon the cattails on the right give way to open water, much of it covered in algae. On the far side of the open water, look for waterbirds perched on fallen logs. Underneath another set of wooden railings, Brewster Creek passes under the path.

As the Elgin Spur of the Prairie Path runs through a collection of forest preserves, a remote ambience prevails.

The final several miles of the path take you past former and current gravel mining operations and chunks of farmland. The trail ends at the Fox River Trail. Taking the Fox River Path right brings you to Elgin and eventually to the Wisconsin border along the Prairie Trail. Turning left takes you back to Aurora.

Local Information

- Aurora Area Convention and Visitors Bureau, 43 West Galena Blvd., Aurora 60506; (630) 897-5581; www.enjoyaurora.com

- Chicago Convention and Tourism Bureau, 2301 South Lake Shore Dr., Chicago 60616; (312) 567-8500; www.choosechicago.com

- DuPage Convention and Visitors Bureau, 915 Harger Rd., Suite 240, Oakbrook 60523; (800) 232-0502; www.discoverdupage.com

- Elgin Area Convention and Visitors Bureau, 77 Riverside Dr., Elgin 60120; (847) 695-7540; www.northernfoxrivervalley.com

Local Events/Attractions

- Aurora Regional Fire Museum, 53 North Broadway, Aurora; (630) 892-1572; www.auroraregionalfiremuseum.org. Vintage firefighting equipment; located across the street from the trailhead in downtown Aurora.

- Blackwell Forest Preserve, Butterfield Road, just west of Winfield Road; (630) 933-7200; www.dupageforest.com. Boat rentals, campground, and lots of trails.

- Kline Creek Farm; 1 mile south of North Avenue (IL 64); (630) 876-5900; www.dupageforest.com/education/klinecreek.html. Living-history farm with animals, education programs, and a visitor center.

- St. James Farm, Butterfield Road east of Blackwell Forest Preserve, Wheaton; (630) 933-7200; www.dupageforest.com/news/stjames isopen0708.html. Equestrian facilities; trails for hiking and riding; open seasonally on weekends.

Restaurants

- La Quinta de Los Reyes, 36 East New York St., Aurora; (630) 859-4000; http://laquintadelosreyesaurora.com. Live music; courtyard area; located at the end of the trail in Aurora.

- Pad Thai Etc. Restaurant, 563 West Liberty Dr., Wheaton; (630) 653-5337. Basic Thai offerings; located on the Prairie Path Main Stem in Wheaton.

Accommodations

- Comfort Suites, 111 North Broadway Ave., Aurora; (630) 896-2800. Located close to the trailhead in downtown Aurora and 1 block from the Hollywood Casino.

9 ILLINOIS PRAIRIE PATH—MAIN STEM

The Illinois Prairie Path, one of the first rail trails in the nation, runs along the route of the former Chicago, Aurora, and Elgin Railway, an electric railroad line that carried commuters and freight between Chicago and its western suburbs. Stretching from Wheaton to Maywood, the main stem of the Prairie Path takes you through wooded parks and greenways and offers a taste of a handful of communities that grew up alongside this route.

Activities:

Start: In Elmer J. Hoffman Park on the east side of Wheaton

Length: 13.4 miles one-way

Surface: Crushed gravel for the 9.4-mile-long DuPage County section of the trail; asphalt for much of the 4.0-mile-long Cook County section

Wheelchair access: The trail is wheelchair accessible.

Difficulty: The trail is easy.

Restrooms: There are public restrooms and water at Elmer J. Hoffman Park and the Villa Park Museum.

Maps: USGS Elmhurst, River Forest, and Wheaton; *DeLorme: Illinois Atlas and Gazetteer:* Pages 28 and 29

Hazards: Sections of this trail can get busy; be mindful of other trail users. Watch for broken glass on the paved sections. The trail crosses a few streets with very heavy traffic. Waiting to cross sometimes requires patience.

Access and parking: From I-355 head west on Roosevelt Road (IL 38). Turn right onto Lorraine Street. Turn left onto Hill Avenue and then right onto Prospect Avenue. Park at Elmer J. Hoffman Park and catch the trail just north of the parking area. UTM coordinates: 16T, 409942 E, 4635804 N

In DuPage County, parking is available in all the communities along the trail. On weekends most leased parking spaces near the Metra stations are free, as are most metered parking spaces. Farther east in Cook County the path runs through residential areas where free parking is often available.

To park at the trailside parking area in Lombard, head north on Westmore Avenue from IL 38 (Roosevelt Road). The parking lot is on the left.

To park at the trailside parking lot in Elmhurst, head north from IL 38 (Roosevelt Road) on York Road. Turn left onto Madison Street and then right onto Spring Road.

Transportation: Take the Metra's Union Pacific West line to either the Wheaton or College Avenue stop. The trail runs alongside the tracks. In Lombard and Villa Park, catch trains on the same Metra line several blocks north of the trail.

Rentals: Midwest Cyclery; 117 Front St., Wheaton; (630) 668-2424; www .midwestcyclery.com; located next to the trail

Contact: DuPage County Division of Transportation, Jack T. Knuepfer Administration Building, 421 North County Farm Rd., Wheaton 60187; (630) 682-7318

Illinois Department of Natural Resources, One Natural Resources Way, Springfield 62702; (312) 917-2070; www.dnr.state.il.us

Illinois Prairie Path, P.O. Box 1086, Wheaton 60187; (630) 752-0120; www.ipp.org

||||||||||||||||||||||||||||||||||||||||||||||||||||||||||||||||||||||||||||||

Before heading east on the trail, consider taking the 1.5-mile trip west along the path into downtown Wheaton, where restaurants, bars, and shops line the streets. Along the way you'll pass Wheaton College, which contains a museum focusing on the school's most famous alumnus, the evangelist Billy Graham. The trail also passes a large Romanesque-style courthouse built in 1896 that is now on the National Register of Historic Places. The building, topped off by a large clock tower, was recently remodeled and now contains high-priced condos. The west side of Wheaton is where the Prairie Path splits into two main branches; one goes to Aurora, the other to Elgin.

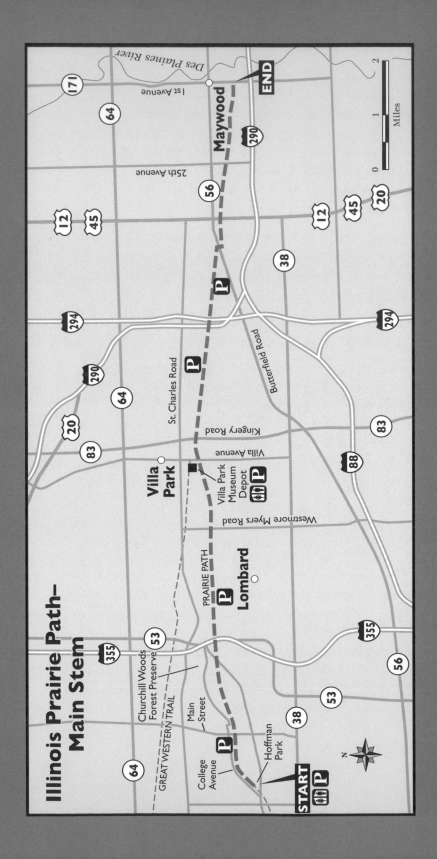

Illinois Prairie Path–
Main Stem

Heading east on the path you'll encounter another pleasant downtown area in Glen Ellyn. Smaller than Wheaton, Glen Ellyn also has a collection of shops and restaurants within sight of the trail. On the way out of Glen Ellyn, the trail passes through a little ravine before shooting under I-355. In Lombard a leafy residential atmosphere dominates as the trail crosses numerous side streets.

The trail is accompanied by an attractive greenway as it proceeds through Villa Park, the next town along the route. At Ardmore Street you'll sweep past an old Prairie-style train depot built with river rock in 1910. Just ahead, another former depot contains a museum with a few small exhibits focusing on local rail history, including the electric railroad that operated on these tracks. The depot was built in 1929 of cut stone and stucco with wood trim. The station has large windows, most notably on the east end, which was designed to house a pharmacy. Inside you'll learn that this rail line stopped service in the late 1950s and that the line was abandoned altogether in 1961. Signs near the museum point to the eastern terminus of the Great Western Trail, which starts just 1 block north.

In Elmhurst the many patches of trailside greenery will likely catch your eye. Well-tended flower gardens decorate the residential backyards along the path, and cottonwood, sumac, and oaks occasionally conspire to create a tunnel of trees that encloses the trail. Near Spring Road community volunteers maintain a swath of restored prairie thick with such plants as milkweed, baby's breath, compass plants, shooting star, and goldenrod.

Passing under I-290 and I-294 signals your departure from DuPage County and your entry into Cook County. In Berkeley the path again runs through a wide greenway sprinkled with picnic tables, playgrounds, and ball diamonds. After a brief on-street section of the trail in the community of Hillside, small industrial facilities multiply. For the remainder of the path through Bellwood and the much larger town of Maywood, residential neighborhoods with modest, well-kept homes intermingle with industrial districts. Through much of this area, the path shares the route with a power line right-of-way.

Major Milepoints

10.2 Cross IL 56 and keep straight ahead on Forest Avenue.

10.3 Turn left onto Warren Avenue.

10.5 Cross Mannheim Road and resume traveling on the Prairie Path.

Local Information

- Chicago Convention and Tourism Bureau, 2301 South Lake Shore Dr., Chicago 60616; (312) 567-8500; www.choosechicago.com

- DuPage Convention and Visitors Bureau, 915 Harger Rd., Suite 240, Oakbrook 60523; (800) 232-0502; www.discoverdupage.com

- Elmhurst Visitor and Tourism Department, 209 North York St., Elmhurst 60126; (630) 530-3312; www.elmhurst.org/index.asp?nid=59

Local Events/Attractions

- Elmhurst Art Museum, 150 Cottage Hill Ave., Elmhurst; (630) 834-0202; www.elmhurstartmuseum.org. Nice collection of contemporary art.

- York Theatre, 150 North York Rd., Elmhurst; (630) 834-0675. An impressive Spanish-style film theater first opened in 1924; the pipe organ is played before some shows.

Restaurants

- Dairy Queen, 205 South Main St., Lombard; (630) 627-6364. Ice cream only; look for the vintage neon sign a few blocks north of the trail.

- Pad Thai Etc. Restaurant, 563 West Liberty Dr., Wheaton; (630) 653-5337. Basic Thai offerings; right on the trail in Wheaton.

- Roberto's Ristorante and Pizzeria, 483 Spring Rd., Elmhurst; (630) 279-8474; www.robertosristorante.net. Slightly upscale, classic Italian food and thin-crust pizzas; located next to the trail.

10 MAJOR TAYLOR TRAIL

The first section of the Major Taylor Trail curves through Dan Ryan Woods Forest Preserve into the historic neighborhood of Beverly. On Longwood Avenue in Beverly, you'll see a string of sprawling historic mansions of various styles. After touring the neighborhoods of Morgan Park and West Pullman, a soaring pedestrian bridge takes you over the Little Calumet River to the Whistler Forest Preserve.

Activities:

Start: Dan Ryan Woods Forest Preserve, parking lots 15 and 16; near the intersection of Western Avenue and 83rd Street

Length: 8.6 miles one-way

Surface: Asphalt

Wheelchair access: The trail is wheelchair accessible; however, on-street sections may not all have ramped sidewalks.

Difficulty: This trail is easy.

Restrooms: There are public restrooms and water at Dan Ryan Woods and Whistler Forest Preserves.

Maps: USGS Blue Island; *DeLorme: Illinois Atlas and Gazetteer:* Page 29; Chicagoland Bicycle Map, Active Transportation Alliance, www.activetrans.org

Hazards: Broken glass appears regularly on the trail. A handful of busy street crossings must be approached with caution.

Access and parking: Take I-94 south from downtown Chicago. Exit at 79th Street and head west to Damen Avenue. Turn left onto Damen Avenue and then right onto 83rd Street. Park in the Dan Ryan Woods Forest Preserve's lots 15 and 16, located on the right. Head north on the trail from the parking area and then follow it as it takes a sharp turn right, heading south. UTM coordinates: 16T, 443582 E, 4621316 N

To park at the south end of the trail, take I-57 south to 127th Street. Turn left onto 127th Street and then right onto Halsted Avenue. After crossing the river, turn left onto Forestview Avenue. Enter Whistler Forest Preserve on the left. The trail starts at the end of the park road.

Transportation: Take the Rock Island Metra train line to the 91st Street station in Beverly. The Major Taylor Trail runs along the east side of the railroad tracks.

Rentals: Bike Chicago, 740 East 56th Place, Chicago; (773) 404-2500
DJ's Bike Doctor, 1500 East 55th St., Chicago; (773) 955-4400

Contact: Chicago Department of Transportation, 30 North LaSalle St., Suite 1100, Chicago 60602; (312) 744-3600
Chicago Park District, 541 North Fairbanks Court, Chicago 60611; (312) 742-7529; www.chicagoparkdistrict.com

The Major Taylor Trail honors an African-American athlete who dominated track cycling at a time when it was the most popular spectator sport in the country. Taylor was lauded for his strength and speed on a bike, especially for his tactical ability and his dazzling last-minute sprints. He made triumphant tours of Europe and Australia, defeating everyone he competed against. The title of his autobiography, *The Fastest Bicycle Rider in the World,* was no exaggeration. The book cites the many speed records he set and the handful of world championship races he won in 1899, 1900, and 1901. Despite harassment and frequent attempts to ban him from cycling because of his race, Taylor's prowess on the cycling track made him the wealthiest African-American athlete in America.

Taylor lived in Chicago the final two years of his life after, sadly, losing his wealth on bad business deals. He died in 1932 while living at a YMCA in Chicago's Bronzeville neighborhood and is buried west of the trail in the Mount Greenwood Cemetery.

The first section of the Major Taylor Trail follows an old railroad embankment that gradually curves along the eastern edge of the Dan

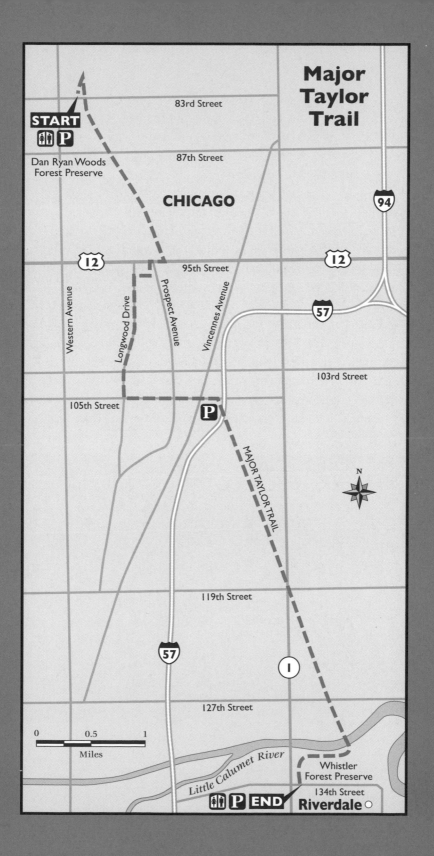

Ryan Woods Forest Preserve. Dense stands of trees rise high above the trail and lean overhead, creating a tunnel of branches and leaves. When the trail leaves the 20-foot-high embankment and returns to street level, the forest preserve continues to sprawl on the right, occasionally dotted with wetlands and marsh grasses.

Known for its historic homes, tree-lined streets, and racially integrated population, Beverly is one of the most attention-grabbing neighborhoods in Chicago. The large lawns, hilly topography, and close-knit community atmosphere add to the area's appeal. Along Longwood Drive you'll encounter a progression of mansions built in various styles, many with wooded, carefully landscaped yards and gardens. The first block on Longwood Avenue takes you past a couple of houses built in the Prairie style, one of which (9914 South Longwood Dr.) was designed by Frank Lloyd Wright. At 10200 South Longwood Ave. sits a mansion built in 1890 in the Colonial Revival style by Horace E. Horton, founder of the Chicago Bridge and Iron Co. Probably the best-known community landmark is a replica of an Irish castle built in 1886 by real estate developer Robert C. Givins at 103rd Street and Longwood Avenue. As the story goes, Givins built the limestone castle in an effort

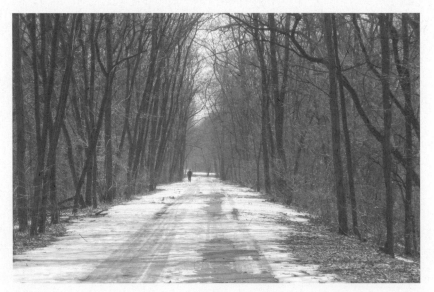

The Major Taylor Trail as it shoots through Dan Ryan Woods.

to woo a bride from Ireland. Owned by the Beverly Unitarian Church since 1942, the structure has an assortment of ghost stories attached to it.

Once reunited with the trail, you'll start a several-mile-long journey through Morgan Park and West Pullman, a couple of Chicago's southern-most neighborhoods. After the trail crosses I-57, it angles alongside a power line right-of-way and through neighborhoods with modest working-class homes. There are grassy areas and occasional patches of woodland; less appealing are the occasional patches of broken glass on the surface of the trail and spots where trash has been dumped. At 118th Street the trail passes a stone-cutting business where big blocks of limestone sit on the side of the trail awaiting the carver's tools.

The final leg of the trail crosses a pedestrian bridge 60 feet above the Little Calumet River. The river, wider than the length of a football field, marks the boundary between Chicago and the suburban town of River-dale. Looking west from the bridge, a string of riverside houses occupy the leafy north bank; the dense woods of Whistler Forest Preserve border the south bank.

Just before entering the forest preserve, the trail skirts the edge of a huge steel mill. Keep an eye peeled for the resident deer population scur-rying into the shrubbery as you follow the trail into the dense woods of Whistler Forest Preserve.

Major Milepoints

2.0 From here, you'll need to travel 2.2 miles along city streets to reach the second part of the trail. Where the trail abruptly ends at the fence, continue south through the grocery store parking lot. Turn right at 95th Street. Proceed with care; 95th is busy. (**Option:** For a shorter but less scenic on-street route, turn left onto Charles and left again onto 105th Street to return to the trail.)

2.2 Turn left onto Vanderpoel Avenue.

2.3 Turn right onto 96th Street.

2.5 Turn left onto Longwood Avenue.

3.6 Turn left onto 105th Street.

4.4 Turn right onto the trail.

Local Information

- Chicago Convention and Tourism Bureau, 2301 South Lake Shore Dr., Chicago 60616; (312) 567-8500; www.choosechicago.com

- Chicago Southland Convention and Visitors Bureau, 2304 173rd St., Lansing 60438; (708) 895-8200 or (888) 895-8233; www.visitchicago southland.com

Local Events/Attractions

- Beverly Arts Center, 2407 West 111th St., Chicago; (773) 445-3838; www.beverlyartcenter.org. Gallery exhibitions and a gift shop. The center hosts films and live music.

- Beverly Hills Cycling Classic, Beverly Area Planning Association; (773) 233-3100; www.bapa.org. Annual 100K criterium (bike race) through the pleasant environs of Beverly. The race is paired with the annual Tour de Beverly Family Ride; both held in July.

Restaurants

- Maple Tree Inn, 13301 South Old Western Ave., Blue Island; (708) 388-3461. Serves Cajun and Creole cuisine. Located west of the southern end of the trail.

- Koda Bistro and Wine Bar, 10352 South Western Ave.; (773) 445-5632; http://kodabistro.com. Well-regarded upscale eatery in Beverly.

- Southtown Health Foods, 2100 West 95th St.; (773) 233-1856; www .southtownhealthfoods.com. Offers groceries and a smoothie bar.

Accommodations

- J. Ira and Nicki Harris Family Hostel, 24 East Congress Parkway, Chicago; (312) 360-0300; www.hichicago.org. A huge, clean, and affordable hostel located downtown; dorm-style rooms and a limited number of private rooms.

- The Benedictine Bed and Breakfast, 3111 South Aberdeen St., Chicago; (773) 927-7424; www.chicagomonk.org. Run by a Catholic monastery in the Bridgeport neighborhood on Chicago's south side.

11 NORTH BRANCH TRAIL

If you look at a map of Chicago's northern suburbs and follow the routes of several streams that merge to form the North Branch of the Chicago River, it looks like strands of a rope gradually coming together. While much of the North Branch and its tributaries have fallen victim to campaigns to straighten the many bends, the sections of river along the North Branch Trail wriggle and twist through a glorious 15.0-mile-long corridor of county-owned forest preserves. Small bluffs, woodland, ponds, prairie, open grassy parkland, and little streams trickling into the Chicago River greet trail users along the way.

Activities:

Start: Bunker Hill Forest Preserve, located on Caldwell Avenue north of Devon Avenue

Length: 15.1 miles one-way

Surface: Asphalt

Wheelchair access: The entire trail is wheelchair accessible.

Difficulty: The length and the small river bluffs give this trail an easy-to-medium level of difficulty.

Restrooms: There are public restrooms at Bunker Hill (water), Miami Woods, Linne Woods (water), Harms Woods, and Blue Star Memorial Forest Preserves and at the Chicago Botanic Garden (water).

Maps: USGS River Forest, Park Ridge, and Highland Park; *DeLorme: Illinois Atlas and Gazetteer:* Pages 21 and 29; North Branch Trail Map, Cook County Forest Preserve, www.fpdcc.com/tier3.php?content_id=68; Chicagoland Bicycle Map, Active Transportation Alliance, www.activetrans.org

Hazards: There are multiple road crossings along the North Branch Trail. Be alert—some of these crossings are very busy with traffic. Fortunately traffic lights and overpasses simplify the busiest crossings. This trail can become congested on summer weekends.

Access and parking: Follow I-94 to Caldwell Avenue (exit 41A) and head north. Enter Bunker Hill Forest Preserve on the left and park in any of the lots on the left near the entrance. Catch the paved trail as it winds along the top of the small bluff south of the park road. Bear right at the three-way junction with the trail that leads to the Caldwell Woods Forest Preserve parking area. UTM coordinates: 16T, 435064 E, 4650205 N

To park at Miami Woods Forest Preserve, take I-94 to Touhy Avenue (exit 39A). Head west on Touhy Avenue, and then turn right onto Caldwell Avenue. Enter on the right.

To reach Linne Woods Forest Preserve, take I-94 to Dempster Street (exit 37A). Head west on Dempster Street and enter the forest preserve on the right.

To park at Harms Woods Forest Preserve, take I-94 to Dempster Street (exit 37A). Head west on Dempster Street and then turn right onto Central Avenue. Continue ahead as Central Avenue becomes Harms Road. There are several parking areas on the left.

To catch the trail at Blue Star Memorial Woods, take I-94 north to Lake Street (exit 34B). Head west on Lake Avenue to the forest preserve entrance on the left.

To park at the Tower Road/Skokie Lagoons parking area, take I-94 to Willow Road (exit 33A). Head west on Willow Road and turn right onto Central Avenue. Bear left as Central Avenue becomes Frontage Road. Turn right onto Tower Road and enter the parking area on the right.

To park at the Chicago Botanic Garden, head north on I-94. At exit 29, remain on the Edens Expressway (US 41) then take the next exit for Lake Cook Road. Head east and travel for 0.5 mile to the botanic garden. Follow signs to the parking areas (fee).

Transportation: From downtown Chicago take the Milwaukee District North Line Metra train from Union Station to Edgebrook. From the Edgebrook station turn right onto West Devon Avenue and catch the beginning of the North Branch Trail less than a block away at the intersection of Devon and Caldwell Avenues.

Rentals: Smart Cycling, 2300 Lehigh Ave., Suite 100, Glenview; (847) 998-0200

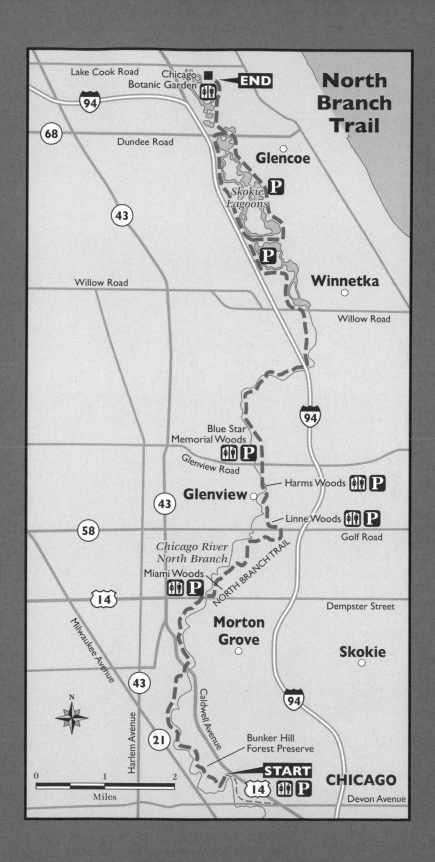

Contact: Forest Preserve District of Cook County, 536 North Harlem Ave., River Forest 60305; (800) 870-3666; www.fpdcc.com

||||||||||||||||||||||||||||||||||||||||||||||||||||||||||||||||||||||||||||||||||||||||||

Like the river that it runs beside, the North Branch Trail never cuts a straight course for long: The trail continuously curves around little ravines, winds through picnic areas, and snakes along the tops of small river bluffs. After the Chicago Lakefront Path, the North Branch Trail gets the second-place prize for the most beloved scenic long trail in Chicagoland. At the north end of the trail, the river flows through a 4.0-mile-long string of tree-fringed lakes called the Skokie Lagoons. The path cruises alongside the lagoon's open water and through acres of bottomland woods.

Like many of the forest preserves along the North Branch Trail, Bunker Hill Forest Preserve, where the route starts, contains big strips of open, grassy picnic areas bordered by dense groves of oak and maple. The first mile or so north of Bunker Hill sets the tone for much of the path to come: The North Branch of the Chicago River is not always visible, but it regularly peeks out from behind clusters of trees, through thick stands of brushes, and over the edges of small ravines. Sometimes the path follows the top of a small bluff; sometimes it runs down alongside the water. During spring and fall, in the absence of leafy cover, more miles of the twisting river will be visible along the path.

Crossing Touhy Avenue, the path winds along the top of a small bluff above the river's earthen banks; trees hang lazily over the river. As you enter the restored prairie at Miami Woods Forest Preserve, watch for hawks as they hunt for prey from above. After the prairie the path cuts through a gently rolling, wooded landscape and over a couple of trickling streams that drain into the river.

With seven street crossings during the 6.0 miles between Dempster Street and the Skokie Lagoons, this stretch of trail gets interrupted regularly. Fortunately, there's plenty of visual charm along the way, such as the section north of Dempster Street, where the trail runs through dense woodland strewn with deadfall and sprinkled with ponds and little ravines.

North of Beckwith Road the landscape becomes less welcoming along a 1.0-mile stretch of trail that is bounded on each side with high chain-link fence. This is also where you'll start to see gravel bridle paths paralleling the main trail. At the pedestrian bridge that crosses to the west side of the river, look downriver to see the spot where the North Branch's Middle Fork joins up with its East Fork, often called the Skokie River.

Crossing Willow Road brings you into the wooded refuge of the Skokie Lagoons. To the right is Willow Road Dam—a favorite spot for local anglers. The county has worked hard over the years to keep the fish biting in these waters. After the lagoons were dug in the 1940s, the land started slowly returning to its original state of marshland. Eventually both the stocked and native fish were unable to survive winters in water that was only 5 or 6 feet deep. To solve this problem, in 1988 the U.S. Environmental Protection Agency (EPA) deepened many of the lagoons to 12 feet, dredging one million cubic yards of sediment. Now the lagoons are some of Cook County's most productive fishing spots for bass, pike, and walleye.

The North Branch Trail concludes at the Chicago Botanic Garden.

The Skokie Lagoons have undergone many changes since the area was a marshland that local Potawatomi Indians called *Chewab Skokie,* meaning "big wet prairie." Like so many other wetlands in the area, the marsh was drained by early residents. Their efforts to create farmland fell flat, however. During wet years the land still flooded. During dry years the peat contained in the marsh would actually catch fire.

When Cook County acquired the marshlands in 1933, the Civilian Conservation Corps (CCC) started digging a series of connected lakes for flood control and recreation. Using mostly wheelbarrows, picks, and shovels, workers excavated four million cubic yards of earth in what became the largest CCC project in the nation. When work finished in 1942, 7 miles of waterway connected seven lagoons. Fed and drained by the Skokie River, three low dams and a main dam at Willow Road were added to control the water level in the lagoons.

As the trail curves left, the traffic noise of I-94 increases and you get farther into the wetlands and bottomland woods that border the lagoons. After crossing the bridge along Tower Road and embarking upon a rolling section of the path alongside Forest Way, you'll encounter big views of the lagoon's open water peppered with islands and fringed with dense woodland. Grassy picnic areas situated along the shore provide spots for viewing waterbirds that hang out in the shallows or float on the open water.

If you love to see carefully selected flowers, trees, and bushes growing in perfectly landscaped environments, the final portion of the route as it passes through the Chicago Botanic Garden will be sure to quicken your pulse. Among the garden's 305 acres of artfully landscaped grounds are twenty-three distinct gardens, including Japanese- and English-style gardens, rose and bulb gardens, fruit and vegetable gardens, and gardens specially designed for children and for persons with limited mobility. Along with the gardens, attractive bridges, statues, fountains, and plenty of scenic spots are situated among the nine islands and the surrounding shoreline.

At the end of this route, benches set within pleasant grassy lawns overlook a few of the many captivating islands containing flowering trees, bridges, and a waterfall. Before returning to the start point of the trail, consider a visit to the pleasant restaurant within the main building at the botanic garden.

Local Information

- Chicago Convention and Tourism Bureau, 2301 South Lake Shore Dr., Chicago 60616; (312) 567-8500; www.choosechicago.com

- Chicago's North Shore Convention and Visitors Bureau, 8001 Lincoln Ave., Suite 715, Skokie 60077; (866) 369-0011; www.cnscvb.com

Local Events/Attractions

- Baha'i House of Worship, 100 North Linden Ave., Wilmette; (847) 853-2300; www.us.bahia.org. The most impressive structure on Chicago's North Shore—a huge, intricately carved dome surrounded by rose gardens.

- Chicago Botanic Garden, 1000 Lake Cook Rd., Glencoe; (847) 835-5440; www.chicagobotanic.org. Visitor center, cafe, restrooms, gift shop. Pick up maps at the visitor center. No entry fee for botanic garden; parking fee per vehicle.

- Chicagoland Canoe Base, 4019 North Narragansett Ave.; (773) 777-1489; www.chicagolandcanoebase.com. Offers rentals for paddling the Skokie Lagoons; a few low dams require portaging.

- Ravinia Music Festival, 418 Sheridan Rd., Highland Park; (847) 266-5000; www.ravinia.org. In operation for more than one hundred years, the festival hosts live concerts all summer long, primarily in its open-air theater. Lawn seats are a great deal.

Restaurants

- Gale Street Inn, 4914 North Milwaukee Ave., Chicago; (773) 725-1300; www.galestreet.com. Located a couple miles south of the trail. Moderately priced; well known for its ribs.

- Garden Café, 1000 Lake Cook Rd., Glencoe; (847) 835-3040; www.chicago-botanic.org/cafe. At the Chicago Botanic Garden; bakery items, soups, sandwiches, salads, pizzas, paninis, and snacks.

- Pampanga's Cuisine Restaurant, 6407 North Caldwell Ave., Chicago; (773) 763-1781. Filipino restaurant located across the street from the south end of the trail.

- Superdawg Drive-in, 6363 North Milwaukee Ave., Chicago; (773) 763-0660; www.superdawg.com. Located close to the trail. A Chicago institution since 1948 serving all the menu items you'd expect, most of which are prefaced with the word "super."

Accommodations

- J. Ira and Nicki Harris Family Hostel, 24 East Congress Parkway, Chicago; (312) 360-0300; www.hichicago.org. A huge, clean, and affordable hostel located downtown; dorm-style rooms and a limited number of private rooms.

- Ravinia Guest House, 264 Oakland Dr., Highland Park; (847) 433-3140. An English Colonial–style B&B; within walking distance of the Ravinia Music Festival.

12 NORTH SHORE CHANNEL AND GREEN BAY TRAILS

This route starts on Chicago's northwest side and follows the North Shore Channel's wooded banks through the communities of Lincolnwood, Skokie, and Evanston. In Skokie the route winds for 2.0 miles through an outdoor sculpture park before meeting up with the Green Bay Trail. The Green Bay Trail launches you on a tour of Chicago's swankiest North Shore suburbs of Wilmette, Kenilworth, Winnetka, Glencoe, and Highland Park.

Activities:

Start: Ronan Park, located at the south end of the North Shore Channel Trail on Lawrence Avenue between California and Sacramento Avenues

Length: 17.7 miles one-way

Surface: Hard-packed gravel on the northern 3.0 miles; asphalt and concrete on the rest

Wheelchair access: The trails are wheelchair accessible. Sidewalks accompany nearly all the on-street sections, but some may not have ramped curbs.

Difficulty: The length may present a challenge to some trail users. Otherwise, it's easy.

Restrooms: There are portable toilets between Howard Street and Touhy Avenue and at the parking area near Dempster Street; public restrooms and water at the Metra stations in Glencoe and downtown Highland Park.

Maps: USGS Chicago Loop, Evanston, and Highland Park; *DeLorme: Illinois Atlas and Gazetteer:* Pages 21 and 29; Chicagoland Bicycle Map, Active Transportation Alliance, www.activetrans.org

Hazards: A few on-street sections of this route follow quiet roads. The longest section by far is the 1.5 miles between the north end of the North Shore Channel Trail and the south end of the Green Bay Trail in Wilmette. While following several short on-street sections through parking areas near train stations, watch for cars pulling out of parking spots.

Access and parking: From the corner of Western and Lawrence Avenues in Chicago, head west on Lawrence Avenue and proceed to California Avenue. Turn right onto California Avenue and then left onto Argyle Avenue. Park at West River Park on the right. Pick up the trail as it heads north along the North Shore Channel on the east side of the channel. UTM coordinates: 16T, 441659 E, 4646745 N

To reach the trail by bicycle, from the south head north on California Avenue. At Montrose Avenue follow the signs to the North Shore Channel Trail by turning left onto Montrose Avenue and then right onto Mozart Street. Bear left onto Manor Avenue. The trail starts to the right on Lawrence Avenue.

There are several parking areas situated along McCormick Boulevard as it parallels the path. Take I-94 north to Touhy Avenue and follow Touhy east to McCormick Boulevard. Turn left onto McCormick Boulevard. There are three trail parking areas on the right over the next 2 miles.

The ten Metra stations along the Green Bay Trail provide many parking options. If station lots are full, consider parking on nearby side streets. Most stations are easily accessed from Green Bay Road. Take I-94 north to Lake Avenue. Head east on Lake Avenue and then turn left onto Green Bay Road.

Transportation: Take the Brown Line CTA train to the Francisco stop. Head northwest on Manor Avenue. The trail starts to the right on Lawrence Avenue. Metra users can start the route at one of the many Union Pacific North stations along the Green Bay Trail between Central Street and Highland Park.

Rentals: T. L. Fritts Sporting Goods, 560 Chestnut St., Winnetka; (847) 446-6694

Contact: Cook County Forest Preserve District, 536 North Harlem Ave., River Forest 60305; (800) 870-3666; www.fpdcc.com

Glencoe Park District, 999 Green Bay Rd., Glencoe 60022; (847) 835-3030; www.glencoeparkdistrict.com

Kenilworth Park District, 419 Richmond Rd., Kenilworth 60043; (847) 251-1666

Wilmette Park District, 1200 Wilmette Ave., Wilmette 60091; (847) 256-6100; www.wilmettepark.org

Winnetka Park District, 540 Hibbard Rd., Winnetka 60093; (847) 501-2040; www.winpark.org

||||||||||||||||||||||||||||||||||||||||||||||||||||||||||||||||||||||||||||||||||||||||||||||||

For much of its recent history, the shores of the Chicago River's North Branch were home to steel mills, brickyards, tanneries, and soap plants. During a time when environmental regulations were nonexistent, easy access to the river simplified the waste-disposal process. Over time, though, industries discovered that the natural flow of the North Branch was not enough to carry the industrial waste downriver. The North Shore Channel was built to remedy this problem.

Constructed in 1910, the channel carried water from Wilmette Harbor south to increase the flow of the North Branch of the Chicago River. A secondary use of the 8-mile channel was to divert sewage from North Shore communities. Instead of shunting sewage into Lake Michigan, these towns sent their waste through Chicago and down to the Chicago Sanitary and Ship Canal and on to the Mississippi River. Thanks to environmental regulations and the development of sewage processing plants, the North Shore Channel is no longer a giant flushing system. In recent decades the channel has blossomed into a pleasant patch of greenery where people go to paddle, bicycle, walk, and watch wildlife.

The trail starts along the North Branch of the Chicago River just south of where the North Branch and the North Shore Channel join forces. Across the river from the starting point in Ronan Park is the Lawrence Avenue Pumping Station, a large Art Deco–style building that distributes runoff during storms and sends wastewater to treatment facilities. Continuing north through River Park, the path weaves through ball diamonds, playgrounds, open grassy lawns sprinkled with trees, and a patch of restored prairie alongside the channel. The path passes under busy streets along the way.

As the path starts to run alongside the busy thoroughfare of North McCormick Boulevard, you'll pass a few outdoor sculptures along the 1.0-mile-long Channel Runne Park. North of Pratt Avenue, the sprawling Lincolnwood Town Center mall sits to the left and the huge structures of the Winston Towers apartment complex occupy the east bank of the channel. Soon you'll pass under the high "L" tracks of the Chicago Transit Authority's Skokie Swift line.

Touhy Avenue marks the south end of the Skokie North Shore Sculpture Park, a 2-mile-long series of sixty outdoor sculptures within a landscaped environment overlooking the North Shore Channel. The pathway weaves among artworks created by a mix of regional, national, and international contemporary artists. Large-scale pieces dominate; many are made of metal. The trees on the banks of the channel provide a pleasing background for viewing the works. Some sculptures tantalizingly appear against the industrial backdrop on the opposite shore of the channel.

One sculpture with a strong midwestern appeal—*Hero* by John Charles Cowles—looks like a piece of John Deere farm equipment designed by a space alien. Another compelling sculpture—*Votive Head 2000* by Stacy Latt Savage—uses steel and wood to create an enormous head that brings to mind the giant sculptures on Easter Island. Unfortunately this remarkable collection of outdoor art has a drawback: The persistent traffic beside the park on McCormick Boulevard tends to diminish the experience. For a quieter, less traffic snarled experience at the sculpture park, visit early on a weekend morning.

North of Golf Road, the trail runs through a small arboretum, which contains many dozen varieties of trees and shrubs arranged by families. Growing on small knolls alongside the trail are five varieties of pine and seven varieties of maple trees. You'll also see specimens of ginkgo, Ohio buckeye, and paper birch trees and prairie grasses growing along the banks of the channel. Several small gardens focus on prairie plants, cherry trees, nut trees, and rose bushes.

From the arboretum, you'll travel for 1.5 miles on side streets before connecting with the Green Bay Trail in downtown Wilmette. From Wilmette the trail rises up above the street-level offering views of the surrounding the leafy neighborhoods and nearby commercial strips. To the north in Winnetka, the path drops down below street level. While running through this narrow 30-foot-deep trench created for the railroad, the path ducks under numerous busy roads—out of the wind and away from street sounds. While the route is uninterrupted and peaceful, the scenery is limited to the wooded banks of the railroad ditch.

By now you've noticed that the Green Bay Trail never strays far from the commuter train tracks of the Union Pacific North Metra Line. Along the 9.0 miles of the Green Bay Trail, you'll also notice an abundance of train stations that serve this route between Chicago and Kenosha, Wisconsin. Many of these stations are attractive wood, brick, and stone structures, often located near the quaint downtown strips and sometimes set within a small park.

Many small parks decorate the sides of the Green Bay Trail. In Glencoe the path passes a small bandstand in Henry J. Kalk Park, as well as a couple of other small parks with playgrounds. Across the street from the Ravinia Metra station in Highland Park is a small park designed by Jens Jensen, the famous landscape architect responsible for some of Chicago's most famous public places, such as Garfield, Humboldt, and Columbus Parks. Some of Jensen's calling cards are evident in this tiny park, including native trees, plants, and shrubs and the circular stone bench known as a council ring. Jensen had a studio and a retreat in Highland Park from 1908 to 1934.

Before reaching Jens Jensen Park, the big brown wooden gates mark the entrance to Ravinia Park, a one-hundred-year-old live music venue. The wide-ranging music program has included such varied artists as Itzhak Perlman, Ramsey Lewis, and Frank Zappa. It's not unusual to see people bring folding chairs, a collapsible table, wine, appetizers, and a several-course meal to enjoy while listening to live music on the sprawling lawn.

Before the trail ends at the Highland Park Metra station, its final few miles guide you along a thin strip of land sprinkled with small community gardens. Trail users with an itch to continue north can follow the green bikeway signs through Highland Park to catch the Robert McClory Trail. From Highland Park, trail users can follow uninterrupted pathway for about 23.0 miles north to Kenosha, Wisconsin.

Major Milepoints

7.1 Begin this 1.5-mile on-street section of the route by turning left onto Green Bay Road. The 0.2-mile stretch on Green Bay Road can be busy—consider using the sidewalk on the left.

7.3 Turn right onto Lincoln Avenue. Pass under the railroad tracks and then turn left onto Poplar Avenue, a quiet side street.

7.8 Stay on Poplar Avenue as it curves right. Immediately turn left onto Woodbine Avenue.

8.0 Turn left onto Isabella Street and then resume your route north on Poplar Avenue.

8.6 When Poplar Avenue ends at Wilmette Avenue, continue straight to start on the Green Bay Trail.

9.6 Turn right onto Melrose Street.

9.7 Turn left onto Abbotsford Road.

9.9 Turn left onto Ivy Court and follow the green bikeway signs to resume your trip on Green Bay Trail.

Local Information
- Chicago Convention and Tourism Bureau, 2301 South Lake Shore Dr., Chicago 60616; (312) 567-8500; www.choosechicago.com

- Chicago's North Shore Convention and Visitors Bureau, 8001 Lincoln Ave., Suite 715, Skokie 60077; (866) 369-0011; www.cnscvb.com

Local Events/Attractions
- Baha'i House of Worship, 100 North Linden Ave., Wilmette; (847) 853-2300; www.us.bahia.org. The most impressive structure on Chicago's North Shore—a huge, intricately carved dome surrounded by rose gardens.

- Chicago Botanic Garden, 1000 Lake Cook Rd., Glencoe; (847) 835-5440; www.chicagobotanic.org. Visitor center, cafe, restrooms, gift shop. Pick up maps at the visitor center; located 1 mile west of the trail. No entry fee for botanic garden; parking fee per vehicle.

- Ravinia Park, 418 Sheridan Rd., Highland Park; (847) 266-5000; www .ravinia.org. For more than one hundred years, the park has hosted live summer concerts, primarily in its open-air theater. Lawn seats are a great deal.

- Skokie North Shore Sculpture Park, P.O. Box 692, Skokie 60076; (847) 679-4265; www.sculpturepark.org. Free public tours offered.

Restaurants

- Cafe Central, 455 Central Ave., Highland Park; (847) 266-7878; www .cafecentral.net. A cozy, midprice French bistro just a couple blocks from the north end of the trail.

- Garden Café, 1000 Lake Cook Rd., Glencoe; (847) 835-3040. At the Chicago Botanic Garden; bakery items, soups, sandwiches, salads, pizzas, paninis, and snacks.

- Homers Ice Cream & Restaurant, 1237 Green Bay Rd., Wilmette; (847) 251-0477; www.homersicecream.com. Located blocks away from the south end of the Green Bay Trail, Homers has been making the creamy good stuff since 1935. Allegedly Al Capone's favorite ice-cream parlor.

- Java Love, 723 St. Johns Rd., Highland Park; (847) 266-0728. Serves coffee, espresso, and sweets just yards from the trail.

Accommodations

- J. Ira and Nicki Harris Family Hostel, 24 East Congress Parkway, Chicago; (312) 360-0300; www.hichicago.org. A huge, clean, and affordable hostel located downtown; dorm-style rooms and a limited number of private rooms.

- Margarita European Inn, 1566 Oak Ave., Evanston; (847) 869-2273; www.margaritainn.com. European-style hotel; some rooms are more affordable than others.

- Ravinia Guest House, 264 Oakland Dr., Highland Park; (847) 433-3140. An English Colonial–style B&B; within walking distance of the Ravinia Music Festival.

13 OLD PLANK ROAD TRAIL

This long suburban trail offers a surprising array of scenic spots—many of them surrounded by development. You'll see cattail-fringed ponds, patches of prairie, numerous parks, and small suburban towns with quiet, wooded neighborhoods. At about the halfway point you'll take a side trail through Hickory Creek Forest Preserve, where the route bounds over wooded hills and makes a couple of crossings of Hickory Creek. In the town of Frankfort, check out the historic architecture and the interesting shops before investigating several good dining options.

Activities:

Start: At Logan Park in Park Forest at the corner of Orchard Drive and North Street

Length: 25.7 miles one-way

Surface: Asphalt

Wheelchair access: The trail is wheelchair accessible; some parking areas are surfaced with gravel.

Difficulty: The length gives this trail a medium level of difficulty.

Restrooms: There are public restrooms at the Logan Park trailhead (water), Governors Trail Park (water), Ridgeland Avenue (portable toilet), trailside park (portable toilets) and the trolley barn on White Street in Frankfort, Hickory Creek Forest Preserve, Lions Den Park, and the trail's western terminus (portable toilets).

Maps: USGS Steger, Frankfort, Manhattan, Mokena, and Joliet; *DeLorme: Illinois Atlas and Gazetteer:* Pages 28, 36, and 37; Old Plank Road Trail Management Commission online map, www.oprt.org; Chicagoland Bicycle Map, Active Transportation Alliance, www.activetrans.org

Hazards: A handful of the road crossings have heavy traffic.

Access and parking: Heading south of Chicago on I-57, get off at exit 340A and head east on US 30 (Lincoln Highway). After passing US 54, turn right onto Orchard Drive and then right onto North Street. Park at Logan Park on the right. UTM coordinates: 16T, 442896 E, 4594085 N

To reach the parking area in Matteson, head east on US 30 from I-57. Turn right onto Main Street and right again onto 215th Street. The parking area is on the right.

Parking is available in the northeast corner of the Target store parking lot on Cicero Avenue. From I-57 drive east on US 30 and turn right onto Cicero Avenue.

To park in Frankfort, head west from I-57 on US 30. Turn left onto La Grange Road (US 45) and left again onto White Street. Turn right onto Kansas Street and park in the lot on the right.

To park at Hickory Creek Junction, drive east on US 30 from I-80. The parking area is on the left.

To reach the Lions Den Park parking area, take I-80 to US 30. Head east on US 30 and turn right onto Cedar Road. Continue south after making a slight jog to the left. Lions Den Park is on the left.

To park at the lot at the trail's western terminus, drive west from I-80 on US 30. Turn left onto Hillcrest Road and left onto Park Road. The lot is on the left.

Transportation: The Matteson station on Metra's Electric District Line is located right on the trail, not far from the eastern terminus. The Rock Island District Metra stops about 6 blocks north of the trail in New Lenox.

Rentals: The Wheel Thing, 15 South La Grange Rd., La Grange; (708) 352-3822

Contact: Forest Preserve District of Will County, 17540 West Laraway Rd., Joliet 60433; (815) 727-8700

Old Plank Road Trail Management Commission, www.oprt.org

The Old Plank Road Trail was never actually a plank road. A plank road is a dirt road covered with a series of planks, similar to wooden sidewalks seen in Western films. During the first half of the nineteenth century, when plank roads were wildly popular in the Northeast and Midwest, a plank road was slated to be built between Joliet and the Indiana border. But railroads began to boom, so train tracks were laid down instead. Finished in 1855, the rail line was called the Joliet Cutoff because it allowed trains to avoid going through Chicago. The Joliet Cutoff served as one of the first rail connections between Illinois and East Coast cities like Boston and New York.

During the early years of the twentieth century, the railroad right-of-way also was home to an interurban trolley line. While on the trail, look for Michigan Central Railroad concrete mile markers still in place. Etched with the letters "EG," the markers likely refer to East Gary, the dividing point on this section of the railroad.

Heading west on the Old Plank Road Trail from the starting point at Logan Park, the first section of the trail runs through the downtown area of Matteson, by a couple of parks, and through some scenic wetlands that sit behind a sprawling shopping mall. In Matteson the Metra station on the left and the red caboose permanently parked alongside the trail both point to the town's rich rail history. After passing Governors Trail Park, you'll see the first trail that branches off from Old Plank Road Trail. This is Preservation Trail, which heads north for 1.5 miles to Oakwood Park on the north side of Matteson. Before crossing Cicero Avenue on the Old Plank Road Trail, the path squeezes between the backside of the huge Lincoln Mall on one side, and a series of ponds and wetlands on the other. Expect to see more of these startling juxtapositions between the wild and the urbanized before the route is done.

Across Cicero Avenue, patches of prairie show up on the edges of the trail. One motivating factor for establishing this trail was the variety of prairie plants growing in the vicinity. Only a couple decades after the first settlers arrived in Will and Cook Counties, agencies began buying property for this right-of-way. As a result, plows never touched much of

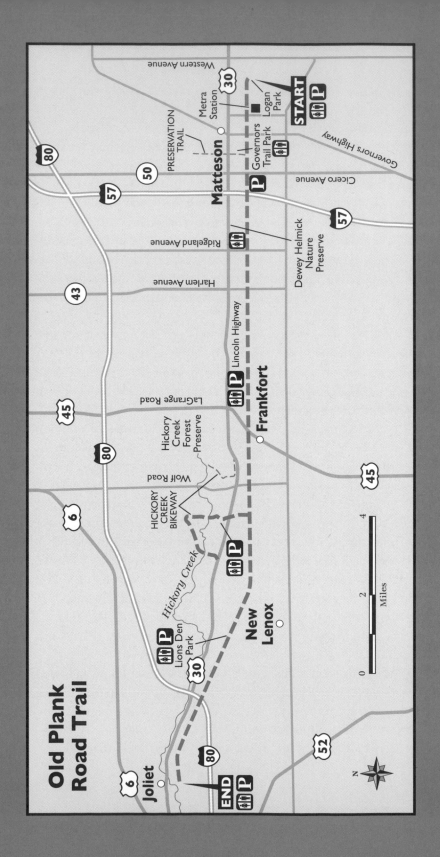

Old Plank
Road Trail

the land alongside the trail. Of the 200 types of prairie plants identified along the trail, you'll find not only common species like goldenrod, compass plant, shooting star, and butterfly weed but also rarer specimens like scurfy pea, prairie lily, savanna blazing star, and silky aster. Pockets of prairie appear scattered along the trail between Cicero Avenue west all the way to New Lennox. Most, however, are located on the mile-long stretch between Cicero and Central Avenues, even under I-57.

Like other spots along this trail, the twelve-acre Dewey Helmick Nature Preserve offers a surprising patch of wildness within a thoroughly built-up landscape. West of Central Avenue the trail traverses a thin strip of land that cuts through the middle of a big pond. On the left, watch for great blue herons standing like statues on the shore of a small wooded island; on the right, a cattail-fringed pond contains a graveyard of still-standing dead trees. Refocusing your eyes beyond the edges of this small wetland reveals dense housing subdivisions blanketing the surrounding landscape.

After crossing Harlem Avenue, the trail gradually descends through a leafy landscape thick with elm, hickory, and maple—it's one of several

The Old Plank Road Trail runs beside a handful of ponds and wetlands.

stretches of trail that deserve a visit during fall color displays. Before entering Frankfort you'll pass a couple of small parks, including Prairie Park, which is primarily a wetland that the town uses to clean and recycle its stormwater runoff. In Frankfort, the first landmarks that come into view are the grain elevator, a trailside park, and a handsome iron sign for Old Plank Road Trail above the trail. Frankfort requires some exploration: A number of well-kept old buildings with interesting shops sit within the compact downtown area. Just south of the trail on White Street, stop in at the trolley barn, a building that once housed the trolleys that operated on the trail. Now it contains an ice-cream shop, a deli, a comic book store, and a coffee shop, as well as displays about the interurban trains and trolleys that ran through Frankfort at the beginning of the twentieth century.

West of Frankfort the trail mounts the appropriately named Arrowhead Bridge over LaGrange Road. The bridge boasts an unusual design, with a pair of legs that straddle the highway and suspend the walkway with a series of four cables coming from the center of the joined struts. The struts come together at the top like the point of an arrowhead. Before the bridge, the trail passes plantings of ash trees, witch hazel, and pine; just after the bridge, Elsner Road provides access north to the Hickory Creek Bikeway East Branch.

Nearly 2.0 miles ahead, don't miss the turnoff for Hickory Creek Junction. After crossing the pedestrian bridge, the path leads you through a picnic area at Hickory Creek Forest Preserve and through its groves of hickory and oak. While following the West Branch of the Hickory Bikeway, you'll cross Hickory Creek twice on the 3.3-mile trip to the trail's endpoint. Once you've reached the one-room schoolhouse museum at the end of the trail, turn around and retrace your path back to the Old Plank Road Trail.

Much of the final 7.5 miles of trail runs through the community of New Lennox. After crossing Spencer Road, the Old Plank Road Trail intersects a 1.0-mile-long paved trail leading to the local high school. Farther ahead on the Old Plank Road Trail are the New Lennox Village Hall, library, and police department. Residential areas come and go. Many of the homeowners' backyards mingle with the path—no fences or shrubbery separates people's backyards from the path. Shortly after brushing against the backside of the sports stadium at Providence High School, you'll arrive at the end of the trail at Park Road.

Major Milepoints

11.2 Turn right for an out-and-back side trip through Hickory Creek Forest Preserve. Once you've reached the end of the trail within Hickory Creek, retrace your path back to the Old Plank Road Trail.

18.2 Back at the Old Plank Road Trail, turn right to continue on the path.

Local Information

- Chicago Southland Convention and Visitors Bureau, 2304 173rd St., Lansing 60438; (708) 895-8200 or (888) 895-8233; www.visitchicago southland.com

- Village of Frankfort, 432 West Nebraska St., Frankfort 60423; (815) 469-2177; www.villageoffrankfort.com

Local Events/Attractions

- Frankfort Country Market; www.frankfortcountrymarket.org. Sunday farmers' market operates along the trail.

- Joliet Area Historical Museum, 204 North Ottawa St., Joliet; (815) 723-5201; www.jolietmuseum.org. The museum provides a thorough introduction to the Joliet area.

- Joliet-area rail trails. Three other long rail trails can be accessed in Joliet. Get route advice for on-street connections at www.oprt.org/maps/westcon.html.

Restaurants

- Francesca's Fortunato, 40 Kansas St., Frankfort; (815) 464-1890; www .miafrancesca.com/restaurants/fortunato. Northern Italian fine dining; part of the popular chain of Francesca restaurants that began with the original Mia Francesca in Chicago's Lakeview neighborhood.

- Frankfort Deli and Meats, 11 South White St., Frankfort; (815) 469-1145. Offers sandwiches and homemade soups; located in the trolley barn just south of the trail.

14 PRAIRIE AND HEBRON TRAILS

As the Prairie Trail spans nearly the entire north–south length of McHenry County, it shoots past some of the most scenic spots within northeast Illinois. In between towns such as Crystal Lake, McHenry, Ringwood, and Richmond, the trail takes you through stunning natural areas at Sterne's Woods, Glacial Park, and Nippersink North Branch Conservation Area. After finishing the Prairie Trail, the route heads west for 6.7 miles along the Hebron Trail.

Activities:

Start: In Algonquin, located in southeast McHenry County

Length: 30.9 miles one-way

Surface: Asphalt between Algonquin and Ringwood; crushed gravel north of Ringwood

Wheelchair access: The trail is wheelchair accessible, but the entire route north of Ringwood is crushed gravel.

Difficulty: The trail is difficult due to the length and the long sections where trail users are fully exposed to wind and sun.

Restrooms: There are public restrooms at the Algonquin Road trail access, Main Street parking area in Crystal Lake, Hillside Road parking area, Petersen Park, Glacial Park parking area, and Nippersink North Branch parking area; portable toilet at Seaman's Road parking area in Hebron.

Maps: USGS Crystal Lake, McHenry, Hebron, and Richmond; *DeLorme: Illinois Atlas and Gazetteer:* Pages 19 and 20; Chicagoland Bicycle Map, Active Transportation Alliance, www.activetrans.org

Hazards: Watch for traffic at busy street crossings. Use caution while following the short on-street section in Crystal Lake. Keep your eyes peeled for bike trail signs that guide you through McHenry.

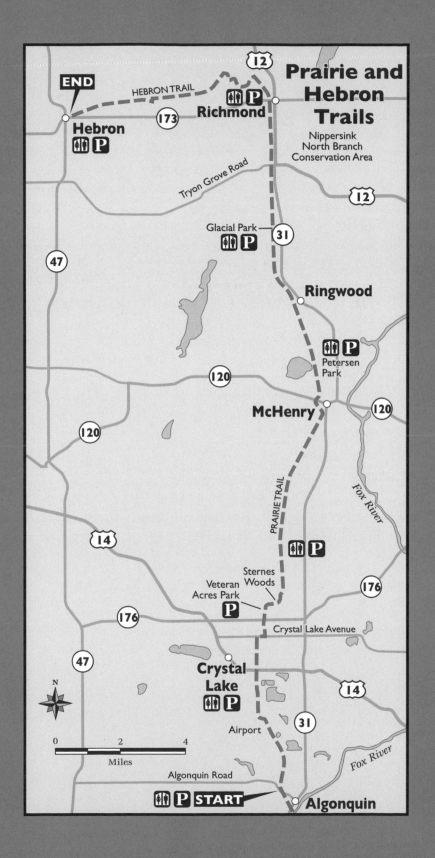

Prairie and Hebron Trails

Nippersink
North Branch
Conservation Area

END

HEBRON TRAIL

173

Richmond

Hebron

Tryon Grove Road

12

47

Glacial Park

31

Ringwood

Petersen
Park

120

120

McHenry

120

Fox River

PRAIRIE TRAIL

14

Sternes
Woods

Veteran
Acres Park

176

Crystal Lake Avenue

47

**Crystal
Lake**

14

Airport

31

N

0   2   4
Miles

Algonquin Road

START **Algonquin**

Fox River

Access and parking: From I-90 west of the Fox River, head north on IL 31. In Algonquin turn left onto Algonquin Road. Turn right onto Meyer Drive and then take a left into the Algonquin Road Trail access parking area. During winter, when this trailhead parking area is closed, use one of the parking areas listed below. UTM coordinates: 16T, 392651 E, 4669502 N

To reach the Main Street parking area in Crystal Lake, head north on IL 31. Turn left at James Rakow Road and then right onto Pyott Road. Turn left onto Berkshire Drive and then immediately right onto Eastgate Avenue.

To park at Veteran Acres Park, head north on IL 31. Turn left onto IL 176 and then right onto Lorraine Drive.

To access the trail at Petersen Park, head north on IL 31. North of McHenry turn left onto McCullom Lake Road and left again onto Petersen Park Road.

To park at the Glacial Park parking area, head north on IL 31 from McHenry. North of Ringwood turn left onto Harts Road. The parking area is on the right.

To park at the Nippersink North Branch Park parking area, head west on IL 173 from I-94. After passing Richmond, turn right onto Keystone Road. The parking area is on the right.

To park in Hebron, keep heading west on IL 173 and turn right onto Seaman Road. The parking area is on the right.

Transportation: The Crystal Lake Metra station on the Union Pacific/Northwest Line is less than 1 mile from the Veteran Acres parking area. The McHenry station on the same Metra line is just 1 block from the Prairie Trail in McHenry.

Rentals: The Bike Rack, 2930 Campton Hills Dr., St. Charles; (630) 584-6588

Contact: McHenry County Conservation District, 18410 US 14, Woodstock 60098; (815) 338-6223; www.mccdistrict.org

||||||||||||||||||||||||||||||||||||||||||||||||||||||||||||||||||||||||||||||||||||||||||||

S tarting from the south end of the Prairie Trail, the trip between Algonquin and Crystal Lake leads you through a landscape once dominated
by gravel mining operations. In many spots residential developments have
been built on top of the former gravel pits. But not all the gravel mining
is gone: As you pass the long conveyer belts and industrial buildings that
are part of an active gravel mining operation, look for a couple of small
creeks flowing on either side of the trail. On the way into Crystal Lake, the
path passes Lake of the Hills Airport and accompanies Main Street, which
is fairly busy.

Once you've left the bustle of Crystal Lake behind and completed the
1.0-mile-long on-street section of the route, Sternes Woods will take you
by surprise. The trail wriggles like a snake over steep hills and underneath
arthritic limbs of big oak trees. Even though this hilly section is brief, those
on bicycles should ride the steep, curving downhill sections with care—
wipeouts are frequent at the bottom of these steep hills. A tiny stream
runs through a small ravine on the right; benches along the path invite
you to sit down to admire the hills and fragrant groves of pine.

Continuing north toward McHenry, the trail shadows a set of railroad
tracks through a wide-open landscape that leans strongly toward agriculture. The gently rolling terrain contains patches of wetlands. After passing
through McHenry, the trail brushes against Petersen Park, which contains
a number of fine picnicking spots on the shore of McCullom Lake. If you're
a fan of small-town architecture from the early twentieth century, turn left
at Bernard Mill Road in Ringwood to visit an eye-catching post office just
1 block off the trail.

For those with an interest in learning the ways that glaciers sculpted
the landscape in northeastern Illinois, be sure to visit Glacial Park, which
you'll encounter at 19.2 miles. The park is chock-full of kames—essentially
mounds—which are formed when glacial meltwater deposits heaps of sand
and gravel in depressions in the ice or at the edge of the glacier. The park's
bog and marshes also offer a visual link to the area's geologic past. These
wetlands began to take shape when large chunks of ice detached from a
receding glacier: As ice melted, a pond formed in the depression; eventu-

ally vegetation overtook the pond. More than 5 miles of hiking trails allow you to explore the kames, dry and wet prairie, woodland, and a creek.

Between Glacial Park and Richmond, the gently rolling terrain surrounding the trail contains swaths of attractive wetland. In some spots, ravines rise up on the sides of the trail, but most often you're granted long views of the surrounding landscape. On the way into Richmond, duck under a one-hundred-year-old wooden railroad bridge. The main drag in Richmond is lined with a collection of buildings from the turn of the twentieth century containing a small assortment of shops focused on items such as jewelry, handmade crafts, and antiques. Further explorations of the the village will reveal attractively restored Victorian homes and several *Sears Catalog* homes.

After Richmond you'll cross the North Branch of Nippersink Creek and then encounter more sprawling wetlands. One-third mile before the end of the Prairie Trail, turn left onto the crushed gravel path that leads into Nippersink North Branch Conservation Area. This winding trail runs through many acres of rolling terrain covered with restored prairie and

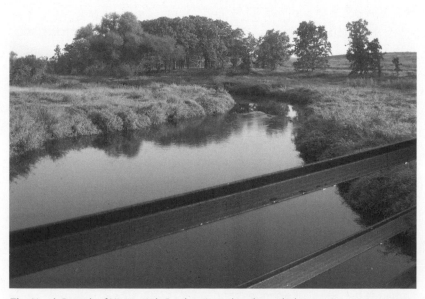

The North Branch of Nippersink Creek as it snakes through the prairie.

stands of hardwood. You'll cross the Nippersink North Branch again as it winds through the prairie.

The first mile or so on the Hebron Trail is dominated by cropland with patches of intermittent woodland alongside the trail. After a very short on-street section, you'll know you're approaching wetlands when you hear the uneven honking of sandhill cranes, a large gray bird that is a rare sight in Illinois. Streets Lake offers a trailside viewing platform where you can survey a collection of muskrat lodges, big stands of sedge grasses and cattails, and rafts of waterbirds. The trail ends at the edge of the tiny town of Hebron.

Major Milepoints

5.1 Start the 0.8-mile-long on-street section by turning right onto Crystal Lake Road. This road is busy; take the sidewalk on the left side of the road if necessary.

5.4 Turn left onto East Street.

5.7 Turn right onto Glenn Avenue.

5.9 Turn right onto Terra Cotta Avenue.

6.0 Turn left onto Lorraine Drive.

6.1 Resume the Prairie Trail from the parking area.

24.1 Leave the Prairie Trail and start the Hebron Trail by turning left into Nippersink North Branch Conservation Area.

Local Information

- Chicago Convention and Tourism Bureau, 2301 South Lake Shore Dr., Chicago 60616; (312) 567-8500; www.choosechicago.com

- Lake County Convention and Visitors Bureau, 5455 West Grand Ave., Suite 302, Gurnee 60031; (847) 662-2700; www.lakecounty.org

- McHenry County Convention and Visitors Bureau, 5435 Bull Valley Rd., Suite 324-B, McHenry 60050; (815) 363-6177; www.visitmchenry county.com

Local Events/Attractions

- Lake Geneva is a charming—if somewhat touristy—town situated on a beautiful lake just across the Wisconsin border about 10 miles north of the trail. For information contact the Walworth County Visitors Bureau, 9 West Walworth St., P.O. Box 1015, Elkhorn, Wisconsin 53121; (262) 723-3980; www.visitwalworthcounty.com.

- North Wall, 824 South Main St., Suite 106, Crystal Lake; (815) 356-6855; www.climbnorthwall.com. An indoor climbing facility alongside the trail in Crystal Lake.

- Royal Oak Orchard, 15908 Hebron Rd., Harvard; (815) 648-4141; www.royaloakfarmorchard.com. In addition to the orchard, there's a bakery, a gift shop, and a restaurant; located west of Hebron.

- Woodstock claims one of the most attractive town squares in all Illinois; plenty of shopping and eating opportunities. For information contact the City of Woodstock, 121 West Calhoun St., Woodstock; (815) 338-4300; www.woodstock-il.com.

Restaurants

- Doyle's Pub and Eatery, 5604 Mill St., Richmond; (815) 678-3623; http://doylespubrocks.com. Located in the former mill in Richmond.

- JW Plateks Restaurant and Brewery, 8609 US 12, Richmond; (815) 678-4078; www.plateks.com. Serves bar food and microbrews.

- Wild Orchid Thai Bistro, 6000 Northwest Hwy, Crystal Lake; (815) 788-0633; www.wildorchidthaibistro.com. Located across Main Street from the trail in Crystal Lake.

Accommodations

- Super 8 Motel, 577 Crystal Point Rd., Crystal Lake; (815) 788-8888. Clean and affordable; located just 1 block off the trail.

15 ROBERT MCCLORY TRAIL

As this route runs from Fort Sheridan to the south edge of Kenosha, Wisconsin, you'll see the nation's largest Navy training center, parks such as Lyons Woods Forest Preserve, and the far north shore towns of North Chicago, Waukegan, and Zion.

Activities:

Start: The north parking lot at the Fort Sheridan Metra station, located at Old Elm and Sheridan Roads

Length: 22.8 miles one-way

Surface: Crushed gravel with occasional paved sections

Wheelchair access: The trail is wheelchair accessible.

Difficulty: Be ready for an easy-to-medium level of difficulty due to the length and the stretches where trail users are fully exposed to the elements.

Restrooms: There are public restrooms and water at the Fort Sheridan, Lake Bluff, and Great Lakes Metra stations; Lyons Woods Forest Preserve (follow signs through the forest preserve for about 1 mile to the main entrance near the corner of Blanchard and Sheridan Roads); and Anderson Park (at the northern end of the trail in Kenosha).

Maps: USGS Highland Park, Kenosha, Waukegan, and Zion; *DeLorme: Illinois Atlas and Gazetteer:* Page 21; Chicagoland Bicycle Map, Active Transportation Alliance, www.activetrans.org

Hazards: Watch for cars pulling in and out of parking spaces as the trail cuts through Metra station parking lots. The trail crosses busy roads in a number of places.

Access and parking: From I-94 north of Chicago, head north on US 41 (the Skokie Highway). Turn right onto Old Elm Road. Park on the north side of Old Elm Road at the Fort Sheridan Metra station. (Bring quarters—you may have to feed the meters.) Catch the trail as it heads north from the parking lot. UTM coordinates: 16T, 432212 E, 4674134 N

To park at the Lake Bluff station, take US 41 north from I-94. Turn right onto IL 176/Rockland Road. Turn left onto Sheridan Road and park in the station on the left.

In North Chicago and Waukegan, on-street parking options are frequently available alongside the trail. Follow Sheridan Road north and then take any major street west to reach the trail.

To park at Lyons Woods Forest Preserve, exit from I-94 on IL 120 heading east. Turn left onto Sheridan Road/IL 137 and look for the entrance to Lyon Woods on the left.

To park at Anderson Park, located at the northern end of the trail, take I-94 north into Wisconsin. Exit at 104th Street and head east. Turn left at 39th Avenue and then right onto 89th Street. Turn left onto 30th Avenue and then right onto 87th Place. Park in the lot between the high school and Anderson Park. Catch the trail heading south from the intersection of 30th Avenue and 89th Street.

Transportation: Take a Union Pacific District North Metra train to the Fort Sheridan station. The Union Pacific North Line runs parallel to this entire route. The first 7.0 miles of the trail run next to four Metra stations. Continuing north, another five Metra stations are within 1 to 2 miles east of the trail.

Rentals: T. L. Fritts Sporting Goods, 560 Chestnut St., Winnetka; (847) 446-6694

Contact: Kenosha County Division of Parks manages the Kenosha County Bike Trail; 19600 75th St., Bristol, WI 53104; (262) 857-1869

Lake County Division of Transportation manages the Robert McClory Trail; 600 West Winchester Rd., Libertyville 60048; (847) 377-7400; www .lakecountyil.gov/transportation

Robert McClory Trail

Kenosha

END

(31)

(165)

(32)

KENOSHA COUTY TRAIL

WISCONSIN
ILLINOIS

(131)

(173)

Zion
29th Street

ROBERT MCCLORY TRAIL

Lyons Woods
Forest Preserve

(41)

Waukegan
P

(120)

10th
Street

North Chicago

Great Lakes
Naval Training Center

Metra Station

(137)

(94)

(131)

Metra Station

(176)

NORTH SHORE
BIKE PATH

**Lake
Bluff**

LAKE
MICHIGAN

N

0   2   4
Miles

(41)

McKinley Road

ROBERT MCCLORY TRAIL

**Lake
Forest**

Old Elm
Road
Metra Station

START

Fort Sheridan

||||||||||||||||||||||||||||||||||||||||||||||||||||||||||||||||||||||||||||||||||||||

The first section of this trail is alternately wooded and grassy as the route parallels train tracks on one side and Sheridan Road on the other. After about 1.0 mile, you'll encounter a stately building that once housed Barat College. The college, which first opened in 1858 as a Catholic girls' school, was shuttered in 2005 and sold to a condominium developer.

Peeking through the trees on the right is Lake Forest High School, where the 1980 film *Ordinary People* was filmed. The school claims a handful of alumni involved in creative pursuits, such as musician Andrew Bird, writer Dave Eggers, and actor Vince Vaughn.

Before arriving at the Lake Bluff Metra station, you'll see the North Shore Bike Path branching to the left alongside IL 176/Rockland Road. The North Shore Bike Path intersects the Des Plaines River Trail about 4.0 miles to the west.

Lake Bluff was one of the communities represented by the trail's namesake, Robert McClory, a Republican member of the U.S. House of Representatives for twenty years. The national spotlight shone on McClory when he served on the House Judiciary Committee and became a key figure in the impeachment proceedings against President Richard Nixon.

Next up along the trail is the Great Lakes Naval Training Center, the largest military facility in Illinois and the largest Navy training center in the nation. The eighty-year-old naval base has more than 1,000 buildings throughout 1,600 acres. In the Great Lakes Metra station that sits alongside the trail, you'll likely see some train passengers sporting brush cuts and bright white sailor hats.

As the route follows a perfectly straight course through North Chicago, the trailside scenery offers a mix of industrial developments and working-class neighborhoods. Vegetable gardens planted alongside the trail give a dash of vitality to the right-of-way that is mostly open, grassy, and treeless. Continuing through North Chicago and entering Waukegan reveals more of the bustling industry for which these North Shore cities are known.

As the pockets of industry retreat, suburban residential neighborhoods take over and several community parks appear alongside the trail.

A few parks are situated near the shiny new Lake County Family YMCA in Waukegan. At about 13.0 miles into the trail, a sign marks the entrance to Lyons Woods Forest Preserve, which contains 3.0 miles of trails that wind through savanna, oak woodland, and restored prairie.

North of Lyons Woods, residential neighborhoods come and go; small parks offer a respite from the trail. The path gets lush and leafy before reaching Zion and then becomes open and grassy again once you've entered the city.

In Zion a few trails and bike lanes will allow you to explore this community founded in 1890 by Scottish faith healer John Alexander Dowie. The church owned the town's commercial establishments and forbade liquor, playing cards, pork, clams, and tan shoes, among other proscribed items. The community collapsed financially in 1939, and private individuals began acquiring the property that belonged to the church.

After entering the Badger State at Russell Road, all that remains is 3.5 miles to the trail's northern terminus in Kenosha, Wisconsin. As you travel these final few miles—now along the Kenosha County Bike Trail—the greenery becomes more prominent and housing developments fade. The trail ends at 89th Street, across the road from a patchwork of soccer fields at Anderson Park.

Local Information

- Kenosha Area Convention and Visitors Bureau, 812 56th St., Kenosha, Wisconsin 53140; (262) 654-7307; www.kenoshacvb.com

- Lake County Convention and Visitors Bureau, 5455 West Grand Ave., Suite 302; Gurnee 60031; (847) 662-2700; www.lakecounty.org

- Lake County Forest Preserve District, 2000 North Milwaukee Ave., Libertyville 60048; (847) 367-6640; www.lcfpd.org

- Zion Park District operates 4.0 miles of trails and a few miles of bike lanes; 2400 Dowie Memorial Dr., Zion 60099; (847) 746-5500; www.zionparkdistrict.com

Local Events/Attractions

- Illinois Beach State Park, 701 North Point Dr., Winthrop Harbor; (847) 746-2845; http://dnr.state.il.us/lands/landmgt/parks/r2/ilbeach.htm.

Popular among local beachgoers; quieter stretches of beach can be found south of the conference center.

- Green Bay Trail, on the south side of Highland Park. Catch the Green Bay Trail heading south through Chicago's swankiest North Shore suburbs of Wilmette, Kenilworth, Winnetka, Glencoe, and Highland Park.

- Shiloh House, 1300 Shiloh Blvd., Zion; (847) 746-2427; www.zionhs .com. Elegant 25-room mansion built by Zion's founder, John Alexander Dowie; open for tours on weekends.

Restaurants
- The Silo, 625 Rockland Rd., Lake Bluff; (847) 234-6660; www.silopizza .com. Known for its deep-dish pizza.

- Bluffington's Cafe, 113 East Scranton Ave., Lake Bluff; (847) 295-3344. Good sandwiches and salads.

Accommodations
- Ravinia Guest House, 264 Oakland Dr., Highland Park; (847) 433-3140. English Colonial–style B&B within walking distance of Ravinia Park.

- Sunset Motel, 511 Rockland Rd., Lake Bluff; (847) 234-4669; www.sunsetmotelroute41.com. Affordable motel accessible from the North Shore Trail.

16 SALT CREEK TRAIL

The Salt Creek Trail is a fun, winding route that passes through a series of forest preserves straddling Cook and DuPage Counties. While much of the route closely follows the arboreal banks of Salt Creek, you'll frequently meander through the adjoining floodplain among tangles of deadfall and stands of shrubs. The final leg of the route introduces you to the islands, high banks, and dense woodlands of Fullersburg Forest Preserve, one of the most eye-catching parks in DuPage County.

Activities:

Start: Brookfield Woods Forest Preserve on 31st Street in Brookfield

Length: 10.9 miles one-way

Surface: Asphalt on the Salt Creek Trail and the bike path along York Road; crushed gravel on the trail through Fullersburg Woods

Wheelchair access: The trail is wheelchair accessible.

Difficulty: Despite the occasionally rolling terrain, the trail is mostly easy.

Restrooms: There are public restrooms at the Brookfield Woods parking area (portable toilets), 26th Street Woods, Brezina Woods, Bemis Woods North, and near the Fullersburg Forest Preserve Visitor Center (water).

Maps: USGS Berwyn and Hinsdale; *DeLorme: Illinois Atlas and Gazetteer:* Page 29

Hazards: This route crosses five major streets. Use caution while crossing.

Access and parking: Driving from Chicago, take I-290 to IL 171 (First Avenue). Head south on IL 171 and then turn right onto 31st Street. Look for Brookfield Woods Forest Preserve on the right. Park at the far back of the lot, where the trail starts. UTM coordinates: 16T, 430147 E, 4631718 N

To park at Brezina Woods Forest Preserve, take I-290 from Chicago to US 12 (Mannheim Road). Follow US 12 south. The entrance to the forest preserve is on the left. The trail crosses the park road just before the parking area.

To park at Fullersburg Forest Preserve, take I-290 west from Chicago to I-88. Follow I-88 until reaching IL 83 (Kingery Highway). Follow IL 83 south. Turn left onto 31st Street and then right onto Spring Road. Turn left at the sign for Fullersburg Park.

Transportation: Take the BNSF Metra line to the Brookfield station. From the station follow Prairie Avenue north for about 1 mile to 31st Street. At 31st Street turn right, cross Salt Creek, and pick up the trail at the back parking area of Brookfield Woods.

Rentals: The Wheel Thing, 15 South La Grange Rd., La Grange; (708) 352-3822

Contact: Forest Preserve District of Cook County, 536 North Harlem Ave., River Forest 60305; (800) 870-3666; www.fpdcc.com

DuPage County Forest Preserve District, 3S580 Naperville Rd., Wheaton 60189; (630) 933-7200; www.dupageforest.com

||||||||||||||||||||||||||||||||||||||||||||||||||||||||||||||||||||||||||||||||||

For most of its 50-mile-long route, Salt Creek winds through a series of densely populated western Chicago suburbs. The section of the creek that you'll see on the Salt Creek Trail, however, flows through a handful of county-operated forest preserves that feature gently rolling topography, thick bottomland woods, and plenty of spots to sit and enjoy the meandering creek.

As the story goes, Salt Creek got its name when a nineteenth-century farmer's wagon was stuck in the creek while hauling a barrel of salt. Leaving the wagon in the creek overnight, the farmer returned the next morning and found the salt had dissolved. Even though early maps labeled the waterway the Little Des Plaines River, the name Salt Creek eventually took hold.

Starting at the east end of the Salt Creek Trail in Brookfield Woods, the path takes you on a curving route through a small savanna before meeting up with Salt Creek. When you reach the creek, you'll pass over several large concrete bank-side openings that channel floodwaters east to the Des Plaines River. As you trace the riverbank, you'll notice that this 30-foot-wide creek occupies a shallow ravine that is wide in some places, narrow in others. After the first road crossing (Maple Avenue), you'll see one of Salt Creek's only major tributaries, Addison Creek, merging from the north.

Now on the south side of the creek, the trail wiggles back and forth between the creekbank and the nearby floodplain strewn with woody vegetation. As your view of the creek comes and goes, it's usually easy to determine the proximity of the water. Closer to the creek, the landscape tends to undulate gently. Away from the creek, the landscape is flat bottomland dense with shrubs, deadfall, and small trees. Of course you'll have better views of the creek and the surrounding landscape when the trees are bare.

After an awkward crossing of La Grange Road, the trail shoots straight alongside the creek and passes by a riffled shallow spot where the creekbed is bisected by a set of old bridge supports made from limestone blocks. These old bridge supports tend to collect fallen trees swept along by floodwaters. After squeezing between a string of houses on the right and the creek on the left, you'll reach a small, 1-foot-high dam that provides one of many pleasant spots along the trail to sit and enjoy the creek's swirling eddies.

Between 31st Street and Wolf Road, the trail mounts a few small bluffs overlooking bends in the creek. From these small bluffs, look for the sharp turns where this portion of the creek is in the process of getting cut off from the rest. (A couple of small islands have been created by the creek's changing course.) The final leg of the Salt Creek Trail cuts through Bemis Woods Forest Preserve, where you'll see a couple of tiny streams that feed into Salt Creek and a trailside golf course before passing under I-394.

At Fullersburg Forest Preserve, Salt Creek meanders beneath more small bluffs and around more islands on its way to the historic watermill at the south tip of the park. While following the creek through the park, you'll pass a series of impressive stone picnic shelters with benches and a fireplace. Many of the Fullersburg picnic shelters, as well as the log visitor center and the Graue Mill, were built or restored by the Civilian Conservation Corps, which had a camp here in the 1930s.

For anyone with an interest in local history, the Graue Mill, originally built in 1852, is well worth a visit. For a small admission fee, a white-aproned miller will explain the 15,000-year-old practice of grinding grain and how it was done at the mill. In the basement you'll learn that the mill served as a stop on the Underground Railroad. Along with other local stops in Plainfield, Aurora, Sugar Grove, Joliet, and Hinsdale, the Graue Mill was a part of

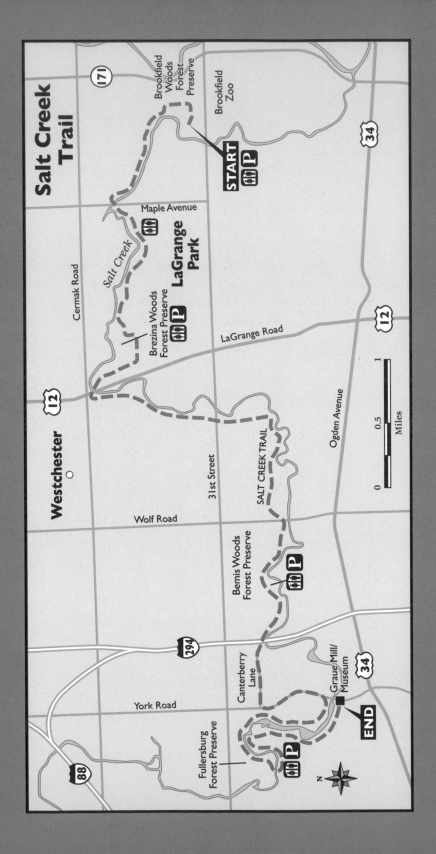

Salt Creek Trail

Westchester

LaGrange Park

Brookfield Woods Forest Preserve

Brookfield Zoo

START

Maple Avenue

Salt Creek

Brezina Woods Forest Preserve

Cermak Road

LaGrange Road

31st Street

Wolf Road

SALT CREEK TRAIL

Ogden Avenue

Bemis Woods Forest Preserve

Canterberry Lane

York Road

Fullersburg Forest Preserve

Graue Mill/Museum

END

171

34

12

12

294

88

34

Miles

0   0.5   1

N

the clandestine network of places where escaped slaves could rest and be fed on their way to Chicago and then to Canada. On the second and third floors of the mill is a collection of artifacts from 1850 to 1890, including room settings, farm implements, and a re-created general store.

Major Milepoints

7.0 After passing under I-394, head to the right through a small nature sanctuary to Canterberry Lane. Go left on Canterberry Lane.

7.5 Turn left onto York Road. Follow the bike path on the right side of the road. The bike path soon switches to the other side of the road.

8.1 Turn right before crossing Salt Creek on the crushed gravel path into Fullersburg Forest Preserve.

9.5 In Fullersburg cross the Salt Creek on the second bridge to the left. Stay to the left to reach the visitor center.

Local Information

• Chicago Convention and Tourism Bureau, 2301 South Lake Shore Dr., Chicago 60616; (312) 567-8500; www.choosechicago.com

• DuPage County Convention and Visitors Bureau, 915 Harger Rd., Suite 240, Oak Brook 60523; (630) 575-8070; www.dupagecvb.com

The Salt Creek Trail provides a good helping of natural beauty close to downtown Chicago.

Local Events/Attractions

- Brookfield Zoo, First Avenue and 31st Street, Brookfield; (708) 485-2200; www.brookfieldzoo.org. One of the largest zoos in the world; more than 2,500 animals.

- Fullersburg Forest Preserve Visitor Center, 3609 Spring Rd., Oak Brook; (630) 850-8110; www.dupageforest.com. The visitor center has on display a 13,000-year-old wooly mammoth skeleton uncovered locally in 1977. If visiting in April or May, ask for a wildflower guide.

- Graue Mill, at the corner of York and Spring Roads, Fullersburg Forest Preserve; (630) 655-2090. A National Historic Landmark, now a living-history museum.

- Riverside Historic District. Enjoy winding streets, many parks, and attractive historic neighborhoods and public buildings in this community designed by Frederick Law Olmstead. Start your visit at the Riverside Historical Museum; 10 Pine Ave., Riverside; (708) 447-2574.

Restaurants

- Little Bohemian Restaurant, 25 East Burlington St., Riverside; (708) 442-1251. Hearty affordable fare of pierogi, Cornish hen, and potato pancakes.

- Grumpy's Coffee and Ice Cream, 35 East Burlington, Riverside; (708) 443-5603. A lovely, cluttered atmosphere.

- York Tavern, 3702 York Rd., Oak Brook; (630) 323-5090. Reliable spot for burgers and beer; located next to Fullersburg Forest Preserve.

- Benjarong Thai Restaurant, 2138 Mannheim Rd., Westchester; (708) 449-9291; http://benjarong.us. Well-regarded Thai restaurant located yards from the trail near the La Grange Road crossing.

Accommodations

- Colony Motel, 9232 West Ogden Ave.; Brookfield; (708) 485-0300; www.colonymotelbrookfield.com. Basic, very affordable rooms.

- Under the Gingko Tree Bed and Breakfast, 300 North Kenilworth Ave., Oak Park; (708) 524-3237; www.undertheginkgotreebb.com. Private baths; affordable prices.

17 VIRGIL GILMAN TRAIL

This trail offers a perfect chance to get to know Aurora and its nearby residential and rural environs. West of the city, the trail repeatedly crosses Blackberry Creek and occasionally runs alongside its wooded banks. After crossing a new 100-yard-long trestle bridge over IL 56, the trail bobs and weaves through stunning woodland at Bliss Woods Forest Preserve.

Activities:

Start: The Hill Avenue parking area east of Aurora

Length: 11.3 miles one-way, with an option for extending the trip

Surface: Asphalt

Wheelchair access: The trail is wheelchair accessible, but there is no sidewalk for a portion of the on-street section. This is also where there's a bit of heavy industry and truck traffic.

Difficulty: The trail is easy.

Restrooms: There are public restrooms at Copley Park (water), the Orchard Road parking area, and Bliss Woods Forest Preserve (water; follow the park road left after crossing Bliss Road).

Maps: USGS Aurora South and Sugar Grove; *DeLorme: Illinois Atlas and Gazetteer:* Pages 27 and 28; Chicagoland Bicycle Map, Active Transportation Alliance, www.activetrans.org

Hazards: Watch for traffic—especially trucks—while following the brief on-street section.

Access and parking: Head south on IL 31 from I-88. In downtown Aurora turn left onto Galena Boulevard. Continue ahead on Galena Boulevard as the street curves right and becomes Hill Avenue. Look for the parking area on the right. UTM coordinates: 16T, 393130 E, 4619671 N

To park at Copley Park, head south on IL 31 (Lake Street) from I-88. After passing Aurora's central downtown area, look for the park on the right.

To park at the Blackberry Farm parking area, head south on Orchard Road from I-88. Turn right onto Galena Boulevard and then left onto Barnes Road. There's a trailhead parking area on the right.

To park at the Merrill Road parking area at the west end of the trail, take I-88 west from Aurora. Exit at IL 56 and follow IL 56 to IL 47. Take IL 47 north to Bliss Road. Turn right onto Bliss Road and then left onto Merrill Road. Look for the parking area on the left.

Transportation: The BNSF Metra line stops in Aurora a mile or so north of the trail.

Rentals: Mill Race Cyclery, 11 East State St., Geneva; (630) 232-2833

Contact: Fox Valley Park District, 712 South River St., Aurora 60506; (630) 897-0516; www.foxvalleyparkdistrict.org

The first few miles of this trail offer an introduction to the modest leafy neighborhoods on the east side of Aurora. After an initial stretch where the trail traces an embankment that rises about 6 feet above the surrounding cropland and bottomland woods, residential neighborhoods take over. At 2.7 miles the trail crosses the Fox River on an old latticed train bridge. Before taking in fine views of the Fox from the high bridge, you may consider a side trip south on the 4.6-mile riverbank trail to the town of Oswego.

On the way to Oswego, this south section of the Fox River Trail passes through several parks, the best of which is a long, thin island in the river. While the river along this stretch is persistently eye-catching, the atmosphere is not terribly peaceful because the trail closely follows IL 25. Oswego contains a pleasant riverside park, as well as good dining options close to the trail.

Continuing west along the Virgil Gilman Trail, you'll duck under several bridges and skirt the edge of Copley Park. After passing the park, watch for trucks on Rathbone Street as the trail drops you off in the middle of a not-too-welcoming industrial area for a short on-street stretch.

The beginning of the next section of the trail is marked by a handsome limestone sign and concrete benches. As the trail parallels a swath of bottomland woods, you'll see occasional small ponds, some blanketed with algae. You'll also catch glimpses of the Aurora Country Club through the trees on the right. After crossing Orchard Road, look for waterbirds as the trail passes a lake and a couple more ponds. If you enjoy exploring grassland, turn left onto the trail near the ponds for a quick loop through the adjoining prairie and savanna.

After crossing Blackberry Creek on an old steel bridge, you'll arrive at Blackberry Farm Historic Village, a county park that offers kiddy rides, an arboretum, and several museum exhibits. One exhibit displays forty carriages, sleighs, and vintage commercial vehicles. Another exhibit contains a display of eleven late Victorian-era stores, including a music shop, pharmacy, general store, photography shop, and toy store. The water park across the street is another popular stop for local families.

A mile or so west of Blackberry Farm, the ramp of a steel bridge spanning IL 56 gradually rises from the prairie in front of you. The 100-yard-long powder-blue trestle bridge recently replaced a flood-prone tunnel that went under the highway (the tunnel is still visible south of the bridge).

After crossing IL 56, the trail crosses Blackberry Creek again and then runs beside the creek as it cuts a straight course northwest. At Bliss Woods Forest Preserve, the path runs through a lovely swath of state-protected woodland thick with sugar maple and basswood trees. In early spring you'll see flowers such as hepatica, bloodroot, and rue anemone. A sprinkling of houses appear on the right; on the left is a hill called an esker—a winding ridge of gravel deposited by a subglacial river. Crossing Bliss Road takes you into a grove of bottomland woods largely comprised of oak and maple.

Just before crossing Blackberry Creek one last time, a spur trail on the right leads to a trailhead parking area. The final section of the Virgil Gilman Trail takes you through a large prairie on the campus of Waubonsee Community College. The college operates several campuses in the area, but this is the main one, open since 1967. If you feel like exploring the campus, you'll find a pleasant little pond behind the first set of buildings.

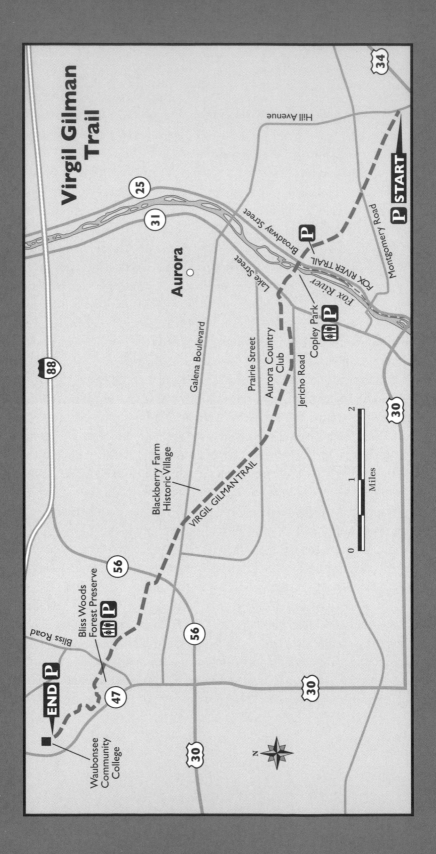

Major Milepoints

3.4   Start brief on-street section by turning right onto Rathbone Street.

3.8   Turn left onto Terry Avenue.

3.9   Pick up the trail on the right.

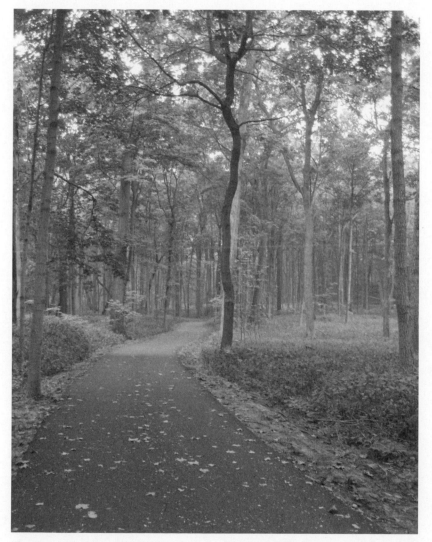

The west end of the Virgil Gilman Trail winds through enchanting woodland at Bliss Woods Forest Preserve.

Local Information

- Aurora Area Convention and Visitors Bureau, 43 West Galena Blvd., Aurora 60506; (630) 897-5581; www.enjoyaurora.com

- Kane County Forest Preserve District, 719 South Batavia Ave. G, Geneva 60134; (630) 232-5980; www.kaneforest.com

Local Events/Attractions

- Aurora Regional Fire Museum, 53 North Broadway, Aurora; (630) 892-1572; www.auroraregionalfiremuseum.org. Vintage firefighting equipment; located in downtown Aurora, across the street from the trailhead for the Aurora Branch of the Prairie Path.

- Blackberry Farm, 100 South Barnes Rd., Aurora; (630) 892-1550; www.foxvalleyparkdistrict.org/?q=node/2

Restaurants

- La Quinta de Los Reyes, 36 East New York St., Aurora; (630) 859-4000; http:// laquintadelosreyesaurora.com. Live music and courtyard area in downtown Aurora.

- Orchard Valley Restaurant, 2411 West Illinois Ave., Aurora; (630) 907-0600; http://foxvalleyparkdistrict.org/?q=node/190. American food; located at a public golf course, fairly close to the trail.

Accommodations

- Comfort Suites, 111 North Broadway Ave., Aurora; (630) 896-2800. Located in downtown Aurora, 1 block from the Hollywood Casino.

18 WAUPONSEE GLACIAL TRAIL

One of the newest rail trails in the state, the Wauponsee Glacial Trail runs from Joliet to the Kankakee River, mostly through wide-open farmland. After passing the town of Manhattan, the trail skirts the eastern edge of the sprawling Midewin National Tallgrass Prairie, formerly the largest ammunition-production plant in the world. The trail ends at the Kankakee River, where you'll enjoy long views from a former railroad bridge.

Activities:

Start: On the south side of Joliet on Rowell Road

Length: 22.3 miles one-way

Surface: Paved surface for first several miles; crushed gravel for the remainder

Wheelchair access: The trail is wheelchair accessible.

Difficulty: The trail borders on the difficult category because of the lack of trail amenities and lack of protection from the wind and sun.

Restrooms: There are public restrooms and water at Sugar River Forest Preserve and the trail parking area in Manhattan.

Maps: USGS Bonfield, Elwood, Joliet, and Symerton; *DeLorme: Illinois Atlas and Gazetteer:* Pages 28 and 36

Hazards: Bring plenty of water; there is no drinking water available on the trail south of Manhattan.

Access and parking: From I-80 go south on Briggs Street (exit 134). Immediately turn right onto New Lenox Road and right again onto Rowell Avenue. Look for the beginning of the trail on the left. There is no parking lot at the trailhead—you must park on the road's ample shoulder. (The closest access spot with off-street parking is the Sugar Creek Forest Preserve—see below.) UTM coordinates: 16T, 411360 E, 4595923 N

To catch the trail at Sugar Creek Forest Preserve, take Briggs Street (exit 134) south from I-80. Continue ahead as Briggs Street merges with US 52. Turn right onto Laraway Road; the entrance to the forest preserve is on the right.

To park at the Manhattan Road parking area in Manhattan, continue south on US 52 and then right onto Manhattan Road. The trail parking area is on the left.

To reach the parking area in Symerton, head south on I-55. Exit east on River Road (exit 241). Turn right onto IL 53 and then left onto Peotone Road. Turn left onto Symerton Road and right onto Commercial Street. Look for the trail parking area 2 blocks ahead.

To park at the south end of the trail, take IL 53 south to IL 102. Turn left onto IL 102 in Wilmington. Turn right onto Rivals Road. Park on the side of the road near the trail crossing.

Transportation: Metra's Southwest Service goes to Manhattan, but service is very limited. The Rock Island District and Heritage Corridor Metra lines serve Joliet. Both train lines are located a few miles north of the trailhead.

Rentals: The Wheel Thing, 15 South La Grange Rd., La Grange; (708) 352-3822

Contact: Will County Forest Preserve District, 17540 West Laraway Rd., Joliet 60433; (815) 727-8700; www.fpdwc.org

‖‖‖

This trail is named for a glacial lake that covered much of the local terrain some 16,000 years ago. Lake Wauponsee reached a depth of 100 feet but lasted for a relatively short period of time before draining away into the Illinois River Valley. The glacial lake takes its name from Chief Waubonsee, an influential Potawatomi chief who lived near Aurora in the early 1800s.

Leafy residential neighborhoods and a dash of light industry show up on the first few miles of the trail. At Mill Street you'll pass the manufacturing facility and retail store for the Mancuso Cheese Company, local purveyors of mozzarella and ricotta since 1907. After crossing Sugar Creek, the trail briefly accompanies the creek through adjoining bottomland woods.

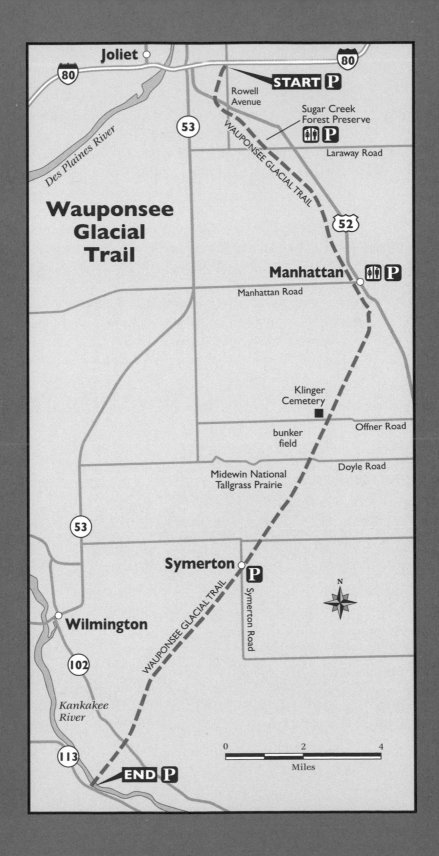

Wauponsee Glacial Trail

Joliet

START P

Rowell Avenue

Sugar Creek Forest Preserve

Laraway Road

Des Plaines River

Manhattan

Manhattan Road

Klinger Cemetery

bunker field

Offner Road

Doyle Road

Midewin National Tallgrass Prairie

WAUPONSEE GLACIAL TRAIL

Symerton P

Symerton Road

Wilmington

Kankakee River

N

END P

0   2   4
Miles

The Will County Forest Preserve administration building sits alongside the trail at Sugar Creek Forest Preserve. This environmentally friendly structure was built using recycled materials and has solar energy panels mounted on the roof. Southwest of the Sugar Creek Preserve, the 75,000-seat Chicagoland Speedway rises from the cropland. Across the road from the speedway is another smaller car racing venue, the Route 66 Raceway, with seating for around 30,000.

With a few exceptions, farmland dominates the landscape for the remainder of the trail. Farmhouses, silos, and barns often appear in the distance. Patches of trees sometimes offer shade, and small creeks regularly meander across the trail, flowing from one field to another. New housing developments spring up as you enter the town of Manhattan. The trail angles southwest as you leave Manhattan and pass the local commuter train station and a cluster of oil storage tanks.

South of Hoff Road, the Wauponsee Trail intersects the Bailey Bridge Trail at the edge of the Midewin National Tallgrass Prairie. Formerly the largest ammunition-production plant in the world, Midewin is now the biggest—

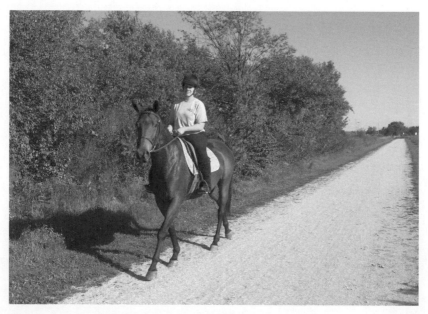

The rural setting along the Wauponsee Trail attracts equestrians.

and perhaps the most tranquil—piece of protected land in northeastern Illinois. The park contains woodland, savanna, prairie, and many remnants of the former arsenal, but mostly it's composed of farmland that is slowly being converted back to prairie and woodland. Today Midewin encompasses more than 15,000 acres. After the U.S. Army finishes its cleanup efforts, the park will add another 4,000 acres and eventually some 40 miles of trails. About 7,200 acres containing nearly 15 miles of trails are now open to the public. (A 5.2-mile hike at Midewin is described in my book *60 Hikes within 60 Miles: Chicago*, published by Menasha Ridge Press.)

At its peak, the Joliet Arsenal employed some 14,000 people and produced 5.5 million tons of TNT a week. The arsenal—in operation from World War II through the Korean and Vietnam Wars—was shut down in 1975, leaving some 1,300 structures, including 392 concrete bunkers that were used to store the TNT.

If you take a quick side trip on the Bailey Bridge Trail, you'll immediately pass a small pioneer cemetery established 1877 by a local homesteader from Pennsylvania. Just after the cemetery you'll enter a swath of land containing many dozens of the earth-covered bunkers designed to withstand explosive blasts and conceal the location of the TNT in case of an enemy attack.

Before and after the village of Symerton, shade trees thin out along the trail and a carpet of cropland unrolls for miles in every direction. Before reaching Ballou Road, the path crosses a small stream and passes through a patch of woodland that offers a needed break from the yawning open space. More woodland develops as the trail hops over Forked Creek and crosses IL 102. Just before reaching the Kankakee River, you'll brush against a sizable wetland on the right. As you cross the Kankakee River on a rehabbed railroad bridge, breathtaking views of the wide river and its wooded banks open up on each side. The trail ends on the south bank of the Kankakee River.

Local Information
- Chicago Southland Convention and Visitors Bureau, 2304 173rd St., Lansing 60438; (708) 895-8200 or (888) 895-8233; www.visitchicago southland.com

- Joliet Visitors Bureau, 30 North Bluff St., Joliet 60435; (815) 723-9045; www.visitjoliet.org

- Manhattan Chamber of Commerce, P.O. Box 357, Manhattan 60422; (815) 478-3811; www.manhattan-il.com

Local Events/Attractions

- Joliet Area Historical Museum, 204 North Ottawa St., Joliet; (815) 723-5201; www.jolietmuseum.org. Offers a thorough introduction to the history of the Joliet area.

- Joliet-area rail trails; www.oprt.org/maps/westcon.html#iandm. Three other long rail trails can be accessed in Joliet. Check the Web site for route advice and on-street connections.

- Kankakee River State Park, 5314 Highway 102, Bourbonnais; (815) 933-1383; http://dnr.state.il.us/lands/landmgt/parks/r2/kankakee. htm. Hiking trails, horse rentals, and 10.5 miles of crushed gravel bike trails.

- Midewin National Tallgrass Prairie, 30239 Highway 53, Wilmington; (815) 423-6370; www.fs.fed.us/mntp. The visitor center has exhibits and maps of the park.

Accommodations

- Chester Manor, 116 South Kankakee St., Wilmington; (815) 476-1055; www.chestermanor.net. Italianate mansion from 1871; offers lunch; a few miles from the trail.

- Kankakee River State Park, 5314 Highway 102, Bourbonnais; (815) 933-1383; http://dnr.state.il.us/lands/landmgt/parks/r2/kankakee. htm. The park contains a couple of campgrounds.

NORTHERN ILLINOIS

In northwest Illinois, the dominant natural feature is the Mississippi River. This upper portion of the river contains many square miles of wetlands, bottomland woods, and open water sprinkled with islands. Ambitious trail users can voyage upstream for 30 miles along the Mississippi River Trail. Starting in the Quad Cities, the trail runs north through a string of river towns and ends in Albany, where you'll encounter one of the largest collections of American Indian mounds in the nation.

East of the Quad Cities, the 60-mile-long Hennepin Canal Trail runs through the rural landscape between the Mississippi and Illinois Rivers. At its halfway point, the Hennepin Feeder Canal Trail comes down from the north to join up with the main Hennepin Canal Trail. Similar to the I&M Canal on the other side of the state, the Hennepin Canal stopped serving as a transportation route many years ago. The Hennepin Canal Trail is a great place to explore for anyone with even a modest interest in local history.

In addition to these longer trails, there are a handful of shorter but no less interesting rail trails in the area. As the Jane Addams Trail runs north from Freeport to the Wisconsin state line, it parallels the route of a creek that once powered mills in several small towns along the way. In the town of Dixon, the Lowell Parkway Trail takes you by the shore of the lovely Rock River on the way to a park situated on a high bluff above the river. The Long Prairie and Stone Bridge Trails offer unlimited solitude as you tour a landscape containing small farm towns, open cropland, and gently rolling woodland.

A rural landscape generally dominates north-central and northwest Illinois. While exploring the rail trails in this region, you'll find that the towns tend to be spread apart. Amenities such as restaurants and convenience stores are sometimes hard to come by. This part of the state often feels remote and out of the way, but you're never terribly far from population centers like Chicago, Rockford, and the Quad Cities. Nor are you far from interesting places like the historic town of Galena in the far northwest corner of the state or Mississippi Palisades State Park, which offers some of the best views in the state from atop the wooded river bluffs.

Overview

19 HENNEPIN CANAL TRAIL

In the late nineteenth and early twentieth centuries, the I&M and Hennepin Canals were dug in northern Illinois to speed up transportation between Lake Michigan and the Mississippi River. The Hennepin Canal, which runs from the Illinois River nearly to the Mississippi, is the lesser known of the two. Long closed to barge traffic, the canal now is essentially a long, narrow pond that stretches nearly halfway across the state.

While following the former towpath alongside the canal, you'll encounter many miles of open space and agricultural land, as well as patches of woodland and prairie. Since the route runs through only one town, cultural attractions are limited, but there are old railroad bridges, thirty-two locks (many with the original mechanical hardware intact), and six aqueducts that carry the canal over streams and rivers.

Activities:

Start: In Bureau, located about 40 miles north of Peoria

Length: 60.3 miles one-way

Surface: Crushed gravel on much of the trail; some sections have "tar and chip"—tar base covered with very small rocks.

Wheelchair access: The route is wheelchair accessible.

Difficulty: This trail sits solidly in the difficult category: It's incredibly long, with a dearth of amenities and frequent exposure to wind and sun.

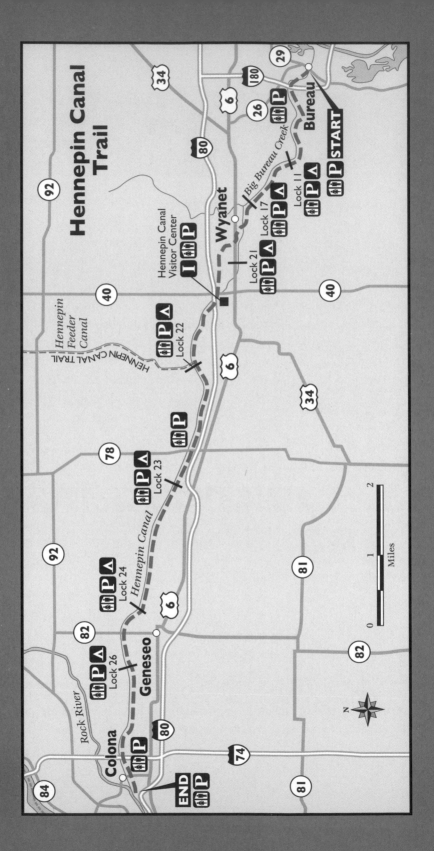

Restrooms: There are public restrooms at the trailhead, Lock 6 (vault toilet), Lock 11, Lock 17, Lock 21 (water), Hennepin Canal State Park Visitor Center (water), Lock 22 (water), boat launch (vault toilet), Lock 23 (vault toilet), Lock 24 (vault toilet), Lock 26 (vault toilet), alongside the trail in Colona (vault toilet), and at the end of the trail at Rock River (vault toilets).

Maps: USGS Annawan, Geneseo, Green Rock, Manlius, Mineral, Princeton South, and Wyanet; *DeLorme: Illinois Atlas and Gazetteer:* Pages 31, 32, and 33. The Hennepin Canal Visitor Center has a basic line-drawn map that shows all locks, bridges, picnicking and camping areas, and boat ramps (see contact information below).

Hazards: Large portions of the route are unsheltered, leaving trail users exposed to wind and sun. Restaurants and stores are nonexistent on the first half of the trail; they're few and far between on the second half.

Access and parking: From I-180 west of Princeton, take IL 26 south. In Bureau look for the trailhead parking area on the right. UTM coordinates: 16T, 301117 E, 4573188 N

Parking is abundant all along the trail. Among the dozens of road crossings, only a few do not have parking spots for trail users. Following are a few of the picnic areas along the trail:

To park at Lock 11, head south on IL 26 from I-80. Follow IL 26 as it curves left, becomes Main Street, and then becomes Tiskilwa Bottom Road. Turn right onto Princeton-Tiskilwa Road (CR 1250 North).

To park at Lock 17, go south on IL 40 from I-80. Turn left onto US 34/6. In Wyanet, turn right onto Wyanet-Walnut Road (CR 8). Turn left onto Canal Street (CR 1410 North). Turn right onto CR 1550 East.

To park at Lock 21, go south on IL 40 from I-80. Turn left onto US 34/6. After crossing the canal, look for the entrance to the camping/picnic area on the right.

To park at Hennepin Canal State Park, go south on IL 40 from I-80. Follow the sign on the right to the visitor center.

To park at Lock 22, exit south on IL 78 from I-80. Turn left onto US 6. After passing through Mineral, turn left onto 1550 North Ave. and then right onto 300 East St.

To park at lock 23, go north on IL 78 from I-80 and turn left onto CR 22 (Baker School Road).

To park at the west end of the trail in Colona, exit I-80 west on Cleveland Road just north of Colona. Turn right onto IL 84 and then left onto Fifth Street. At Fifth Avenue turn right and follow the park road out to the boat launch on the Rock River. Catch the trail on the other side of the pedestrian bridge.

Transportation: Amtrak trains stop in Princeton, located about 5 miles north of the east end of the trail.

Rentals: Quad Cities Convention and Visitors Bureau rents bikes at four locations, 1601 River Dr., Suite 110, Moline, (309) 277-0937; www.visitquad cities.com

Contact: Hennepin Canal Visitor Center, 16006 875 East St., Sheffield 61361; (815) 454-2328; http://dnr.state.il.us/lands/landmgt/parks/r1/hennpin.htm

Bureau to Lock 22

Finished in 1907, the Hennepin Canal was envisioned as a shortcut between Lake Michigan and the Upper Mississippi, specifically the Quad Cities. Supporters of the canal hoped to replicate the success of the I&M Canal, which turned Chicago into a transportation epicenter. But as the last long-distance canal built in the United States, the Hennepin Canal arrived too late in the game to find success. Riverboat traffic was already on the decline, and railroads had become the preferred method of transportation. In addition, a widening of the locks on both the Illinois and Mississippi Rivers made larger riverboats the standard of the day. With lock chambers much narrower than the rivers it connected, the canal was obsolete almost immediately. By the 1930s, the Hennepin was already used primarily for recreation.

Starting the trail in Bureau, the first few miles reveal intermittent stretches of Big Bureau Creek as it winds through a considerable plot of bottomland woods. Shortly after passing under I-180, wooded bluffs rise up from the Bureau Creek floodplain on the north side of the canal. Woods continue to sprawl to the south. In the first 6.0 miles of the canal, you'll encounter nine locks that raised and lowered boats nearly 45 feet as they traveled the canal. After Lock 10, Bureau Creek closely parallels the canal for a long stretch. At Lock 11 sycamore and fir trees provide shade for the pleasant picnic grounds that sit at the foot of an old trestle bridge.

Between Lock 15 and US 6, the trail runs through a 4.2-mile historic area. Along this stretch you'll encounter an aqueduct and six locks, many with the original mechanical devices still intact. At Lock 17 you'll see another old trestle bridge and the remains of a bridge built on a system of rollers so that it could be moved aside for canal boats. After Lock 18 a railroad bridge—now a pedestrian bridge—takes you over the canal toward Wyanet. (A convenience store and diner are located in Wyanet, nearly 1 mile north of the trail.) Another mile up the trail, near US 6, Lock 21 has a large shaded picnic area, areas for tent and equestrian camping, and one of several lift bridges left along the canal. The lines of concrete blocks near the camping area are the remnants of a canal boat repair shop.

Nearly 21 miles along the trail, you'll reach the rolling grassy lawn of the Hennepin Canal Visitor Center. The visitor center contains a few

Thirty-two locks raised and lowered boats along the 60-mile-long Hennepin Canal.

exhibits focusing on the history of the canal, including a model of a lock and an aqueduct and a display of tools used to build the canal. Take a breather from your life on the trail by visiting the park's small wildflower prairie, the wooded hiking trails, and wetlands.

Once you've racked up some miles on this trail, you'll likely realize that at its heart, the canal is little more than a pond immeasurably stretched. As with any area pond, observers will see great blue herons, white egrets, kingfishers, and red-winged blackbirds. You may see hawks loitering in the top branches of the huge cottonwood trees at the edge of the canal. If good fortune allows, you may catch a glimpse of a beaver or muskrat moving through the water before ducking out of sight. On summer evenings you'll likely see swallows careening over the surface of the canal in search of insects.

The slender canal widens into a lake-size basin at the point where the Hennepin Feeder Canal and its accompanying trail join from the north. As the largest expanse of open water along the canal, the Feeder Basin, as it's called, often hosts local anglers casting from their boats. From the basin the feeder canal and its trail shoot north for 28.9 miles to the Rock River in the town of Rock Falls. The feeder canal was never built for barge traffic; instead, as the name suggests, its purpose was to fill the canal with water from the Rock River.

Lock 22 to the Rock River

At Lock 22 visitors can gain a better understanding of how the locks along the canal functioned. Lock 22 is one of the few locks that are largely intact, with wooden gates, metal gears, pulleys, and counterweights that lifted the small drawbridge over the canal. At the edge of the canal, a picnic area offers an inviting spot to take a break. Canoeists like to put in at Lock 22 because they can paddle nearly 10 miles west to Lock 23 with no portages.

For such a long trail, there are surprisingly few traces of civilization. The best opportunity in the trail's midsection to patronize a convenience store, a restaurant, or a hotel rears up near Annawan at 32.9 miles. (Turn left at IL 78; the amenities are just 0.5 mile south of the trail.)

Beyond Lock 23, it can feel as though you're piling up some long and lonely miles on the windswept prairie. A veil of trailside trees restricts the scenery for long stretches. Periodically, when the greenery drops away, normally ho-hum views beyond the canal suddenly seem deeply interesting. Vast tracts of corn and soy plants are occasionally interrupted by farmhouses and small patches of woodland. Every mile or so you're shuttled under a road and through a short metal tunnel about 6 feet in diameter. Also along this stretch, keep watch for the equestrians using the mowed path on the opposite side of the canal.

Anglers often launch their boats near Geneseo, where the canal grows wide and the shores are thick with woodland. Nearby you'll catch glimpses of the Green River, which has been channelized with levees on each side. West of Geneseo, near Lock 25, the trail follows an embankment that offers views of the surrounding countryside. A few houses sit along the road on the opposite side of the canal. Beyond Lock 26, thicker woodland continues after crossing over the Green River. The aqueduct over the Green River was one of a handful of aqueducts along the canal that were removed.

In the town of Colona, residential neighborhoods border the canal, as do a series of pleasant community parks with benches, picnic tables, and pavilions. A row of big cottonwood trees escorts you along the final stretch of canal to its confluence with the Rock River.

Local Information

- Annawan village offices, 203 West Front St., Annawan 61234; (309) 935-6226; www.annawanillinois.org

- Bureau County Tourism Council; (815) 915-3192; www.bureau county-il.com

- Henry County Tourism Bureau, 307 West Center St., Cambridge 61238; (309) 937-1255; http://visithenrycounty.com

Local Events/Attractions

- Bishop Hill Museum State Historic Site, Bishop Hill Street, Bishop Hill; (309) 927-3345; www.bishophill.com. This well-preserved village once hosted a religious commune in the mid-1800s. It now contains interesting shops, galleries, and several historic structures.

- Johnson-Sauk Trail State Recreation Area, 28616 Sauk Trail Rd., Kewanee; (309) 853-5589; http://dnr.state.il.us/lands/landmgt/parks/ r1/johnson.htm. Contains one of the largest round barns in the nation; hiking trails; nearly 100 campsites.

Restaurants

- Lavender Crest Winery, 5401 US 6, Colona; (309) 949-2565; www .lavendercrest.com. Good selection of sandwiches, salads, and wine; lunch only.

- The Loft Restaurant and Lounge, 310 North Canal St., Annawan; (309) 935-6666. Basic country diner fare; 0.5 mile south of the trail on IL 78.

Accommodations

- Best Western Annawan 315 North Canal St., Annawan; (309) 935-6565. Pool and a spacious lounging/breakfast area; located 0.5 mile south of the trail.

- Camping along the canal is available at Locks 11, 17, 22, 23, and 26 and at Bridges 14, 23, and 37. Ask for the map showing the location of all locks and bridges along the trail. For more information visit http://dnr.state.il.us/lands/landmgt/parks/r1/hennpin.htm#camping.

20 HENNEPIN FEEDER CANAL TRAIL

Shooting south from Rock Falls, this historic towpath attracts cyclists, hikers, and anglers who come to enjoy the stocked waters, the peaceful wooded banks, and the canal's abundant birdlife. Swallows are often seen wheeling above the surface of the water, and great blue herons stand in the shade of giant cottonwood trees. As the trail takes a series of gentle turns heading south through rural countryside, the number of visitors dwindles, allowing you to have many miles of trail all to yourself.

Activities:

Start: The Jim Arduini Boat Launch in Rock Falls. From the parking area, cross the canal on Second Road. Look for the trailhead on the left just after you cross the bridge.

Length: 28.9 miles one-way

Surface: The first 3.6 miles of the trail is paved before it becomes smooth, hard-packed gravel. At 17.2 miles the surface becomes "tar and chip"—tar base covered with very small rocks.

Wheelchair access: The trail is wheelchair accessible.

Difficulty: This trail is inching toward the difficult category due to its length, lack of amenities and lack of shade.

Restrooms: There are public restrooms at the Jim Arduini Boat Launch in Rock Falls (vault toilets), Nims Township Park (water; from the trail, head over the small bluff), Centennial Park (water), Bridge 50 (crossing for IL 172), Bridge 52 (Hahnaman Road), and Bridge 64 (crossing for 1945 Ave. North).

Maps: USGS Hahnaman, Mineral, Sterling, Tampico, and Yorktown; *DeLorme: Illinois Atlas and Gazetteer:* Pages 24 and 32. The Hennepin Canal Visitor Center has a basic line-drawn map that shows all locks, bridges, picnicking and camping areas, and boat ramps (see contact information below).

Hazards: Bring plenty of water: After the first mile, there is no drinking water along the way—no stores or restaurants, either. (Consider the optional side trip into Tampico for provisions.) The path becomes very narrow when it passes under many of the bridges. Approach these underpasses slowly.

Access and parking: Exit I-88 on IL 40, heading north. In Rock Falls turn right onto Dixon Avenue and then left onto Emmons Avenue. Park on the left in the boat ramp parking lot. UTM coordinates: 16T, 277745 E, 4629478 N

Trail users can choose from numerous places to park and pick up the trail. Nearly all twenty-four bridges along the trail have small parking areas. You may still park if there is no official parking area, but do not block car traffic or the trail. To reach the IL 172 and the Hahnaman Road parking areas (both with restrooms), follow these roads west from IL 40, which runs parallel to the trail.

To park at Bridge 64, the southernmost parking area with restrooms, head west on 2000 North Avenue from IL 40. After curving to the right onto 675 East Avenue, turn onto 1950 North Avenue. Go left onto 450 Street East and right onto 1900 North Avenue.

Transportation: The closest Amtrak stations are in Mendota, Princeton, and Kewanee.

Rentals: No nearby bike rental options

Contact: Hennepin Canal State Park and Visitor Center, 16006 875 East St., Sheffield 61361; (815) 454-2328; located on the main Hennepin Canal Trail about 6 miles east of the Feeder Basin

||||||||||||||||||||||||||||||||||||||||||||||||||||||||||||||||||||||||||||||

Unlike the rest of the Hennepin Canal, the Hennepin Feeder Canal was not built for boat traffic. Instead its main purpose was to harness water from the Rock River to fill the 60-mile-long expanse of the main canal. The feeder canal was originally slated to take water from the Rock River in the town of Dixon, about 10 miles northeast of Rock Falls. But local citizens changed the route of the canal by raising money for a survey to show

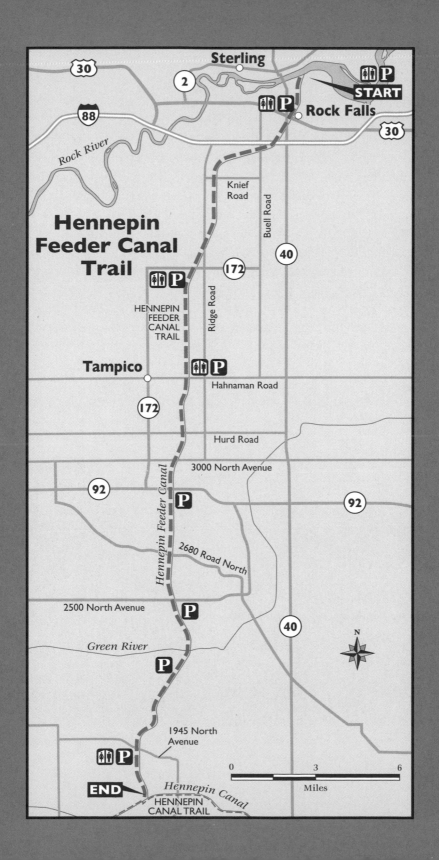

that building the mouth of the feeder canal in Rock Falls would be 6 miles shorter, require one less bridge, and eliminate the need for a lock.

After it was finished in 1907, the Hennepin Canal never grew to become the prominent shipping route it was expected to be. The exponential growth of railroads, the widening of locks in the Illinois and Mississippi Rivers, and the dredging of the Illinois River all conspired to minimize the boat traffic on the canal. In the 1960s state and federal agencies began a lengthy process to transform the entire canal and the path alongside it into a long, narrow recreation area.

The Jim Arduini Boat Launch, where this route starts, sits next to a hydroelectric plant along the Rock River and a newly constructed pedestrian bridge over the river. The first 5.0 miles on the trail heading out of Rock Falls brings you under ten bridges. (Approach the underpasses carefully: The pathway narrows considerably under some of these bridges and becomes rough gravel as it passes under others.) Not far from Rock Falls, a bright red train caboose appears through the trees on the right, marking Centennial Park. The park contains a lagoon, several ponds, and a one-room-schoolhouse museum.

The Hennepin Feeder Canal is lined with greenery as it makes one of its gentle curves.

Enormous cottonwood trees grow on both sides of the canal as the trail takes you farther from Rock Falls. Many of these trees—typically with branches fanning out toward the top—tower 100 feet above the canal. In early spring, the trees' cottony seeds coat the surface of the canal.

It doesn't take long to figure out that birds love the canal: Cardinals, orioles, kingbirds, red-winged blackbirds, red-tailed hawks, and great blue herons are just a few of the birds commonly seen along the way. Keep watch for beavers and muskrats, as well as such reptiles as water snakes, painted turtles, and the much larger softshell turtles—often with shells larger than dinner plates.

If presidential birthplaces give you a thrill, and you're riding a bike, consider a short side trip to the birthplace of Ronald Reagan. At Bridge 52 (Hahnaman Road), you can take a short trip to the town of Tampico, where there's a small museum/gift shop located next to the building where the fortieth U.S. president was born. For the first ten years of Reagan's life, his family lived in an apartment above a restaurant on Main Street. To reach Tampico take Hahnaman Road to the right. Traffic is mellow on the 1.6-mile route into town. Tampico contains restaurants, convenience stores, and a water spigot in the little park on Main Street. The town also contains folksy murals in honor of its most famous resident.

With a few exceptions, the second half of this route is a mirror reflection of the first. The tree-fringed canal is an attractive slice of scenery, to be sure; but with nearly 30 miles of little variation, it can grow monotonous. Fortunately patches of wetland occasionally break up the scenery. Intermittently, the banks on either side of the canal drop down to reveal long views of the rural landscape speckled with garnet-colored barns in the distance.

The highlight of this section appears when the canal is funneled over an aqueduct about 40 feet above the Green River. (Of the nine aqueducts on the Hennepin Canal, only one was built on the feeder canal.) This impressive piece of early-twentieth-century engineering occurs in a pleasant spot with views up and down the sandy-bottomed river. Swallows make their nests underneath the aqueduct and are frequently twirling through the trees and above the river in search of bugs. At the turnaround point on this route, a large basin marks the location where the Hennepin Feeder Canal joins the main canal.

At the Feeder Basin you can turn around and head back to Rock Falls or extend the trip with a visit to the Hennepin Canal Visitor Center, about 6.0 miles to the east along the main canal.

Local Information
- Blackhawk Waterways Convention and Visitors Bureau, 201 North Franklin Ave., Polo 61064; (815) 946-2108 or (800) 678-2108; www .bwcvb.com

- Rock Falls Convention and Visitors Bureau, 601 West 10th St., Rock Falls 61071; (815) 625-4500; www.visitrockfalls.com

Local Events/Attractions
- Ronald Reagan Birthplace, 111 South Main St., Tampico; (815) 438-2130. The family apartment has been restored to its original 1900's style. Next door is a small gift store and museum.

Restaurants
- Arthurs Garden Deli, 1405 First Ave., Rock Falls; (815) 625-0011. Good sandwiches.

- Candlelight Inn, 2200 First Ave., Rock Falls; (815) 626-1897; http:// candlelightinnrestaurant.com. Kebobs and steaks.

- Dutch Diner, 105 South Main St., Tampico; (815) 438-2096. Restaurant named for Tampico's most famous resident; known for its pies.

Accommodations
- Holiday Inn, 2105 First Ave. (IL 40), Rock Falls; (815) 626-5500

21 JANE ADDAMS TRAIL

The Jane Addams Trail offers a satisfying ramble through wetlands, prairie, wooded landscapes, and farmland of northwest Illinois. While following the Richland Creek floodplain, the trail crosses twenty-one wooden bridges and cuts through a handful of small towns and hamlets. An optional side trip to Jane Addams's hometown allows visitors to learn more about this important figure in U.S. history.

Activities:

Start: The Wes Block trailhead, the southern terminus of the trail, located several miles north of Freeport

Length: 13.0 miles one-way. When the trail crosses into Wisconsin, it becomes the 33-mile-long Badger State Trail.

Surface: Smooth crushed gravel

Wheelchair access: The route is wheelchair accessible.

Difficulty: The trail is easy.

Restrooms: There are public restrooms at the Wes Block trailhead and at a trailside park in Orangeville.

Maps: USGS Freeport West, Orangeville, and Monroe; *DeLorme: Illinois Atlas and Gazetteer:* Page 17; Jane Addams Trail Map, Freeport/Stephenson County Convention and Visitors Bureau, www.janeaddamstrail.com/portals/0/fullmap.html

Hazards: No hazards other than a few semibusy roads that must be crossed.

Access and parking: From I-39 south of Rockford, take US 20 west. Follow US 20 past IL 26. Turn left onto Fairview Road and follow signs to the right. Parking is at the end of the road. UTM coordinates: 16T, 280345 E, 4689694 N

In addition to the Wes Block trailhead at the south end of the trail, there is also parking next to the trail on Beaver, McConnell, and Orangeville Roads (the Richland Creek trailhead). All of these parking areas can be reached by heading north on IL 26. From IL 26 turn left onto Beaver, McConnell, or Orangeville Road to reach the respective parking areas.

Transportation: In future years, watch for a new Amtrak route running between Rockford and Chicago.

Rentals: Trailside Bike Rental, 1740 West High St., Orangeville; (815) 291-9316

Contact: Wisconsin Department of Natural Resources (manages the Badger State Trail), 101 South Webster St., P.O. Box 7921, Madison, WI 53707; (608) 266-2621; http://dnr.wi.gov/org/land/parks/specific/badger

For information about the Jane Addams Trail, visit www.janeaddams trail.com.

||||||||||||||||||||||||||||||||||||||||||||||||||||||||||||||||||||||||||||||||

The Jane Addams Trail follows the route of the Illinois Central Railroad as it runs through the floodplain of Richland Creek. Once the tracks were laid down in the area in 1887, a handful of small railroad towns sprouted up in their wake: Scioto Mills, Buena Vista, Red Oak, and Orangeville. The towns also benefited from a series of mills that were built along the creek. As happened in so many other places, the towns shrank as the need for water-powered mills dried up and the use of the railroad declined.

Less than 2.0 miles into the trail, before reaching the hamlet of Scioto Mills, the first glimpses of Richland Creek appear, zigzagging through the bottomland on the left. Scioto Mills was built in the early 1850s around a sawmill and a gristmill. The gristmill, powered by Richland Creek, reportedly did brisk business grinding feed and flour with three millstones.

At Cedarville Road, consider a short detour to the Cedarville Historical Museum, where you can learn about the trail's namesake—the person President Theodore Roosevelt called "America's most useful citizen." Born and raised in Cedarville, Addams is best known for founding and operating the Hull House, an institution on Chicago's near west side that was once recognized around the world. The Hull House spearheaded what was

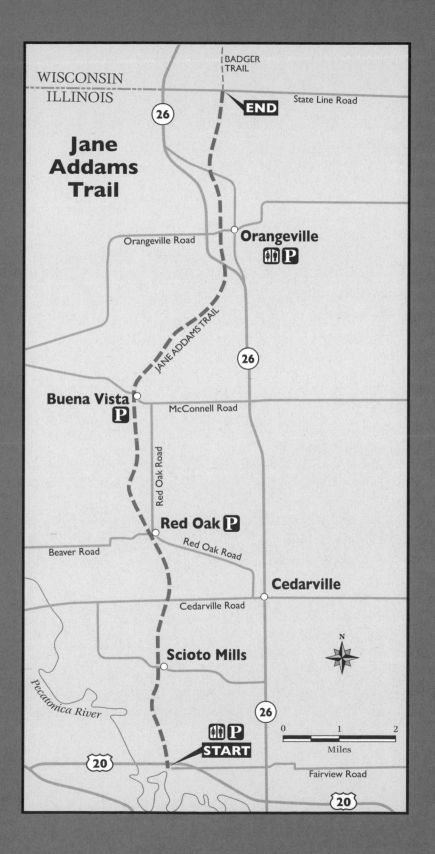

called the settlement house movement, which began in response to problems created by urbanization, industrialization, and immigration.

From the 1890s until her death in 1935, Addams and the Hull House provided many services to people in need—many who were recent immigrants. These services included kindergarten and day care facilities for the children of working mothers, an employment bureau, an art gallery, libraries, and English and citizenship classes, as well as theater, music, and art classes. The complex eventually expanded to include thirteen buildings.

Later in Addams's life, she helped found numerous organizations and advocacy groups that worked on behalf of children, families, and workers. She also became involved in the peace movement. She worked to found the Women's International League for Peace and Freedom in 1919 and was the organization's first president. In 1931 Addams was the first woman to receive the Nobel Peace Prize.

The Cedarville Historical Museum is located 1.8 miles from the trail. From the trail turn right onto Cedarville Road and follow the blue signs to

Heavy clouds hang above the Jane Addams Trail.

the museum (left on Mill Street and then left on Second Street). If you continue ahead on Mill Street after Second Street, you'll see the house where Addams grew up—a large white-brick private residence located on the right at the turn in the road.

Back on the trail and heading north from Cedarville Road brings you through wetlands and bottomlands galore. Along this section you'll pass through the sleepy hamlets of Red Oak and Buena Vista, both of which had mills along Richland Creek. At about 7.0 miles into the trail, just north of McConnell Road, the route cuts through a rocky embankment before crossing a bridge over Richland Creek. For the rest of trail, Richland Creek and most of its accompanying wetlands move from the west side of the trail to the east. While many of the bridges offer pleasant views of the surrounding wetlands and prairie, Bridges J9 and J8, just before and after Brush Creek Road, respectively, allow for particularly eye-catching views of Richland Creek as it winds through swaying grasslands.

On the way into Orangeville, you'll see a quarry to the left and then pass a small pond surrounded by grassland. From Orangeville it's just a short trip up to the state line, where the Jane Addams Trail becomes the Badger State Trail.

The Badger State Trail extends 33 miles north from the Illinois border into the communities of Clarno, Monroe, Monticello, Exeter, Belleville, and Basco. (Bicyclists, cross-country skiers, and equestrians age sixteen and older must have a Wisconsin state trail pass.) About 8.0 miles north of the Illinois border is the town of Monroe, the self-proclaimed Swiss cheese capital of the nation. Stores around the town square will be happy to indulge any cheese-related shopping urges you may have. In the center of the square is an impressive courthouse. In the town of Exeter between Monticello and Belleville, the trail enters a 1,200-foot-long, century-old tunnel.

Currently the Badger State Trail connects with the 40-mile-long Military Ridge State Trail and the 23-mile Sugar River State Trail. Once the state follows through with the plan to extend the trail another 7.0 miles, Badger State Trail users can connect with the 17-mile-long Capital City Trail in Madison.

Local Information

- Freeport/Stephenson County Convention and Visitors Bureau, 4596 US 20 East, Freeport 61032; (815) 233-1357; www.stephenson-county-il.org

- Green County Tourism, N3150 B, Highway 81, Monroe, WI 53566; (888) 222-9111; www.greencounty.org

- Northern Illinois Tourism Development Office, 200 South State St., Belvidere 61008; (815) 547-3740; www.visitnorthernillinois.com

Local Events/Attractions

- Cedarville Historical Museum, 450 West Second St., Cedarville; (815) 563-4485; www.uic.edu/jaddams/hull/cedarville. Contains photos, letters, and personal items that belonged to Jane Addams.

- Jane Addams burial site, Cedarville Cemetery. Located on Red Oak Road 0.25 mile west of Cedar Creek, Cedarville.

Restaurants

- Alber Ice Cream Parlor, 126 East Douglas, Freeport; (815) 232-7099; www.albericecreamparlor.com. Old-fashioned ice-cream parlor located in the Union Dairy Building.

- Café Mondo, 15 North Chicago Ave., Freeport; (815) 233-3423. Sandwiches and soups.

Accommodations

- Lake Le-Aqua-Na State Park, 8542 North Lake Rd., Lena; (815) 369-4282; http://dnr.state.il.us/lands/landmgt/parks/r1/leaquana.htm. Pleasant campground.

22 LONG PRAIRIE AND STONE BRIDGE TRAILS

As you travel from one side of Boone County to the other on the Long Prairie Trail, you'll encounter small winding creeks, a few small railroad towns, and plenty of open space. Entering Winnebago County marks the beginning of the Stone Bridge Trail, where the greenery grows thick and the landscape becomes more rolling. Toward the end of the route, a short trip off-trail brings you to a picturesque landmark—an old double-arched limestone bridge straddling a rocky creek.

Activities:

Start: County Line Road parking area, located about 5 miles west of Harvard

Length: 19.4 miles one-way

Surface: Asphalt on the 14.1-mile Long Prairie Trail; crushed gravel on the 5.3-mile Stone Bridge Trail

Wheelchair access: The route is wheelchair accessible.

Difficulty: The route offers a medium level of difficulty. Some sections leave trail users fairly exposed to sun and wind.

Restrooms: There are public restrooms at the parking area on the east end of the trail (vault toilet), Poplar Grove (portable toilet), Caledonia parking area (portable toilet), and Roland Olson Forest Preserve parking on CR 7 (vault toilet; water).

Maps: USGS Belvidere, Belvidere North, Capron, and South Beloit; *DeLorme: Illinois Atlas and Gazetteer:* Pages 18 and 19; Illinois Bicycle Map, Region 2, Illinois Department of Transportation, www.dot.state.il.us/bike map/state.html

Hazards: None

Access and parking: From I-90 west of Elgin, exit north onto US 20. In Marengo turn right onto IL 23. South of Harvard turn left onto US 14 and

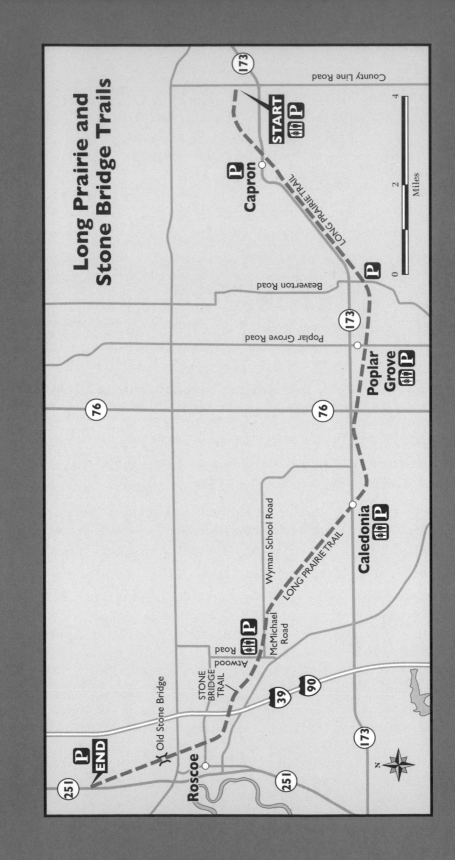

Long Prairie and Stone Bridge Trails

START

END

Capron

Poplar Grove

Caledonia

Roscoe

Old Stone Bridge

STONE BRIDGE TRAIL

LONG PRAIRIE TRAIL

County Line Road

Beaverton Road

Poplar Grove Road

Wyman School Road

McMichael Road

Atwood Road

173

76

251

39

90

0   2   4

Miles

N

left again onto IL 173. Turn right onto County Line Road. The parking area is on the left. UTM coordinates: 16T, 359598 E, 4696263 N

Parking lots are provided in all three villages along the route:

To park in Poplar Grove, head west on IL 173 from Harvard. Turn left onto State Street and look for the trail as it crosses the road.

To park in Caledonia head west on IL 173 from Harvard. Turn left onto Front Street.

To park at the Roland Olson Forest Preserve, head east on Belvidere Road from IL 251. Turn left onto Atwood Road.

Transportation: In future years, watch for a new Amtrak route running between Rockford and Chicago.

Rentals: Side by Side Cycles, 142 West Main St., Capron; (815) 569-2472; www.sidebysidecycle.com; rents bikes and dual trikes

Contact: Boone County Conservation District, 603 Appleton Rd., Belvidere 61008; (815) 547-5432; www.boonecountyconservationdistrict.org; maintains the Long Prairie Trail

Village of Roscoe, 5792 Elevator Rd., Roscoe 61073; (815) 623-7323; www.villageofroscoe.com; maintains the Stone Bridge Trail

The route of the Long Prairie Trail originally served a railroad that the Kenosha, Rockford, and Rock Island Railroad Company started operating in 1858. The company that built the railroad soon sold it to the Chicago and Northwestern Railroad, which maintained it as an active line for nearly a century. As the story goes, the railroad was abandoned when a train crossing Beaverton Road (trail mile 5.6) derailed, leaving behind a torn-up railbed, broken ties, and twisted tracks. In lieu of making costly repairs, the railroad was mothballed. A gouge in the railbed remains today.

As you start toward Capron from the trailhead, the route immediately reaches across an arm of Picasaw Creek. Not far ahead, Picasaw Creek brushes against the trail in a couple of spots, resulting in lush greenery and grassy wetlands fringed with willows. When the number of big oaks leaning over the trail start to dwindle, you're allowed glimpses of horse pastures and the gently rolling agricultural landscape of the surrounding area.

The small town of Capron has been adorned with several different names. Originally called Helgesaw in honor of the many Scandinavians in the area, it was later renamed Long Prairie due to a sizable swath of nearby prairie. Then, like so many other towns in Illinois, it acquired the name of a manager with the local railroad.

South of Capron the trail hugs IL 173 for 2.5 miles. This largely unshaded strip of trail follows a small embankment and crosses a couple of minor streams. Look for Queen Anne's lace, black-eyed Susans, and goldenrod growing alongside the trail. On the way into Poplar Grove, the trail crosses Beaver Creek and then follows a 10-foot embankment above the surrounding landscape. Poplar Grove announces its arrival with a grain elevator and big storage silos alongside the trail.

After Caledonia, oak-hickory woods grow thick and the landscape becomes more textured. In one spot the trail mounts an embankment 30 feet high; in another, 35-foot-high ravines rise up on the sides of the trail. When the greenery opens, farms appear in the distance, but rarely are there structures near the trail. The lack of nearby development, combined with a small number of trail users, lends the trail a distinctly remote feel.

Leaving Boone County and entering Winnebago County at 14.1 miles signals the beginning of the Stone Bridge Trail. In Winnebago County the landscape becomes more rolling and wooded. Long views grow more frequent, and the ravines and embankments built for the railroad multiply.

As the trail passes over North Kinnikinnick Creek, the surrounding shrubs and grasses disguise the fact that you're high up on a bridge. The only features that give away your location are the wooded fencing on the sides of the trail and gurgle of the creek below. A walking path leads you on a series of switchbacks down the ravine to a wooden platform overlooking the creek, adjoining wetlands, and the trail's namesake—a double-arched limestone bridge built in 1882. Local engineers say the bridge (now on the National Register of Historic Places) is unique for its date of construction and its design, which includes an internal drainage system.

For the final couple of miles, the railroad right-of-way carves a straight, level path through open savanna and prairie. Houses speckle the landscape.

The views are wide, but shade is thin. Shortly after crossing the final bridge, which spans Dry Creek, you'll reach the parking area at the end of the trail.

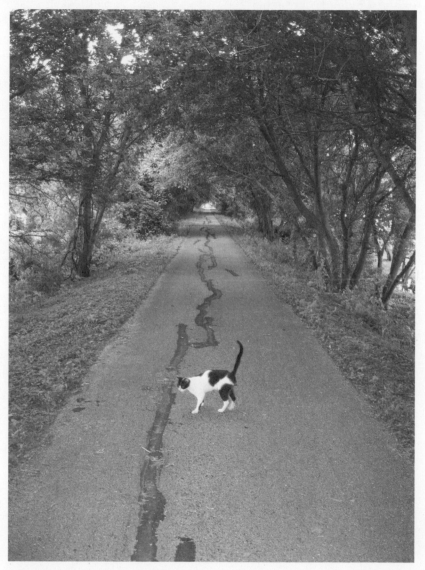

Trail users come in all sizes and species.

Local Information

- Northern Illinois Tourism Development Office, 200 South State St., Belvidere 61008; (815) 547-3740; www.visitnorthernillinois.com

- Rockford Area Convention and Visitors Bureau, 102 North Main St., Rockford 61101; (800) 521-0849; www.gorockford.com

Local Events/Attractions

- Edwards Apple Orchard, 7061 Centerville Rd., Poplar Grove; (815) 765-2234. A petting zoo, pony rides, and a store; locals come mostly for the U-pick apples.

Restaurants

- Thai Basil Fusion, 1531 West Lane Rd., Machesney Park; (815) 633-9400; www.thaibasilonline.com. Good food served in a contemporary atmosphere; located north of Rockford.

- Trail Stop, 105 North State St., Poplar Grove; (815) 765-3799. Trailside ice-cream shop.

Accommodations

- Hononegah Forest Preserve, 80 Hononegah Rd., Rockton; (815) 877-6100; www.wcfpd.org/Preserves/Hononegah.cfm. Camping close to the Rock River; located a couple of miles from the west end of this route.

- Sweden House Lodge, 4605 East State St., Rockford; (815) 398-4130; www.swedenhouselodge.com. Indoor pool.

23 LOWELL PARKWAY TRAIL

Lowell Park has been a cherished landmark in the Dixon area for the past one hundred years. The park's high wooded bluffs, scenic shoreline along the Rock River, and collection of rustic rock shelters have drawn people for generations. On the way to the park from Dixon, you'll take a mile-long ramble along the Rock River and then explore an attractive wooded landscape.

Activities:

Start: At the south end of the Lowell Parkway, at corner of Bradshaw Street and Washington Avenue in Dixon

Length: 8.5 miles one-way

Surface: The route includes paved path, quiet park road, and a 3.3-mile segment on gravel path. The gravel path is not a well-compacted surface, which is great for hiking but not so great for bikes with skinny tires. Medium to wide tires will work best. If you don't have wider tires, this section is easily skipped.

Wheelchair access: The Lowell Parkway Trail is wheelchair accessible; the rest of the route would not be good for wheelchair use.

Difficulty: The route is easy until reaching Lowell Park, where you must go up and down a high bluff.

Restrooms: There are public restrooms at the 0.8-mile trail junction (portable toilet) and the Lowell Park boat ramp (water). There is a trailside water fountain at 0.5 mile.

Maps: USGS Grand Detour and Dixon East; *DeLorme: Illinois Atlas and Gazetteer:* Page 25

Hazards: If walking or running the route through Lowell Park, be careful on the winding, shoulderless park road. Consider investigating some of the park's hiking trails instead.

Access and parking: From I-88 exit to Dixon on IL 26. A half mile after crossing the Rock River in Dixon, turn right onto Bradshaw Street. The parking area for the trailhead is 0.5 mile ahead on the right at the intersection with Washington Avenue. UTM coordinates: 16T, 294277 E, 4636554 N

To reach Lowell Park follow IL 26/US 52 northwest of Dixon. On the way out of Dixon, turn right onto Lowell Park Road. The park entrance is on the right. Park either by the nature center or down by the river.

Transportation: The closest Amtrak stations are in Mendota, Princeton, and Kewanee.

Rentals: No nearby bike rentals are available.

Contact: Dixon Park District, 804 Palmyra St., Dixon 61021; (815) 284-3306

The Lowell Parkway Trail—running from Dixon to Lowell Park—was once part of the Illinois Central Railroad, which initially traveled from Galena in the northwest corner of the state to the southern tip of Illinois. When completed in 1856, it was the longest rail line in the world. This section of the former rail line runs through an attractive, leafy landscape that likely hasn't changed much in the past 150 years.

Nearly 1.0 mile out from the trailhead, turn off the Lowell Parkway and follow the gravel-surfaced Meadows Trail (the first path on the right) through the agricultural fields and down to the bank of the Rock River. As the path parallels the river for nearly 1.0 mile, the benches scattered along the way offer inviting places to rest and admire the intermittently wooded and grassy riverbanks.

The trail eventually curls away from the river and takes a sinuous route through wooded areas, savanna, and patches of cropland back up to the Lowell Parkway. Occasionally the main trail intersects grassy mowed trails used for horseback riding.

Back on the Lowell Parkway, the Dixon Correctional Center, Illinois's largest medium-security prison, peeks through the greenery on the left. Soon, on the right, you'll see bluffs tumbling steeply down toward the Rock River.

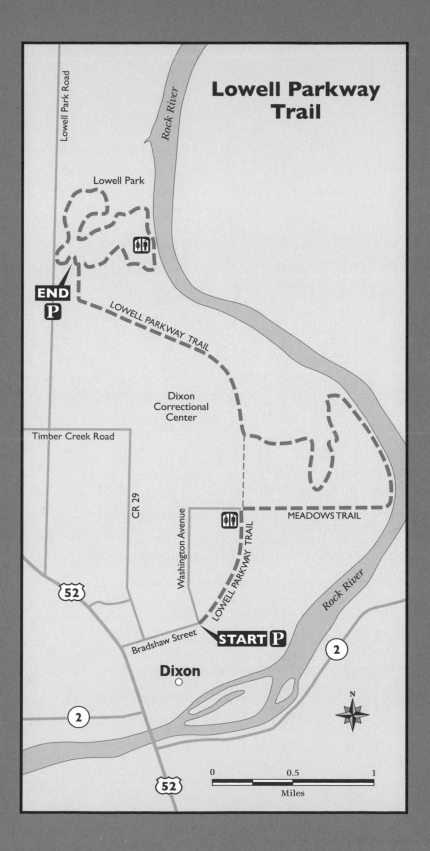

Lowell Parkway Trail

Lowell Park Road

Rock River

Lowell Park

Lowell Park

END
P

LOWELL PARKWAY TRAIL

Dixon
Correctional
Center

Timber Creek Road

CR 29

Washington Avenue

MEADOWS TRAIL

LOWELL PARKWAY TRAIL

Rock River

52

Bradshaw Street

START P

2

Dixon

2

N

52

| 0 | 0.5 | 1 |

Miles

Once in Lowell Park, the route immediately follows an exhilarating descent of the bluff on a squiggly road, cutting through a tunnel of trees. This century-old park was once a popular destination for some of Chicago's upper crust. President Ronald Reagan, while growing up in Dixon, served as a lifeguard at the park for six summers. On the way down the bluff, an overlook located across from the stone picnic shelter offers an expansive view of the Rock River Valley. Descending from the viewing spot, a rocky limestone wall accompanies the road on the right.

After picking the bugs from your teeth at the bottom of the bluff, follow the park road along the wooded shore of the river. If you've brought a picnic, pull up a bench at one of the old stone picnic shelters and enjoy the river view. You'll be glad to know that the route up the bluff isn't excessively steep. Returning to the top of the bluff, take the first right for a quick tour of the north section of the park. Completing the north leaf of the circuitous park road, continue past the nature center for the final leaf that runs through the park's pine plantation. Stay to the right and follow the signs leading back to the Lowell Parkway Trail, which you'll follow back to Dixon.

If you've got energy to burn, you can extend your trip another 0.8 mile north along the Lowell Parkway Trail beyond the turnoff for Lowell Park.

Major Milepoints

0.8 Turn right on the gravel path leading down to the Rock River. The path is unmarked but is easy to identify—it's the first path you'll encounter on the right.

4.1 Turn right when you return to the paved Lowell Parkway.

5.5 Turn right to enter Lowell Park (follow the sign).

5.7 Turn right onto the park road.

7.3 Turn right onto the park road at the top of the bluff.

8.1 Continue straight ahead through the pine plantation.

8.5 Turn right onto the park road (follow signs for the bike trail).

Local Information
- Lee County Tourism, 113 South Peoria Ave., Dixon 61021; (815) 288-1840; www.leecountytourism.com

- Blackhawk Waterways Convention and Visitors Bureau, 201 North Franklin Ave., Polo 61064; (815) 946-2108 or (800) 678-2108; www.bwcvb.com

Local Events/Attractions
- John Deere historic site, 8393 South Main St., Grand Detour; (815) 652-4551; www.deere.com/en_US/attractions/historicsite. Located a few minutes north of Dixon in Grand Detour on IL 2.

- Nachusa Grasslands Preserve, 8772 South Lowden Rd., Franklin Grove; (815) 456-2340; www.nachusagrasslands.org. Large native prairie and wetland area; periodic tours, bird walks, and other special events.

- Ronald Reagan Boyhood Home and Visitor Center, 816 Hennepin Ave., Dixon; (815) 288-5176; www.ronaldreaganhome.com

Restaurants
- Baker Street, 111 West First St., Dixon; (815) 285-2253. Coffee, baked goods, soups, and sandwiches.

- Salamandra Restaurant, 105 West First St., Dixon; (815) 285-0874. Features dishes from various regions of Mexico. Located on main downtown strip.

Accommodations
- White Pines Inn/White Pines Forest State Park, 6712 West Pines Rd., Mt. Morris; (815) 946-3817; www.whitepinesinn.com. One of Illinois's oldest state parks; camping, cabins, and a restaurant.

24 MISSISSIPPI RIVER TRAIL— QUAD CITIES TO ALBANY

This route introduces you to a collection of intriguing Mississippi River towns. Starting in the cities of Rock Island and Moline, the trail hugs the bank of the river as it leads you through parks, industrial areas, and the downtown business districts. Continuing north, a series of small river towns are lined up like pearls on a string: Hampton, Rapids City, Port Byron, and Cordova. The trail ends at a park containing one of the largest collections of Native American burial mounds in the nation.

Activities:

Start: Sunset Park, located in Rock Island at the convergence of the Rock and Mississippi Rivers

Length: 34.5 miles one-way

Surface: Asphalt

Wheelchair access: The route is wheelchair accessible. There are on-street sections in the towns of Hampton, Port Byron, and Cordova, but the route follows quiet streets.

Difficulty: The trail is difficult because of the lack of shade on many portions, the length, and the long stretch where it accompanies traffic on IL 84.

Restrooms: There are public restrooms and water at Sunset Community Park, in downtown Moline, and at the River Harbor parking area, Empire Park, the riverside park in Rapids City, the boat launch in Port Byron, and Albany Mounds State Historic Site.

Maps: USGS Camanche, Cordova, Milan, Port Byron, and Silvis; *DeLorme: Illinois Atlas and Gazetteer:* Pages 23, 30, and 31; Illinois Bicycle Map, Region 2, Illinois Department of Transportation, www.dot.state.il.us/bikemap/state.html; League of Illinois Bicyclists Quad City Bike Map, www.bikelib.org/maps-and-rides/maps/quad-cities

Hazards: Be mindful of other trail users while in Rock Island and Moline. Occasionally the trail crosses busy streets; watch for traffic at these crossings and when traveling along the on-street sections in Hampton and Cordova.

Access and parking: From I-280 south of Rock Island, head north on IL 92. Exit at Sunset Lane and turn left. Enter Sunset Park and park in the first lot on the right. UTM coordinates: 15T, 700168 E, 4595169 N

Heading north on I-74 into Moline, exit at Seventh Avenue and go northeast. Bear left on 23rd Avenue. Turn right on River Drive. The park on the left contains a couple of large parking areas.

To park at Illiniwek Forest Preserve, go north on I-80 from I-280. Just before crossing the Mississippi River, exit onto IL 84 and head south. The park is several miles ahead on the right.

To park in Rapids City, head north on IL 84 from I-80. In Rapids City turn left onto 12th Street and then right onto First Avenue.

To park in Port Byron, go north on IL 84 from I-80. In Port Byron turn left onto Agnes Street and look for the parking area near the boat launch.

To park at the Albany Mounds State Historic Site at the end of the trail, take I-88 to the Albany Road exit northeast of the Quad Cities. Head northwest on Albany Road. As you enter the town of Albany, turn left onto Cherry Street. The parking area is at the end of the road.

Transportation: Amtrak trains stop in Galesburg.

Rentals: Quad Cities Convention and Visitors Bureau rents bikes at four locations; 1601 River Drive, Suite 110, Moline; (309) 277-0937; www.visit quadcities.com

Contact: The Great River Trail Guide; (309) 277-0937, ext. 113; www.great rivertrail.com

||||||||||||||||||||||||||||||||||||||||||||||||||||||||||||||||||||||||||||||||

As the trail strikes out north from Sunset Park in Rock Island, you'll scoot alongside Lake Potter, a backwater lake that hosts a marina. Getting closer to downtown Rock Island, the trail mounts the river levee and passes numerous industrial areas. Up on the levee, you'll catch fine views up and down the river. The first bridge along the way, an old latticed train bridge, has a midsection that rotates to allow river barges to pass. Farther north, the newer Centennial Bridge calls your attention to its series of arched, latticed support sections.

In downtown Rock Island, a garish riverboat casino looks out of place beside the stately architecture of the business district. Downtown Rock Island offers a choice of watering holes and restaurants within blocks of the trail. Like Moline to the east, Rock Island has its roots in manufacturing agriculture implements for midwestern farms. John Deere was located in Moline, and International Harvester was located in Rock Island.

While passing through Rock Island and Moline, you'll see Arsenal Island within the Mississippi River. The first European settlement on this island was Fort Armstrong (a replica of the fort now stands on the island). During the Civil War, the island served as a Confederate prison camp—a cemetery on the island contains the graves of 2,000 prisoners who died at the camp. Not long after the Civil War, an armory was established on the island. Visitors come to see the various types of weapons and firepower on display at the island's Rock Island Arsenal Museum. (*Note:* Photo identification is required to access the island, and guards are notorious for being very strict about who gets access. Don't be surprised if you are turned away.)

Just after passing the bridge to Arsenal Island, you won't miss the 70-foot-tall glass structure of the Quad City Botanical Center on the right. Inside is a tropical garden with a 15-foot waterfall set amidst palm trees, orchids, and bromeliads.

Continuing north, the path passes a smattering of industrial sites while following a levee that puts you about 40 feet above the surface of the river. Tucked among the industrial sites is a pedestrian bridge that leads out to Sylvan Island. Once host to a steel mill and a rock-crushing operation, the thirty-six-acre island now is a wooded park laced with hiking trails.

In downtown Moline the trail brushes against the backside of the I Wireless Center, a 12,000-seat entertainment venue and home rink for the local American Hockey League team, the Quad City Flames. Continuing north of Moline the trail winds through a few parks, including Riverside Park, which is pressed between the Mississippi River and River Drive. The lightly wooded grounds at Empire Park contain a visitor center with dis-

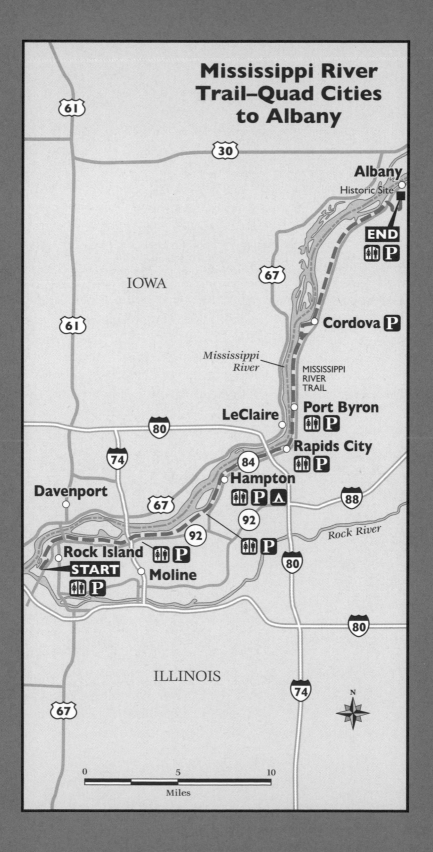

Mississippi River Trail–Quad Cities to Albany

plays focusing on the ecosystem of the Mississippi River and the history of the village of Hampton.

In the sleepy village of Hampton, you may want to visit the small local history museum or the old-fashioned ice-cream shop—both alongside the route during a brief on-street section. Just north of Hampton, you can break out the picnic basket at the Illiniwek Forest Preserve and have lunch at the edge of the river looking out at Lock and Dam 14. Illiniwek provides a perfect spot to watch the progression of river barges moving up and down the 0.5-mile-wide waterway (watch for coal going upriver and grain coming down).

The remaining 20 miles of the trail runs largely alongside IL 84, which is used by a fair amount of traffic. Occasionally the trail strays from the highway for interludes of varying length, most notably in the towns of Rapids City, Port Byron, and Cordova.

A couple miles upstream from Hampton is Rapids City, named for the rapids that once existed on this stretch of river. Before the rapids were removed with dynamite, riverboats had to unload cargo onto a train, trans-

Patches of woodland occasionally appear along the Mississippi River Trail.

port it north, and then load it on another boat upstream. In Rapids City the path cuts through a small riverside park overlooking river wetlands.

In Port Byron the river narrows, offering views of LeClaire, Iowa, located on a bluff across the river. Each August the atmosphere heats up between these two towns. This is when boat traffic on the river shuts down and the townspeople stretch a 2,400-foot, 680-pound rope from one shore to the other for an interstate tug-of-war. Multiple teams compete, and whichever town chalks up the most wins during the day is the winner for the year.

Another few miles upstream, on-street bike route signs guide you from one end of the town of Cordova to the other. Cordova once served as a shipping point for grain grown by local farmers. The main shipping storage facility was eventually turned into a site for manufacturing clamshell buttons.

North of the Cordova, the trail and IL 84 head inland away from the river, passing the Cordova Dragway, the entrance to a nuclear power plant, and a large 3M industrial facility. The final few miles of the trail take you by a sprawling Mississippi backwater and thick bottomland woods that are a part of the Upper Mississippi River National Fish and Wildlife Refuge.

When the trail ends at Meridosia Road, turn right for a few hundred yards of on-street travel. At Bunker Hill Road take the trail left and enter the Albany Mounds State Historic Site. Within the rolling prairie and woodland of this small park are nearly one hundred American Indian mounds—one of the largest collections of such mounds in the nation. A sizable community of Hopewell Indians lived in the area about 2,000 years ago, using the mounds as burial sites for their dead.

Major Milepoints

12.6 To start the 0.8-mile-long on-street section in Hampton, keep straight ahead on First Avenue.

13.0 Turn right on Eighth Street.

13.4 Resume the trail on the left.

23.8 Turn left on Thirteenth Avenue and quickly turn right on Third Street to start a 2.3-mile-long on-street section in Cordova.

24.5 Turn right on Third Avenue.

24.9 Turn left on Ninth Street.

25.4 Turn left on River Road.

26.1 Resume the Mississippi River Trail.

33.5 Turn right on Meridosia Road to reach Albany Mounds State Historic Site.

33.7 Enter the park via the trail on the left.

Local Information

- Mississippi River Visitors Center, overlooking Lock and Dam 15; (309) 794-5338; www.mvr.usace.army.mil/missriver/MRVC/MRVC.htm. Operated by the U.S. Army Corps of Engineers at the west end of Arsenal Island, Rock Island.

- Quad Cities Convention and Visitors Bureau, 1601 River Dr., Suite 110, Moline 61265; (800) 747-7800; www.visitquadcities.com

Local Events/Attractions

- Brettun and Black Museum, at the corner of First Avenue and Sixth Street, Hampton; (309) 755-0362. Small museum with limited hours.

- Celebration River Cruises, 2501 River Dr., Moline; (309) 764-1952; www.celebrationbelle.com. The 800-passenger *Celebration Belle* is one of the largest functioning riverboats on the Upper Mississippi. The trail passes the boarding area.

- Rock Island Arsenal Museum, Rock Island Arsenal, Rock Island; (309) 782-5021; www.riamwr.com/museum.htm. Focuses on firearms and arsenal history.

- Tugfest; www.tugfest.com. Interstate tug-of-war held early August in Port Byron, Illinois, and LeClaire, Iowa. Other events include fireworks, carnival rides, live entertainment, and a parade.

Restaurants

- Bier Stube, 415 15th St., Moline; (309) 797-3049; www.bier-stube.com. German food served in comfortable atmosphere.

- Blue Cat Brew Pub, 113 18th St., Rock Island; (309) 788-8247; www
  .bluecatbrewpub.com. Six different beers brewed on-site; blocks
  away from the trail.

- Remember When Ice Cream and Candies, 625 First Ave., Hampton;
  (309) 752-0362. Old-fashioned ice-cream parlor right on the trail;
  back deck overlooks the Mississippi River.

Accommodations
- Illiniwek Forest Preserve, IL 84 north of Hampton; (309) 496-2620.
  Pitch a tent on the river's edge.

- Stony Creek Inn, 101 18th St., Moline; (309) 743-0101; www.stoney
  creekinn.com. Outdoors-themed hotel in downtown Moline, right
  alongside the path.

- Leisure Harbor Inn Bed and Breakfast, 701 Main Ave., Cordova; (309)
  654-2233; www.leisureharborinn.com. Four guest rooms; located on
  the Mississippi River.

25 MISSISSIPPI RIVER TRAIL— THOMSON TO FULTON

This short trip between the two Mississippi River towns of Thomson and Fulton offers a pleasing collection of scenic riverside spots. Near Thomson the trail brushes against a beautiful, bird-laden wetland area and an unusual sand prairie. Before reaching Fulton, catch expansive views of the Mississippi River with a short side trip to Lock 13. In Fulton the river levee guides you to the town's main attraction, a traditional Dutch windmill located on the bank of the river.

Activities:

Start: Thomson Causeway Recreation Area along the Mississippi River in Thomson

Length: 10.3 miles one-way, with a couple of on-road options for extending the route

Surface: Crushed gravel for the first couple of miles, followed by paved path

Wheelchair access: The trail is wheelchair accessible.

Difficulty: The trail is easy.

Restrooms: There are public restrooms at the Thomson Causeway Recreation Area's main picnic area (water here and at trail's starting point), the gas station on 14th Avenue, and the windmill in Fulton (water).

Maps: USGS Thomson, Clinton NW, and Clinton; *DeLorme: Illinois Atlas and Gazetteer:* Pages 23 and 24

Hazards: None

Access and parking: On I-88 west of Rock Falls take exit 36 (Como Road) north. Keep straight as Como Road merges with US 30 heading west. Turn right onto IL 78 and follow it for nearly 10 miles before turning left onto Thomson Road. Follow Thomson Road as its name changes to Argo Fay Road and then to Main Street. After Thomson, turn left onto Lewis Avenue

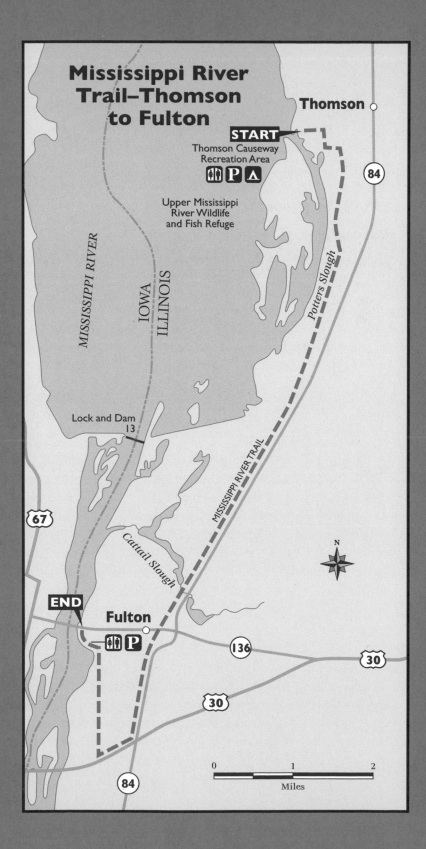

Mississippi River Trail–Thomson to Fulton

Thomson

START
Thomson Causeway
Recreation Area

84

Upper Mississippi
River Wildlife
and Fish Refuge

MISSISSIPPI RIVER

IOWA

ILLINOIS

Potters Slough

Lock and Dam
13

MISSISSIPPI RIVER TRAIL

67

Cattail Slough

N

END

Fulton

136

30

30

84

0   1   2
Miles

and enter Thomson Causeway Recreation Area. Once past the gatehouse, stay to the right, following signs for the River Birch camping area. On the road leading to the camping area, park in the small lot on the right next to the bike path. UTM coordinates: 15T, 739401 E, 4648577 N

The Dutch windmill in Fulton offers parking and access to the trail. From the intersection of IL 84 and IL 136, follow IL 136 east toward the river. Turn right onto Fourth Street and then left onto 10th Avenue.

Transportation: Amtrak trains stop in Galesburg.

Rentals: Arnold's Bike and Embroidery, 319 Main St., Thomson; (815) 259-8289; located blocks from the trailhead

Contact: City of Fulton Chamber of Commerce, P.O. Box 253, Fulton 61252; www.cityoffulton.us; (815) 589-4545

U.S. Fish and Wildlife Service, Savanna District; 7071 Riverview Rd., Thomson 61285; (815) 273-2732

|||||||||||||||||||||||||||||||||||||||||||||||||||||||||||||||||||||||||||||||||||||||

As you reach the end of this route, you'll come across an odd sight: a traditional Dutch windmill on the banks of the Mississippi. But getting a better look, it seems like a natural spot for the 100-foot-tall windmill. The windmill is perched on the flood-control dike in Fulton, a town where Dutch heritage runs deep and wide.

While this fully operational windmill looks old, it's not: It was built in 2000 by Dutch craftsmen using traditional methods. Wind turns the head (or cap) and the sails. The grinding machinery takes up three floors and uses a set of blue basalt millstones that produce flours from buckwheat, corn, rye, and wheat.

Start your way toward the windmill from the much smaller town, Thomson, located a few miles upriver from Fulton. As you start from the trailhead, the crushed-rock trail winds through grassland managed by the U.S. Fish and Wildlife Service. The sandy soil supports plants unusual for the area, such as prickly pear cactus, visible on the side of the trail. At about 1.75 miles the trail rises just enough to provide striking views of the lush wetlands known as Potters Marsh and Potters Slough. With the help of field glasses, you'll likely see ducks, pelicans, and wading birds such as great blue herons and white egrets.

After the trail drops you off on a narrow, very quiet paved road, the route accompanies gently rolling grassland dotted with the occasional pine trees. Like the grassland earlier, an unusual sandy soil is prevalent here. This sand prairie, as it's called, has been designated as a state preserve. At the stop sign, consider taking a side trip to Lock and Dam 13, where you can enjoy views of the widest pool on the Upper Mississippi River. (This will add about 4.0 miles to the route. There are picnic areas, restrooms, water, and great views of lock and dam.)

Continuing toward Fulton you'll cross Johnson Creek just before pulling alongside IL 84. Farther ahead, the route passes a small municipal park and the Fulton Industrial Park.

The parkland along the river in Fulton offers many spots to linger. Kiwanis Park is where the path mounts the levee that keeps back the river's floodwaters. Grab a bench to sit and watch the waterbirds, or just enjoy

This bridge over the Mississippi River connects Fulton, Illinois, with Clinton, Iowa.

the view of the huge steel-truss bridge rising 65 feet above the water, connecting Fulton with Clinton, Iowa. The river is only 0.3 mile across here; upstream by Lock and Dam 13 it swells to about 3 miles across.

Continuing under the bridge along the levee brings you to the Dutch windmill. On street level, you can enter the windmill and drop in at the visitor center housed inside. After completing the trail, consider visiting some of the old storefront buildings that line the town's nearby shopping district. For another option, instead of retracing your route, return to the rail trail by heading east on Ninth Avenue.

Major Milepoints

2.0 Turn right onto the paved road.

7.1 In Fulton the signs direct you to perform a quick zigzag on streets for 0.2 mile. Turn right onto 14th Street (IL 136) and then immediately left onto 14th Avenue.

Local Information

- Blackhawk Waterways Convention and Visitors Bureau, 201 North Franklin Ave., Polo 61064; (800) 678-2108 or (815) 946-2108; www .bwcvb.com

Local Events/Attractions

- The Dutch Windmill, 10th Avenue and First Street, Fulton; (815) 589-4545; www.cityoffulton.us. Milling demonstrations, a gift shop, and Fulton's visitor center.

- Heritage Canyon, 515 North Fourth St., Fulton; (815) 589-4545; www .cityoffulton.us. Re-created historic village within a rock quarry near the Mississippi River.

- Lock & Dam 13 walking tours; (815) 259-3628. Offered Sun at 1:00 p.m. from the end of May to the beginning of Sept.

- Melon Days; www.thomsonil.com/index.html. Thomson, the Melon Capital of the World, hosts this festival on Labor Day weekend.

Restaurants

- Cousin's Subs and Freezer's Ice Cream; 1510 10th Avenue, Fulton; (815) 589-2681

- Harbor Café and Pizzeria; known locally for its pizza; 1901 South 4th Street; (815) 589-4747

Accommodations

- Comfort Inn and Suites, 1301 17th St. (corner of IL 84 and IL 136), Fulton; (815) 589-3333

- Super 8, 101 Valley View Dr., Savanna; (815) 273-2288. Indoor pool.

- Thomson Causeway Recreation Area; (815) 259-2353. Operated by the U.S. Army Corps of Engineers; 131 campsites draw in the RV crowd.

- Mississippi Palisades State Park, 16327 A, Highway 84, Savanna; (815) 273-2731; http://dnr.state.il.us/lands/landmgt/parks/r1/palisade.htm. Camp store and 240 sites; great hiking trails.

CENTRAL ILLINOIS

Contrary to popular belief, central Illinois is not one great expanse of farmland. Sure, there's plenty of corn and soy, but there are also great parks, interesting towns and cites, and a nice collection of rail trails that run through a mix of urban and rural settings. A handful of the rail trails in central Illinois are located in the vicinity of Bloomington, Decatur, Springfield, and Peoria. If you've never visited, now's your chance to get to know these cities that sprouted up on the central Illinois prairie. Expect to see leafy parks, pleasant neighborhoods, and historic downtowns.

The highlight among central Illinois rail trails is the Rock Island Trail, which runs north from Peoria. Along this 30-mile-long trail, you'll encounter a few small towns, wetlands, woods, and plenty of wide-open farmland before crossing the Spoon River on an old train bridge. In the late nineteenth century, trains used this route for transporting grains to the distilleries of Peoria, cementing it's the city's status as the whiskey capital of the world. Another feature of the Rock Island Trail: There's an excellent campground alongside the trail specifically for trail users.

Given that two of the trails in central Illinois have the words "Lincoln" and "Prairie" in their names, it's difficult to miss the local historic connections. While the big prairies are mostly gone, the legacy of the sixteenth U.S. president remains vibrant. Tourism bureaus throughout the area are grateful that Lincoln visited so many local courthouses as an itinerate lawyer. And of course the state capital of Springfield contains museums and a roster of historic landmarks relating to Lincoln's career as a state politician.

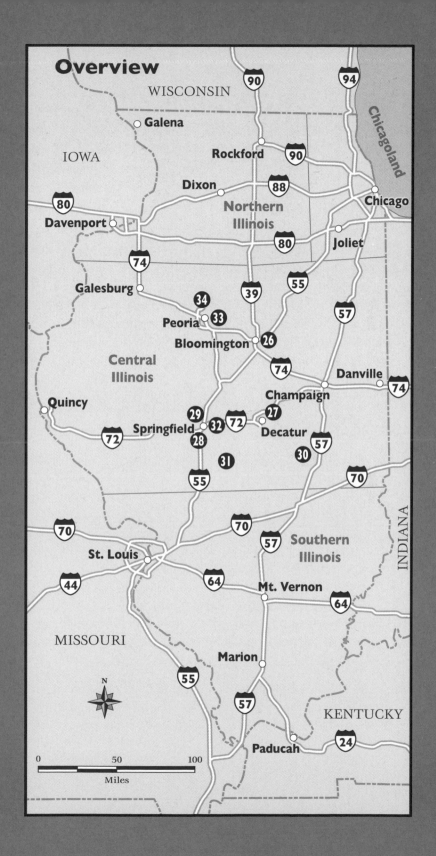

26 CONSTITUTION TRAIL

There's nary a better way to get to know the cities of Bloomington and Normal than following this urban trail as it runs through the center of each town. The tree-lined north section of the trail takes you through Normal's new residential areas, public parks, and downtown. To the south in Bloomington, you'll see the town's old warehouse district and pleasant residential neighborhoods before heading west into the outlying countryside. In between these two sections, you'll follow a 1.0-mile-long on-street section that cuts through a historic neighborhood containing a collection of fine Victorian homes.

Activities:

Start: North end of the trail at the Kerrick Road parking area, north of Bloomington-Normal

Length: 11.0 miles one-way

Surface: Asphalt

Wheelchair access: The entire path is wheelchair accessible.

Difficulty: The trail is easy.

Restrooms: There are public restrooms at Rosa Parks Commons (water), Allers Shelter Wayside (water), Atwood Wayside Herb Garden (water), Alton Depot Park (water only), and the Route 9 Wayside (portable toilet).

Maps: USGS Normal East, Bloomington East, and Bloomington West; *DeLorme: Illinois Atlas and Gazetteer:* Pages 42 and 52; Constition Trail Map, Normal Parks and Recreation, www.normal.org/Files/trailmap.pdf

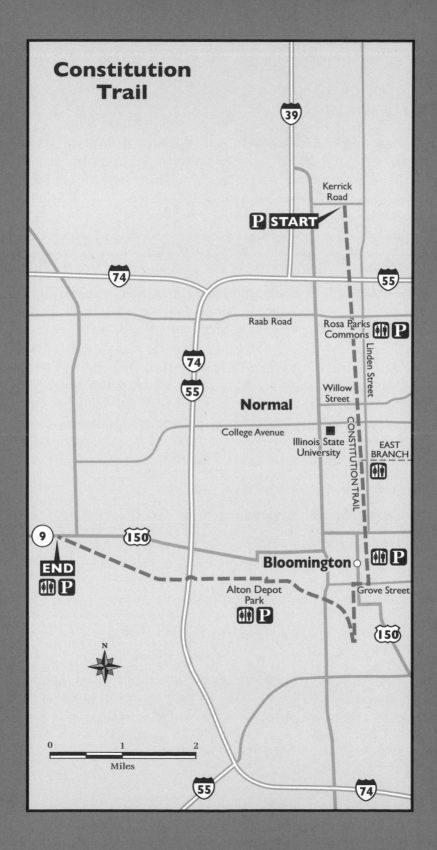

Hazards: During the warmer months, the main section of the trail in Normal can be busy with walkers and cyclists.

Access and parking: From Bloomington-Normal, follow I-55 north to I-39. Continue north on I-39 and then exit south onto US 51. Turn left onto Kerrick Road. The parking area is on the right. Coming from the northeast, take I-55 south to I-39 and follow the directions above. UTM coordinates: 16T, 331640 E, 4490919 N

To reach Rosa Parks Commons, take Main Street (US 51) north from downtown Bloomington or Normal. Turn right onto Raab Road. The parking area is on the right.

To catch the trail in downtown Normal, head south on Linden Street at College Avenue in downtown Normal. Cross the tracks and enter the parking area on the right. (The path runs by the Amtrak station.)

To access the trail at the Atwood Wayside, go to the corner of Washington Street and Clinton Avenue in Bloomington. Head north on Clinton, and then take the first right on Jefferson Street. The wayside is on the left when you reach Robinson Avenue.

To reach the Route 9 Wayside (the endpoint for this route), head west from Bloomington on Market Street (IL 9/US 150). The wayside is on the left just after passing the Mitsubishi Motorway.

Transportation: Amtrak serves Bloomington/Normal.

Rentals: No nearby bike rentals are available.

Contact: Town of Normal, 100 East Phoenix Ave., P.O. Box 589; Normal 61761; (309) 454-2444; www.normal.org/Gov/ParksandRec/Facilities/ConstitutionTrail.asp

S et within the most fertile farmland in Illinois, the twin cities of Bloomington and Normal both claim rich histories and an intriguing mix of people. Farmers of course come to the cities to pick up supplies and unload their harvest. Teachers, students, and administrators come to the sprawling campus of Illinois State University in Normal. And workers come for jobs at places with familiar names such as State Farm Insurance, Mitsubishi, and Beer Nuts . . . yes, Beer Nuts. (More on that later.)

Dedicated in September 1987 in celebration of the 200th anniversary of the U.S. Constitution, the Constitution Trail now includes a half dozen trail segments within the two cities. Some of these are branches connected to the main north–south stem; others are not connected. A couple of the more notable branches of the main stem are mentioned below; learn about the shorter disconnected segments by getting a copy of the Constitution Trail map.

The parking area on Kerrick Road, where this route starts, sits beside a series of monolithic grain silos that look vaguely like silver spaceships ready for liftoff. Heading south along the trail, you'll see the agricultural fields and light industry that adorn the outskirts of every medium-size Illinois city. After the I-55 underpass, you can survey a long progression of residential backyards. Continuing ahead, the trail passes a collection of sports fields at Rosa Parks Commons and a spur trail that heads 1.3 miles east alongside Raab Road.

Getting closer to downtown Normal, the tree-lined trail corridor passes Creek Nature Sanctuary, decorated with wildflowers, prairie grasses, and groves of hardwood. In downtown Normal, things get busy as the trail crosses College Avenue, the town's main business strip, and then runs by the Amtrak station and Normal City Hall. Keep an eye on the route in downtown Normal. It gets fuzzy at times but is easy to figure out.

South of downtown Normal, consider a side trip on the 4.4-mile eastern arm of the Constitution Trail as it runs beside pleasant residential backyards, past two small public gardens, and alongside Sugar Creek. The fun dissipates for the final 2.4 miles of this route as it accompanies General Electric Road: The traffic is relentless, and the suburban sprawl is less than scenic.

Passing the eastern arm of the Constitution Trail, the trail mounts an embankment built for the railroad and then passes beneath a historic bridge. The bridge, listed on the National Register of Historic Places, is the only surviving camelback-style bridge in Illinois. Built with wood in 1904, it was constructed with a distinctive high arch that allowed steam locomotives to pass underneath. During a recent restoration, the bridge's hump was lowered to allow vehicles easier passage on Virginia Street. Continuing south, the camelback theme continues as the trail crosses two newly constructed arched pedestrian bridges. The first provides a view of Sugar Creek down below; the second passes over Emerson Avenue.

Emerging from the short tunnel under Washington Street, you'll see the one and only Beer Nuts factory to the right. This family-owned company has been producing nut snacks under various names since 1937. In the 1950s the company changed its name to Beer Nuts when it was trying to get local bar owners to stock the salty, thirst-inducing treats.

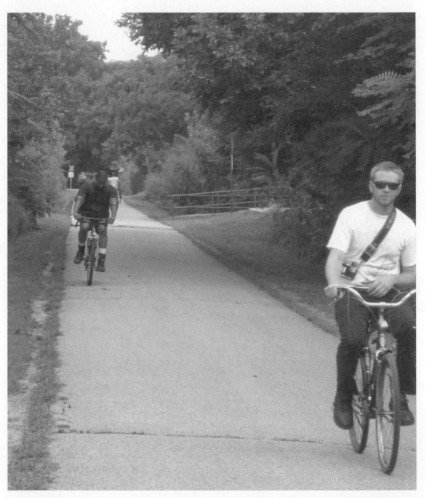

The Constitution Trail is popular with the students at Illinois State University in Normal.

The on-street portion of the route takes you on a brief tour through a neighborhood of attractive Victorian homes on South Clayton Street. One of the most striking is the Vrooman Mansion, now a bed-and-breakfast, at the corner of South Clayton and Taylor Streets.

Getting back on the rail trail at Lincoln Avenue brings you into Bloomington's old industrial area. Interpretive signs along the path explain that many businesses once operated warehouses along this stretch of railroad. An old brown-brick building on the left was built by Illinois's own John Deere Company in 1847. Also operating in the area was a foundry and a National Guard armory, both located close to the tracks for easy transportation.

Leaving the industrial area, you'll see the high steeple of St. Mary's Church, built in 1886 by German immigrants who lived in the neighborhood. After passing through tiny Allen Depot Park, the trail descends a hill and then accompanies Washington Street through a more recently built industrial area.

After passing under I-55/74, the path breaks away from Washington Street and suddenly transports you into the Illinois countryside. The final couple of miles of trail lead you through wooded and grassy stretches with cropland always in the background.

Major Milepoints

5.3 Turn right onto Grove Street to begin the 1.0-mile on-street segment. To visit the Beer Nuts company store, turn right onto South Robinson Street 1 block west of the trail.

5.5 Turn left onto South Clayton Street.

6.3 At Lincoln Street turn right. Pick up the path before the cemetery on the right.

Local Information

•   Bloomington-Normal Area Convention and Visitors Bureau, 3201 CIRA Dr., Suite 201, Bloomington 61704; (309) 665-0033 or (800) 433-8226; www.bloomingtonnormalcvb.org

•   City of Bloomington, 109 East Olive St.; Bloomington 61701; (309) 434-2509; www.cityblm.org/page.asp?show=section&id=2800

Local Events/Attractions

• Beer Nuts Plant and Company Store, 103 North Robinson St., Bloomington; (309) 827-8580; www.beernuts.com

• David Davis Mansion State Historic Site, 1000 East Monroe Dr., Bloomington; (309) 828-1084; http://daviddavismansion.org. Take a tour of this posh historic home once owned by a U.S. Supreme Court judge. Located a few blocks off the trail.

• Illinois Shakespeare Festival, Campus Box 5700, Normal; (309) 438-2535; www.thefestival.org. This popular event takes place in early Aug at the Ewing Manor.

Restaurants

• The Garlic Press Market Cafe, restaurant adjoins a cooking/gift store; heavy emphasis on fresh, healthy ingredients; 106 North St., Normal; (309) 852-0987; www.thegarlicpress.com

Accommodations

• Burr House Bed and Breakfast, 210 East Chestnut St., Bloomington (Located across the street from Franklin Park); (309) 828-4182; http://home.comcast.net/~leighton.cook/BurrHouse

• Comlara County Park, 13001 Recreation Area Dr., Hudson; (309) 726-2025; www.mcleancountyil.gov/Parks/Camping.htm. The best camping in the area. Located fifteen minutes north of Bloomington.

• Vrooman Mansion Bed and Breakfast, 701 East Taylor St.; (309) 828-8816; http://vroomanmansion.com. Impressive Victorian home with 36 rooms on three floors. The on-street portion of this route runs by the front door.

27 DECATUR TRAILS

Explore this patchwork of trails that run through a series of city parks and neighborhoods in southwest Decatur. Along the way you'll encounter plenty of watery attractions, such as Stevens Creek, the Sangamon River and its wetlands, and the Lake Decatur Dam.

Activities:

Start: Fairview Park, located on the west side of Decatur

Length: 5.3 miles one-way, optional side trip to Rock Springs Conservation Area

Surface: Asphalt

Wheelchair access: Most of the route featured here is wheelchair accessible. Although short on-street sections of this route do include sidewalks, not all the sidewalks have ramps for wheelchair users.

Difficulty: The route is easy.

Restrooms: There are public restrooms and water at Fairview, Kiwanis, and Lincoln Parks.

Maps: USGS Decatur and Harristown; *DeLorme: Illinois Atlas and Gazetteer:* Page 62

Hazards: None

Access and parking: From I-72 west of Decatur, head east on US 36. Turn right onto South Fairview Avenue (IL 48) and then right onto Eldorado Street. Enter Fairview Park and park in the lot behind the amphitheatre. Catch the trail as it runs east near the parking area. UTM coordinates: 16S, 330551 E, 4412285 N

To park at the east end of the trail near Lake Decatur, head south on Main Street from US 36. Turn right onto Lincoln Park Drive before crossing the Lake Decatur Dam.

Transportation: The closest Amtrak stations are in Springfield and Mattoon.

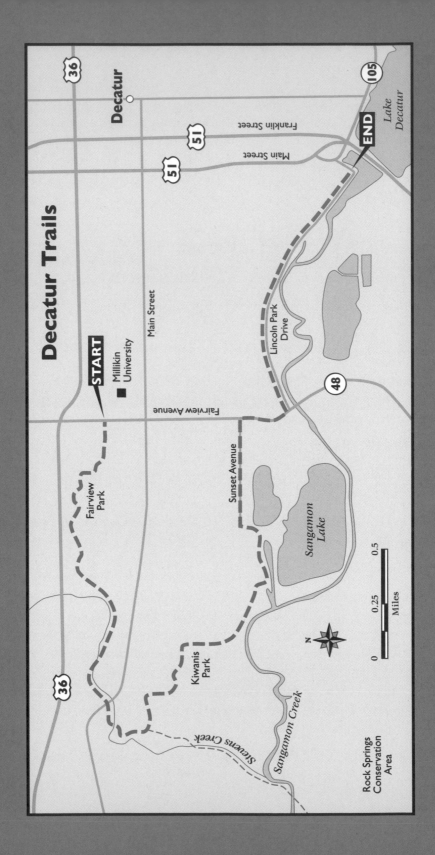

Rentals: No nearby bike rentals are available.

Contact: Decatur Park District, 620 East Riverside Ave., Decatur 62521; (217) 422-5911; www.decatur-parks.org

||||||||||||||||||||||||||||||||||||||||||||||||||||||||||||||||||||||||||||||||||

A s you follow this horseshoe-shaped route west from Fairview Park and then east toward Lake Decatur, you'll get to know the parks, neighborhoods, streams, and wetlands of southwest Decatur. Individually these places are not exactly goose bump–inducing spots of unparalleled beauty or historical interest, but taken together they provide an enjoyable overview of many of the beloved places within this central Illinois community. On this route you'll also have the opportunity for a scenic side trip to the Rock Springs Conservation Area to the southwest.

Fairview Park, where this route starts, is a pleasant urban recreation area with a rolling, grassy landscape. Starting near the music pavilion, you'll scoot past a duck pond and several picnic areas and then cross a bridge over a park road. On the other side of the bridge, the trail gradually descends through lush woodland. Stevens Creek runs at the bottom of a 70-foot-deep ravine on the right; another lesser ravine tumbles downward on the left. At the end of this glorious wooded section, the trail crosses a high pedestrian bridge over Stevens Creek. A steep path takes you down past several creekside picnic spots before ducking under Main Street.

In an area thick with bottomland woods, you'll come to the junction with a trail that leads to Rock Springs Conservation Area. Go to the right for the 2.2-mile side trip (one-way) that takes you over the Sangamon River, though wetlands and a pine forest, and up a series of river bluffs that guide you nearly 100 feet above the river. Rock Springs Conservation Area is chock-full of picnic areas, hiking trails, and historic attractions.

As you continue on the main route (to the left), the trail mounts a gentle rise overlooking a swath of native prairie. Just beyond the entrance to the city's water treatment facility, the trail cuts through Kiwanis Park and then follows a levee protecting Decatur's southwest neighborhoods from the periodic flooding of the Sangamon River. Enjoy the view of the surrounding wetlands as you follow the levee's raised embankment.

From the levee you'll follow a 0.75-mile on-street section in order to connect with the rest of the route. On Lincoln Park Avenue you'll pick up a new trail that follows the upper edge of a bluff above the Sangamon River and its accompanying bottomlands. After skirting the edge of the hilly terrain at Lincoln Park, the bottomland woods grow dense. Getting closer to the dam, the river gets wide and anglers line the rocky banks. This is also where the trail shares its route with a quiet access road along the river. The rushing water at the Lake Decatur Dam marks the end of the route.

Major Milepoints

1.9   Stay left at the trail junction. (**Side trip:** Go to the right to take the 4.4-mile round-trip excursion to Spring Rock Conservation Area.)

3.3   Turn right onto Sunset Avenue.

3.8   Turn right onto Fairview Avenue.

4.0   Turn left onto the trail that runs beside Lincoln Park Drive.

Local Information

- Central Illinois Tourism Development Office, 700 East Adams St., Springfield 62701; (217) 525-7980; www.visitcentralillinois.com

- Decatur Area Convention and Visitors Bureau, 202 East North St., Decatur 62523; (217) 423-7000; www.decaturcvb.com

- Rock Springs Conservation Area, 3939 Nearing Lane, Decatur; (217) 423-7708; www.maconcountyconservation.org. The center contains ponds, hiking trails, and a homestead prairie farm exhibit.

Local Events/Attractions

- Macon County Museum Complex, 5580 North Fork Rd., Decatur; (217) 422-4919; www.decaturcvb.com. Includes a log courthouse where Lincoln tried cases, a one-room schoolhouse, and several other historic buildings.

- Scovill Park, 71 South Country Club Rd., Decatur; (217) 422-5911; www.decatur-parks.org. Park contains a zoo, gardens, and a children's museum. Located on the south shore of Lake Decatur.

Restaurants

- Bizou, 122 North Main St., Decatur; (217) 422-7000. French restaurant with an eclectic atmosphere.

- Doherty's Pub and Pins, 242 East William St., Decatur; (217) 428-5612; www.dohertyspubandpins.com. Irish food and drink.

Accommodations

- Friends Creek Regional Park; (217) 423-7708; www.maconcounty conservation.org. County-owned park with a campground, hiking trails, and a historic schoolhouse.

- Younker House Bed and Breakfast, 500 West Main St., Decatur; (217) 429-9718. Brick home in the historic district.

Lake Decatur was created with this dam along the Sangamon River.

28 GREEN DIAMOND TRAIL

As you follow this short trail between two small rural towns, you'll encounter wide-ranging views of the surrounding farmland. You'll cross Maucopin Creek and its wooded banks on the north end of the trail. At the south end of the trail, cyclists may want to take a side trip to a shrine intended to protect travelers along former Route 66.

Activities:

Start: Veterans Park in Farmersville, located about 25 miles south of Springfield

Length: 4.4 miles one-way

Surface: Small rock chips applied over a tar surface

Wheelchair access: The trail is wheelchair accessible, although sections of South Cleveland Street do not have sidewalks.

Difficulty: The route is easy.

Restrooms: There are no public restrooms on this route.

Maps: USGS Farmersville and Atwater; *DeLorme: Illinois Atlas and Gazetteer:* Page 69; Illinois Bicycle Map, Region 6, Illinois Department of Transportation, www.dot.state.il.us/bikemap/state.html

Hazards: None

Access and parking: From I-55 exit west to Farmersville on Main Street. Turn left onto South Cleveland Avenue. Park at Veterans Park on Knobbe and South Cleveland Streets. From the park head south on South Cleveland Street. The trail starts on the right at the end of the street. UTM coordinates: 16S, 271847 E, 4369003 N

To park at the south end of the trail, exit west on IL 48/127. Immediately turn right onto Frontage Road. Turn left onto Waggoner Road and park next to the old train depot.

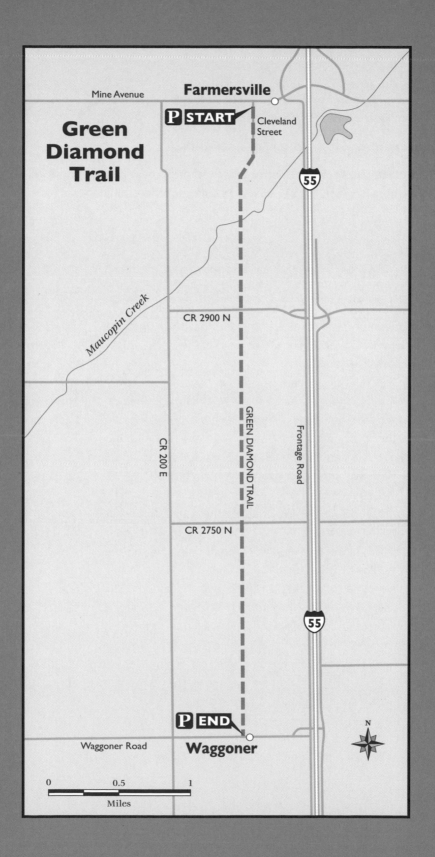

Green Diamond Trail

Mine Avenue

Farmersville

P START

Cleveland Street

I-55

Maucopin Creek

CR 2900 N

CR 200 E

GREEN DIAMOND TRAIL

Frontage Road

CR 2750 N

I-55

P END

Waggoner Road

Waggoner

N

0   0.5   1
Miles

Transportation: The closest Amtrak station is in Carlinville, located about 15 miles southwest of Waggoner.

Rentals: No nearby bike rentals are available.

Contact: Montgomery County Offices, Montgomery County Courthouse, Hillsboro 62049; (217) 532-9530; www.montgomeryco.com

||||||||||||||||||||||||||||||||||||||||||||||||||||||||||||||||||||||||||||||

The Green Diamond was the Illinois Central Railroad's fastest of several trains that ran between Chicago, Springfield, and St. Louis. The train, in operation until 1968, was painted in a two-tone green that led to its nickname, "Tobacco Worm." The train made seven stops during a journey of nearly five hours. This trail follows a short section of the Green Diamond Line as it ran through farm country between Farmersville and Waggoner.

After picking up the minimally marked trailhead on the south edge of the village of Farmersville, you'll pass through a grove of cottonwoods and then cross a small tributary to Maucopin Creek. Once you get on the straight-as-an-arrow railroad right-of-way, dense woodland appears on the left as you cross over the creek's main branch.

The 70-mile-long creek is named for a yellow pond lily—historically a favorite food source of local Native Americans. The lily has a large root that was baked in a fire pit. (In 1677 one European visitor observed that Native Americans in the area regularly gathered and ate fourteen different kinds of root plants, including maucopin.)

After the creek, the big trees dwindle and the shrubs and smaller trees take over. Prairie flowers such as goldenrod, Queen Anne's lace, and phlox decorate the sides of the trail. A half mile to the east is the constantly buzzing I-55. Frontage Road—which served as Route 66 from 1940 to 1977—sits beside the interstate. You'll catch glimpses of these roads now and then, but for the most part the landscape is dominated by agricultural land with a sprinkling of farms in the distance.

At the south end of the trail in the hamlet of Waggoner sits a tiny historic train depot within a small park. Before heading back to Farmersville, take a break on the bench within the park's little wooden gazebo.

If you're on a bicycle and are interested in Route 66 history, you may want to put more miles under your tires with a 3.7-mile trip south from Waggoner to the Shrine of Our Lady of the Highways. Erected by school-children in 1959 along the former Route 66, the shrine's statue of the Virgin Mother is meant to watch over travelers along the Mother Road.

To reach the shrine, head east on Main Street in Waggoner. Turn right onto Frontage Road as it runs on the west side of I-55. The shrine is located south of Goby Road (North 23rd Road) at 22353 West Frontage Road.

The Shrine of Our Lady of Highways is one of a few Route 66 landmarks found in the area. In Farmersville there's Art's Restaurant and Motel. Litchfield, a dozen miles south of Waggoner, hosts Route 66 attractions like the Ariston Cafe, a diner open since 1924, and the still-operating Skyview Drive-In Theatre.

Local Information

- Central Illinois Tourism Development Office, 700 East Adams, Springfield 62701; (217) 525-7980; www.visitcentralillinois.com

- City of Litchfield Office of Tourism, 120 East Ryder St., Litchfield 62056; (217) 324-5253; www.cityoflitchfieldil.com

- Springfield Convention and Visitors Bureau, 109 North Seventh St., Springfield 62701; (217) 789-2360; www.visit-spring fieldillinois.com

Local Events/Attractions

- Mother Jones Monument and Union Miners Cemetery, Lake Street, Mt. Olive; (217) 999-4261. Monument honors the famous labor activist who fought for coal miners' rights. Cemetery contains the graves of miners who were killed in the 1898 mining riots.

- Shrine of Our Lady of the Highways, 22353 West Frontage Rd., Raymond; www.ourladyofthehighways.com. Built in 1959 as a high school project. Located 3.7 miles south of Waggoner.

- Sky View Drive-In Theatre, 150 North Historic Old Route 66, Litchfield; (217) 324-2533; www.litchfieldskyview.com. Last surviving drive-in along the historic roadway.

Restaurants

*   Art's Motel and Restaurant, 101 Main St., Farmersville; (217) 227-3277. Classic Route 66 diner from 1920; recently refurbished and reopened.

*   Ariston Cafe, 413 Old Route 66 North Road, Litchfield; (217) 324-2023; www.ariston-cafe.com. Originally opened in 1924 but relocated when Route 66 was rerouted. Still owned by same family, it is said to be the oldest cafe on Route 66.

Accommodations

*   Best Western Carlinville, I-55 and IL 108, Carlinville, (217) 324-2100. Indoor pool and Jacuzzi; located just a few miles south of the trail.

*   Sangchris Lake State Park, 9898 Cascade Rd., Rochester; (217) 498-9208; http://dnr.state.il.us/lands/landmgt/parks/r4/sangch.htm. Two large campgrounds and one small walk-in camping area.

This old wooden train depot sits at the south end of the Green Diamond Trail in Waggoner.

29 INTERURBAN TRAIL

While exploring this route between southwest Springfield and the nearby town of Chatham, you'll see suburban neighborhoods, attractive woodlands, and the occasional agricultural field. Near Chatham the trail runs for a stretch alongside a lovely section of Lake Springfield and its adjoining wetlands.

Activities:

Start: North trailhead, near the corner of IL 4 and IL 54 in southwest Springfield

Length: 9.2 miles one-way

Surface: Asphalt

Wheelchair access: The entire trail is wheelchair accessible.

Difficulty: The route is easy.

Restrooms: There are portable toilets and water at a park on the left side of the trail at 0.4 mile.

Maps: USGS Springfield West and Chatham; *DeLorme: Illinois Atlas and Gazetteer:* Pages 60 and 61; Illinois Bicycle Map, Region 6, Illinois Department of Transportation, www.dot.state.il.us/bikemap/state.html

Hazards: Use caution while crossing a handful of busy streets.

Access and parking: Head west on I-72 south of Springfield and exit north on Veterans Parkway (IL 4). Turn left onto Lindbergh Boulevard and right onto Robbins Road. The trailhead parking area is on the right. UTM coordinates: 16S, 267630 E, 4403907 N

To park at the trailhead on Park Avenue, head east on Wabash Avenue (IL 54) from IL 4. Turn right onto Park Avenue; the parking area is to the right on Park Avenue.

There is no established parking area at the south end of the trail. The best option is to park at the small town square park at the corner of IL 4 and Mulberry Street. Catch the trail by heading east on Mulberry Street.

Transportation: Amtrak serves Springfield.

Rentals: No nearby bike rentals are available.

Contact: Springfield Park District, 2500 South 11th Street, Springfield 62703; (217) 544-1751; www.springfieldparks.org

||||||||||||||||||||||||||||||||||||||||||||||||||||||||||||||||||||||||||||||||||||||

The Interurban Trail is one of a half dozen rail trails in Illinois built on the former routes of electric passenger trains that stitched together communities in central and southern Illinois. The largest of these interurban train operations was the Illinois Terminal Company. At its peak, the company operated trains on more than 550 miles of tracks connecting cities such as Danville, Champaign, Decatur, Bloomington, Peoria, Springfield, and Edwardsville. In 1910 the McKinley Bridge brought trains across the Mississippi to St. Louis. Before the widespread demise of passenger train service in the mid-1950s, Springfield hosted four different railroad depots that served as stops for the interurban trains.

The trailhead for the Interurban Trail is located in a suburban landscape of shopping malls, chain stores, and office buildings. The environment changes quickly, though, after you cross the pedestrian bridge over Veterans Parkway (IL 4). From the bridge you'll begin a tour of suburban Springfield backyards, some adorned with flower gardens.

After the trail brushes against the commercial strip on IL 54 and then crosses a couple of busy roads, the route shoots south alongside McArthur Road between a residential area on the right and agricultural land on the left. Then you'll duck under I-72 and pass some of its newly built surrounding developments before angling right and shadowing the Union Pacific Railroad. As you accompany the railroad, chokecherry and hickory trees provide leafy curtains on both sides of the trail.

The best part of the trail appears as you cross the west arm of Lake Springfield and then take an extended ramble alongside the lake's wetlands. Near the lake, check out the signs featuring photos of the old interurban rail line and its trains. As you cross the pedestrian bridge, big views open up of the lake's wooded shores and hills that slope down toward the

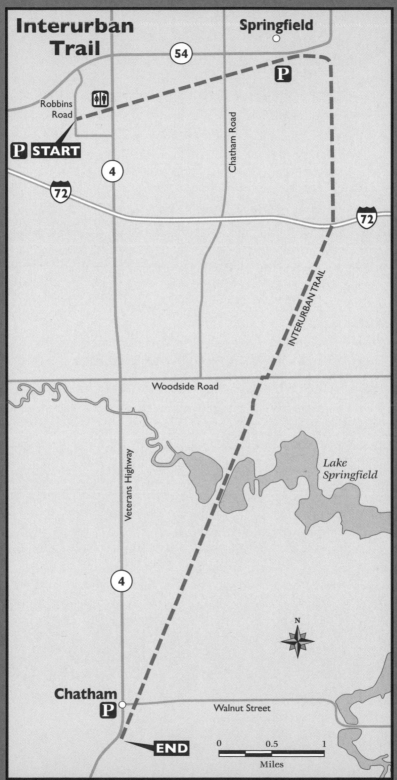

water. You're looking at the west end of the 9-mile-long artificial lake that was created in 1935 by damming Sugar Creek. Continuing south for nearly 0.5 mile, the trail traces an embankment about 20 feet above the open water and wetlands laden with cattails.

On the way into Chatham, the trail scoots alongside several golfing fairways and a swath of newly planted subdivisions. Once in Chatham, be sure to peek into the Chatham Railroad Museum, located in the old train depot alongside the trail. Since the hours are extremely limited, you probably won't find the museum open, but no matter; you can see most of the historic exhibits through the windows. The office contains a potbelly stove, a safe, an early typewriter, and a tabletop printing press and looks like you would imagine the interior of a small train depot to appear when the building was constructed in 1902.

Local Information

• Central Illinois Tourism Development Office, 700 East Adams St., Springfield 62701; (217) 525-7980; www.visitcentralillinois.com

• Springfield Convention and Visitors Bureau, 109 North Seventh St., Springfield 62701; (217) 789-2360; www.visit-springfieldillinois.com

The Interurban Trail spans the west arm of Lake Springfield.

Local Events/Attractions

- Abraham Lincoln Presidential Museum, 212 North Sixth St., Springfield; (800) 610-2094; www.alplm.org. This museum dedicated to Illinois's most-famous figure contains some high-tech attractions.

- Chatham Railroad Museum, 100 North State St., Chatham; (217) 483-7792

- Illinois State Museum, 502 South Spring St., Springfield; (217) 782-7386; www.museum.state.il.us. Permanent and changing exhibits on the state's land, life, people, and art.

- Old State Capitol State Historic Site, 1 Old State Capitol Plaza, Springfield; (217) 785-7960; www.oldstatecapitol.org/osc.htm. Restored with period furnishings.

Restaurants

- Mariah's Restaurant, 3317 Robbins Rd., Springfield; (217) 793-1900; www.mariahsrestaurant.com. Conveniently located across the street from the trailhead parking area.

- Sonic Drive-In, 1312 Wabash Ave., Springfield; (217) 787-8591. This fast-food joint is steps off the trail; cyclists like to hang out at the picnic tables.

- Fulgenzi's Trattoria and Pizzeria, 214 West Chestnut St.; Chatham; (217) 483-6133. Located next to the village square in Chatham.

Accommodations

- The Henry Mischler House, 803 East Edwards St., Springfield; (217) 525-2660; www.mischlerhouse.com

- Carpenter Street Hotel, 525 North Sixth Street, Springfield; (217) 789-9100; www.carpenterstreethotel.com. Affordable; located north of downtown.

- Sangchris Lake State Park, 9898 Cascade Rd., Rochester; (217) 498-9208; http://dnr.state.il.us/lands/landmgt/parks/r4/sangch.htm. Two large campgrounds and one small walk-in camping area.

30 LINCOLN PRAIRIE GRASS TRAIL

Starting out in Mattoon, the west half of this trail runs through sprawling tracts of farmland that are interrupted now and then with ravines, ponds, creeks, and patches of prairie and woods. In Charleston the eastern part of the trail borders several historic points of interest, including the oldest fairground in the state.

Activities:

Start: The Ninth Street baseball/softball fields in Mattoon

Length: 12.1 miles one-way

Surface: Sections of the trail within Mattoon and Charleston paved with asphalt; hard-packed crushed gravel on the rest of the trail

Wheelchair access: The trail and the parking areas are wheelchair accessible, but the parking areas have rough gravel.

Difficulty: This trail is easy; however, if the sun is hot or the wind is strong, this ride could become more difficult because of the lack of protection.

Restrooms: There are public restrooms at the Douglas-Hart Nature Center (water fountain at trailhead).

Maps: USGS Mattoon East, Charleston South, and Charleston North; *DeLorme: Illinois Atlas and Gazetteer:* Page 72; Illinois Bicycle Map, Region 5, Illinois Department of Transportation, www.dot.state.il.us/bikemap/state.html

Hazards: None

Access and parking: From I-57 head west on IL 16 at exit 190B. Turn right onto North 10th Street in Mattoon. The trailhead parking area is at the corner of 10th Street and Richmond Avenue. UTM coordinates: 16T, 382585 E, 4371285 N

To park at the Loxa Road parking area, take IL 16 east from I-57. About halfway between Charleston and Mattoon, go north on Loxa Road (CR North 1100 East). Park on the right where the trail crosses the road.

The easternmost parking area is at North Park in Charleston. From IL 16 in Charleston head north on Fourth Street and continue until it ends. Enter North Park along IL 130 to the right.

Transportation: Amtrak trains stop in Mattoon.

Rentals: No nearby bike rentals are available.

Contact: Charleston Parks and Recreation Department (maintains the east half of the trail), 520 Jackson Ave., Charleston 61920; (217) 345-6897; www .charlestonillinois.org

Mattoon Public Works Department (maintains the west half of the trail), 208 North 19th St., Mattoon 61938; (217) 234-3611; http://mattoon .illinois.gov

|||||||||||||||||||||||||||||||||||||||||||||||||||||||||||||||||||||||||||||||||||

This trail runs east–west between Mattoon and Charleston along a former railroad line built by the New York Central Railroad. On the way out of Mattoon, the trail runs by the town's water tower and a few light industrial buildings before it ducks under I-57. The next road after I-57, Lerna Road, provides access to the Douglas-Hart Nature Center, where you'll find a picnic spot, a collection of nature exhibits, and 2.5 miles of trails that wind through prairie, woodland, and wetland.

To make the 0.2-mile trip to the Douglas-Hart Nature Center from the trail, turn left onto Lerna Road and left again onto DeWitt Avenue. If riding, you may want to walk the bike along this busy stretch of roadway. The nature center is on the right.

Back on the trail, a wooden sign points out that prairie restoration is under way on the land alongside the trail. Indeed, the goldenrod, milkweed, compass plants, black-eyed Susans, morning glories, and trumpet vines provide a welcome buffer to the seemingly endless expanse of corn and soy. But don't get too distracted by trailside prairie plants on this stretch of trail: Every 30 yards or so, the trail squeezes between dual telephone poles. The poles positioned on each side of the trail create the curious effect of a continuous gateway, as if you're constantly entering some new territory.

Sure enough, just ahead new territory turns up. At the trail's halfway point, more trees start to appear on the side of the trail, and soon the route

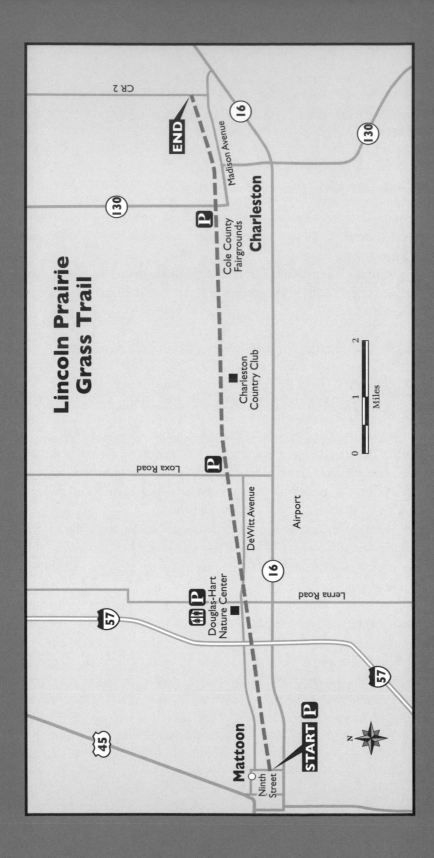

cuts through the middle of the golf course at the Charleston Country Club. After passing the golf course pond on the right, the trail dips below the surrounding landscape and then rises to mount a small ridge within a rural residential area. Up on the ridge, look through the walnut and maple trees on the right to see Cassell Creek flowing at the bottom of a 60- to 70-foot ravine.

Getting farther into Charleston brings you past the grandstand, the track, and the exhibit buildings of the Coles County Fairgrounds. The Coles County Fair has been running continuously since 1854—making it the oldest county fair in the state. In its early years, the fairgrounds hosted popular speakers such as William Jennings Bryan and the evangelist preacher Billy Sunday. In 1858 about 10,000 people showed up at the fairgrounds for one of the seven debates between Abraham Lincoln and Stephen Douglas in a campaign for one of the state's U.S. Senate seats. Although Lincoln lost the election, these debates launched him into national prominence that eventually led to his election as president. A small museum on the fairgrounds explores the debates through film, audio, artifacts, and photos. In the museum you'll learn that Lincoln was a regular visitor to the area—his parents lived south of Charleston at what is now Lincoln Log Cabin State Historic Site.

Not far ahead on the trail you'll see faded lettering on the side of long, squat brick building that once served as a plant for the Brown Shoe Company. If you look closely, you'll make out the huge letters bragging that workers here made "2,000 pairs daily." In the early 1900s the Brown Shoe Company (now owner of brands such as Famous Footwear and Naturalizer) branched out from its headquarters in St. Louis to build many plants such as this one in small Illinois towns that were beyond the reach of the large urban labor unions.

Crossing IL 130 brings you by a large grain elevator and a couple of old train depots. Beyond Olive Avenue, you'll immediately return to the rural landscape that you saw before entering Charleston. The trail ends at CR 2, nearly 1.5 miles past Olive Avenue. While in Charleston, be sure to check out its charming downtown area, located 0.25 mile south of where the trail intersects IL 130.

Local Information

* Charleston Tourism Office, 520 Jackson Ave., Charleston 61920; (217) 348-0430; www.charlestontourism.org

- Mattoon Welcome Center, 500 Broadway Ave., Mattoon 61938; (800) 500-6286; http://mattoon.illinois.gov

Local Events/Attractions

- Charleston's historic downtown; (217) 348-0430; www.charleston tourism.org. Check out the courthouse and murals depicting the community's history.

- Coles County Fair, P.O. Box 225, Charleston; (217) 345-2656; www .colescountyfair.com. The fair runs for a week in early August.

- Douglas-Hart Nature Center, 2204 Dewitt Ave. East, Mattoon; (217) 235-4644; www.dhnature.org. Located 1 block from the trail.

- Lincoln-Douglas Debate Museum, 416 West Madison Ave.; (217) 348-0430. Located at the Coles County Fairgrounds.

Restaurants

- Bangkok Thai, 1140 Lincoln Ave., Charleston; (217) 348-1232; www .bangkokthaicharleston.com. Good food and a pleasant atmosphere.

- Jackson Avenue Coffee, 708 Jackson Ave., Charleston; (217) 345-5283; www.jacksonavenuecoffee.com. Serves up the good stuff in a great downtown location.

- Monical's Pizza, 815 Broadway Ave., Mattoon; (217) 234-6442; www .monicalspizza.com. Regional pizzeria chain.

Accommodations

- Days Inn Charleston, 810 West Lincoln Ave., Charleston; (217) 345-7689. Clean and affordable.

- Fox Ridge State Park, 18175 State Park Rd., Charleston; (217) 345-6416; http://dnr.state.il.us/lands/landmgt/parks/r3/fox/fox.htm. Occupies a beautiful spot south of Charleston along the Embarras River. Plenty of campsites and several small cabins.

- The Osage Inn, 13444 East CR 720 North, Charleston; (217) 345-2622; www.bbonline.com/il/osageinn. Guests stay in an 1860s log home.

31 LINCOLN PRAIRIE TRAIL

The best part of this trail is the north section that runs through bottomland woods, over the Sangamon River, and beside Lake Taylorville. The rest of the trail allows you to clock some mileage on a paved trail while admiring prairie grasses and the wide-open farmland of Central Illinois.

Activities:

Start: The western edge of Taylorville

Length: 14.5 miles one-way

Surface: Asphalt

Wheelchair access: The route is wheelchair accessible.

Difficulty: The trail presents a medium level of difficulty because of the minimal amount of shade along the way.

Restrooms: There are portable toilets and water at Lake Taylorville's Jaycee Park.

Maps: USGS Taylorville, Willeys, Owaneco, and Pana; *DeLorme: Illinois Atlas and Gazetteer:* Pages 61, 62, and 70; Illinois Bicycle Map, Region 6, Illinois Department of Transportation, www.dot.state.il.us/bikemap/state.html

Hazards: Watch for traffic as the trail crosses multiple side roads.

Access and parking: Head southeast of Springfield on IL 29. As IL 29 turns left in Taylorville, continue straight on Webster Street. Turn left onto Main Cross Street and right onto Paw Paw Street. There are no signs and only a few parking spaces near the trailhead on the left. UTM coordinates: 16T, 303722 E, 4379995 N

Coming from the south on I-55, head northeast on IL 48. Outside Taylorville, turn left onto Shumway Street. Turn right onto Main Cross Street and then right onto Paw Paw Street.

Since the trail shadows IL 29 for nearly the entire distance, it's easy to find access points. The many road crossings along the way typically offer a small grassy spot for parking.

The parking area at the south end of the trail is just north of Pana on IL 29, at the junction with CR 12.

Transportation: Amtrak trains serve Springfield.

Rentals: No nearby bike rentals are available.

Contact: Springfield Convention and Visitors Bureau, 109 North Seventh St., Springfield 62701; (217) 789-2360; www.visit-springfieldillinois.com
   Central Illinois Tourism Development Office, 700 East Adams St., Springfield 62701; (217) 525-7980; www.visitcentralillinois.com

|||||||||||||||||||||||||||||||||||||||||||||||||||||||||||||||||||||||||||||||||||||||||

N o one would identify this as one of the most exciting rail trails in the state. On its way from Taylorville to Pana, there's little topographical relief along the trail as it cuts diagonally through an agricultural checkerboard. Long stretches of the trail possess minimal greenery. While the lack of trailside trees allows long views of the surrounding landscape, it can be less than desirable when you need shelter from the sun on a hot day. Another knock against this trail is how nearly all of it runs shoulder to shoulder with IL 29. Although IL 29 isn't overly busy or noisy, it usually hosts a steady flow of traffic.

Drawbacks aside, this trail still provides a good place to walk, run, ride, or skate for a respectable number of miles. The most interesting part of the trail is the north section, which crosses the Flat Branch of the Sangamon River and brushes against Lake Taylorville. First, though, you'll go through Taylorville residential areas, cross IL 48 (very busy, with fast-moving traffic), and then mount an embankment. The embankment leads you through a heavily wooded bottomland. Look for jewelweed and vine-covered hickories as the trail drops from the embankment and the walls of a ravine start to rise on both sides of the trail.

After the second bridge, which spans a waterway connecting Bertinetti Lake with the Sangamon River, look left for a view of Lake Taylorville and its spillway. Attractive parkland occupies the rolling grassy hills bordering the lake. The parking area near the trail overlooks the dam and a 30-foot-high spillway that shunts water toward the Sangamon River. If you

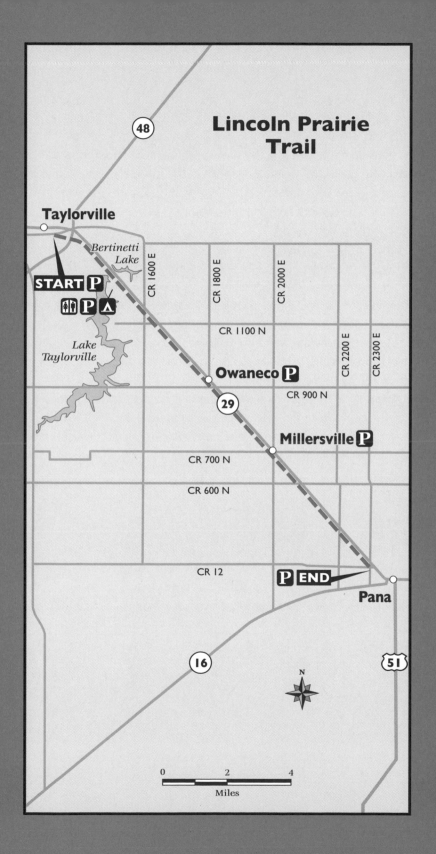

care to log a few extra miles, follow the road past the spillway to explore more parkland and a campground on the opposite shore of the lake.

South of Lake Taylorville, the landscape smoothes out as corn and soybeans take center stage. The slight embankment under the trail, combined with the lack of trees along much of the route, allows for long views of cropland and distant farms. A variety of prairie grasses grow beside the trail, including flowers such as phlox, compass plants, Queen Anne's lace, morning glory, and chicory.

There are occasional interruptions of the vast agricultural fields. One of these is the Taylorville Prison—a minimum-security state facility surrounded by fortified walls topped with razor wire. In Owaneco, bike route signs direct trail users along a couple of side streets and by grain elevators. If it's a hot day, take advantage of Owaneco's "Ped Shed," a small sheltered rest stop with beverage vending machines. After passing more grain elevators in Millersville, you'll cross Locust Creek and a research farm operated by the University of Illinois.

Wrap up at the trailhead parking area just north of Pana. While visiting Pana, keep watch for a few downtown murals depicting the history of the town. Some murals show Pana's history as a major coal producer in the area. Oddly enough, this small town also was a major Midwest flower

A stone sign outside Pana marks the south trailhead of the Lincoln Prairie Trail.

grower. At one time the town hosted five different companies that shipped fifteen million roses annually. Pana still considers itself the City of Roses.

Local Information

- Taylorville Tourism Council, P.O. Box 13, Taylorville 62568; (217) 824-9447; www.visittaylorville.com

- Pana Chamber of Commerce, 120 East Third Street, Pana 62557; (217) 562-4240; www.panaillinois.com

Local Events/Attractions

- Christian County Coal Mine Museum, 115 North Washington St., Taylorville; (217) 823-1819. Features history of local coal mining.

- Christian County Historical Society Museum, East Route 29, Taylorville; (217) 824-6922; www.taylorville.net/historical_society.htm. Contains an 1820 log house and the 1839 courthouse where Lincoln argued cases.

- Taylorville Chautauqua Auditorium, Manners Park, Taylorville; (217) 824-3110. Opened in 1914 and now listed on the National Register of Historic Places.

Restaurants

- One-East Market, Inc., 100 East Market St., Taylorville; (217) 824-5111. Sandwiches, salads, and plenty more. Located in a historic building on the town square.

Accommodations

- The Inn at Oak Terrace Resort, 100 Beyers Lake Rd.; (800) 577-7598; www.oakterraceresort.com. Lodging, golf course, spa, and a restaurant.

- Market Street Inn Bed and Breakfast, 220 East Market St., Taylorville; (217) 824-7220; www.marketstreetinn.com. Lodging in an 1892 Queen Anne Victorian house.

- Sangchris Lake State Park, 9898 Cascade Rd., Rochester; (217) 498-9208; http://dnr.state.il.us/lands/landmgt/parks/r4/sangch.htm. Two large campgrounds and one small walk-in camping area.

32 LOST BRIDGE TRAIL

This well-used trail on the west side of Springfield takes you through a wooded landscape, over a couple bridges, and alongside a handsome community park. In the community of Rochester at the south end of the trail, you'll learn about a historic meeting between a former president and Abraham Lincoln when he served in the Illinois legislature.

Activities:

Start: The east side of Springfield next to the Illinois Department of Transportation building

Length: 6.1 miles one-way

Surface: Asphalt

Wheelchair access: This trail is wheelchair accessible.

Difficulty: This trail is easy.

Restrooms: There are portable toilets and water at the trailhead. There are no public restrooms in Rochester (water at Rochester trailhead), but stores and gas stations may allow you to use their restrooms.

Maps: USGS New City and Springfield East; *DeLorme: Illinois Atlas and Gazetteer:* Page 61; Illinois Bicycle Map, Region 6, Illinois Department of Transportation, www.dot.state.il.us/bikemap/state.html

Hazards: None

Access and parking: From I-55/72 on the east side of Springfield, exit heading west on IL 29. Turn left onto the Dirkson Parkway. Turn into the parking area for the Illinois Department of Transportation. Follow signs to the trailhead. UTM coordinates: 16S, 276796 E, 4405894 N

The south trailhead for the Lost Bridge Trail is at the corner of IL 29 and Main Street in Rochester.

Transportation: Amtrak trains stop in Springfield.

Rentals: No nearby bike rentals are available.

Contact: Springfield Park District, 2500 South 11th St., Springfield 62703; (217) 544-1751; www.springfieldparks.org

The Lost Bridge Trail runs along a railroad corridor between the east edge of Springfield and the nearby village of Rochester. The trail's name refers to an old train bridge over Sugar Creek at the beginning of the route that was sold for scrap metal by the railroad company. Fortunately one of the two old bridges that were once along this stretch of the Baltimore and Ohio Railroad remain. The remaining bridge spans the South Fork of the Sangamon River near Rochester.

The first section of the trail brushes against a reservoir that sits behind the large Illinois Department of Transportation building. While the busy interstate on the opposite shore of the little lake doesn't exactly set the stage for a peaceful environment, the grassy shore of the lake still provides a pleasant spot with an observation platform and picnic tables.

After passing the lake, a series of turns through a wooded area take you to the railroad right-of-way. You'll duck under the interstate and then cross a new wooden bridge over Sugar Creek, which carries the outflow from Lake Springfield, a large reservoir to the south.

Beyond the meanders of Sugar Creek, the surrounding landscape alternately pitches upward and drops downward. For a stretch the trail traces a raised embankment 25 feet above the surrounding landscape. Then the inverse occurs, and hickory-laden embankments rise about 40 feet on both sides of the trail. After passing a small pond and patches of wetland, the trail shoots under a road and through a short tunnel and then makes a gradual descent toward Rochester.

The minimal number of street crossings along this trail allow for a jaunt with rare interruptions. IL 29, a fairly busy road, parallels nearly the entire trail. Thankfully the road doesn't subtract much from the experience because of the heavy woods and the ravines that serve as a barrier between the trail and the highway. Before reaching Rochester, a spur trail

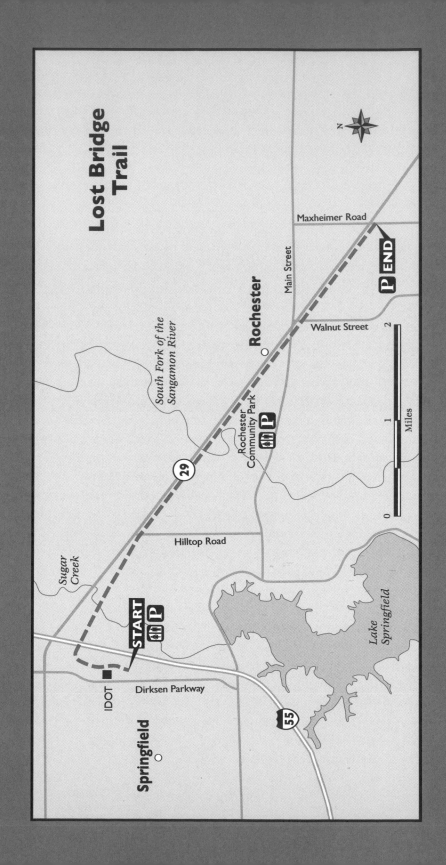

veers to the right into a community park containing a duck pond, sports fields, and a concession stand.

In Rochester you'll pass a trail parking area, as well as a folksy mural on the side of a silo depicting a meeting in 1842 between former U.S. President Martin Van Buren and Abraham Lincoln, who was serving in the Illinois state legislature at the time. As the story goes, Van Buren was sidelined in Rochester while on a journey. Lincoln and his storytelling skills were called upon to entertain the former president for the evening. A friendship arose from the brief meeting, and Van Buren eventually endorsed Lincoln's presidential bid. To learn more about this historic meeting, turn left on John Street in Rochester to see a historic marker and small wayside exhibit.

Local Information
- Central Illinois Tourism Development Office, 700 East Adams St., Springfield 62701; (217) 525-7980; www.visitcentralillinois.com

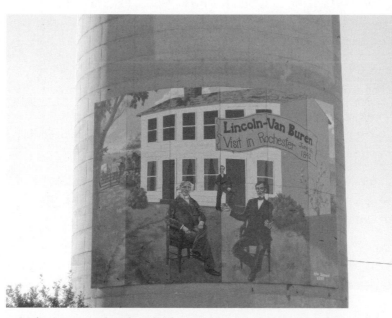

In Rochester, a mural on the side of grain silo commemorates a local meeting between President Martin Van Buren and Abraham Lincoln.

- Springfield Convention and Visitors Bureau, 109 North Seventh St., Springfield 62701; (217) 789-2360; www.visit-springfieldillinois.com

Local Events/Attractions

- Abraham Lincoln Presidential Museum, 212 North Sixth St., Springfield; (800) 610-2094; www.alplm.org. This museum dedicated to Illinois's most-famous figure has some high-tech attractions.

- Illinois State Museum, 502 South Spring St.; (217) 782-7386; www.museum.state.il.us. Permanent and changing exhibits on the state's land, life, people, and art.

- Old State Capitol State Historic Site, 1 Old State Capitol Plaza, Springfield; (217) 785-7960; www.oldstatecapitol.org/osc.htm. Restored with period furnishings.

Restaurants

- Cozy Dog Drive-In, 2935 South Sixth St., Springfield; (217) 525-1992; www.cozydogdrivein.com. Credits itself with inventing the corn dog. Get ready for lots of Route 66 memorabilia.

- Cafe Brio, 524 East Monroe St., Springfield; (217) 544-0574. Downtown restaurant with good food and pleasant atmosphere.

Accommodations

- The Henry Mischler House, 803 East Edwards St., Springfield; (217) 525-2660; www.mischlerhouse.com

- Carpenter Street Hotel, 525 North Sixth St., Springfield; (217) 789-9100; www.carpenterstreethotel.com. Affordable; located north of downtown.

- Sangchris Lake State Park, 9898 Cascade Rd., Rochester; (217) 498-9208; http://dnr.state.il.us/lands/landmgt/parks/r4/sangch.htm. Two large campgrounds and one small walk-in camping area.

33 RIVER TRAIL

The highlight of this route is the ascent up a high bluff heavily laden with maple and oak trees. While it may sound punishing, this 3.0-mile climb is well worth the effort. After passing creeks, ravines, and dense woodland on the way to the top, the final few miles of trail takes you through some nearby Peoria suburbs.

Activities:

Start: The Taylor Street ball diamonds in East Peoria

Length: 6.6 miles one-way, with optional side trip

Surface: Asphalt

Wheelchair access: The trail is wheelchair accessible.

Difficulty: Medium difficulty due to the climb up the bluff

Restrooms: There are public restrooms and water at the Taylor Street ball diamonds and Bunnell Park.

Maps: USGS Peoria East and Morton; *DeLorme: Illinois Atlas and Gazetteer:* Page 41

Hazards: If cycling down the bluff, keep an eye peeled for upcoming street crossings. They arrive quickly.

Access and parking: From Peoria head east on I-74. Exit at US 150/IL 116 and turn right. Just after crossing the channel, turn left onto Springfield Road. Park in the gravel lot on the left just before the ball diamonds. From the parking area, catch the trail up on the levee; proceed to the right alongside the Farm Creek Diversion Channel. UTM coordinates: 16T, 282186 E, 4504744 N

To access the trail at the Fondulac Park District administration building, head southeast on Washington Street from US 150/IL 116. Turn right onto Veterans Drive. The administration building is on the left at 201 Veterans Drive.

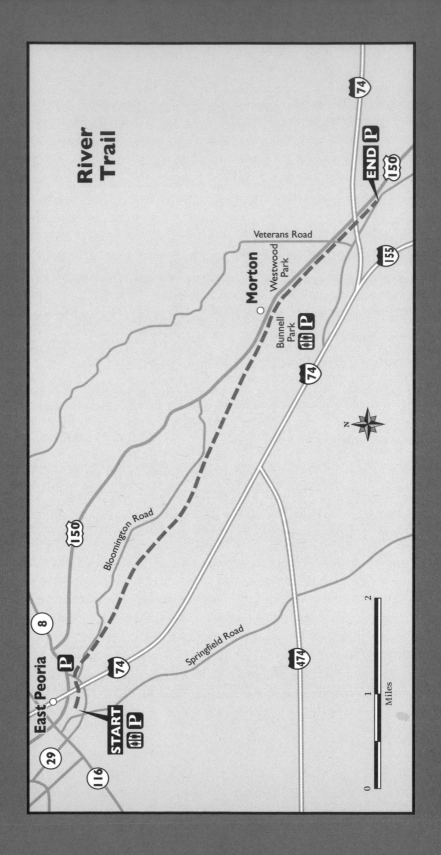

River
Trail

Veterans Road

Morton

Westwood
Park

Bunnell
Park

END

P

74

150

155

74

East Peoria

8

29

116

P

START

P

74

150

Bloomington Road

Springfield Road

474

N

0   1   2

Miles

To park at Bunnell Park take US 150 southeast from East Peoria. Turn right onto Hawthorne Avenue and left onto Lilac Lane.

To park at the east end of the trail, take US 150 to Morton. Park at the picnic shelter at the intersection of US 150 and Detroit Avenue.

Transportation: The closest Amtrak stations are in Bloomington and Galesburg.

Rentals: Bushwhacker, 4700 North University in the Metro Centre, Peoria; (309) 692-4812

Contact: Fondulac Park District, 201 Veterans Dr., East Peoria 61611; (309) 699-3923; www.fondulacpark.com

Morton Park District, 349 West Birchwood St., Morton 61550; (309) 263-7429; www.mortonparkdistrict.com

The River Trail follows a section of railroad that was once part of a 500-mile network of electric passenger trains that linked communities in central and southern Illinois. Run by the Illinois Terminal Company, these interurban trains, as they were known, followed trolley wires to cities like Champaign, Bloomington, Lincoln, Springfield, and St. Louis. The River Trail section of the line angled southeast from Peoria about 15 miles to the town of Mackinaw, where routes split to Bloomington and Springfield. Passenger service operated from 1895 until 1956, when the automobile began to take center stage. After passenger service dried up, the Illinois Terminal Company used the track to haul freight until the early 1980s.

The first 1.0 mile of the trail traces levees along the Farm Creek Diversion Channel and one of its small tributaries. To control the sometimes-heavy flow of water that comes down from the steep bluffs after a strong rain, these creekbeds have been widened, deepened, straightened, and lined with concrete. Often with only a trickle of water running at the bottom of the steep concrete banks, these diversion channels may look like overkill. Apparently they're not: Over the years, the dirt banks that were once built along the creek overflowed on a number of occasions and flooded downtown East Peoria.

On the way to the foot of the bluff, you'll face a few busy cross streets. Just after the diversion channel splits, a green train caboose at Veterans Road marks the spot where the gradual 3.0-mile climb to the top of the bluff begins. Since the route was graded for rail travel, it's never terribly steep, but you will get a workout.

As you ascend, thick greenery on one side of the trail hides a steep ravine. The other side of the trail is open and grassy, allowing views of the nearby bluffs. One of the highlights of this trail is the bridges, some of which are 30 feet above the sandy-bottomed stream and its banks, thick with cottonwoods and sumac. Alongside the trail, little gullies—some containing trickling rivulets and others just dry rocky creekbeds—sometimes cut into the bluff. As the sides of the bluff move closer to trail, tree limbs form a thick canopy overhead.

When the landscape flattens out at the top of the bluff, you'll pass some agricultural fields and a new housing subdivision named "Trailside." (The growing trend of naming apartment complexes and housing subdivisions in honor of nearby rail trails speaks to the growing desirability of living next to these trails.) Along this stretch you'll have the opportunity to ogle a series of grassy backyards. The trail takes a downward dip before pulling alongside US 150, which you'll accompany for the rest of the route.

Unfortunately the final couple miles of the trail offer a minimal amount of charm. You'll pass housing subdivisions, a mobile home park, and a cornfield. (At 6.0 miles consider a 1.0-mile side trip: Take the spur trail left alongside Veterans Road to Westwood Park, which has restrooms and water.) After ducking under I-74 again, the trail ends at a picnic shelter on a depressing traffic island surrounded by anonymous strip malls and a wide road with fast-moving traffic. If you're cycling back down the bluff to West Peoria, you'll find pedaling is optional for most of the way.

Local agencies will soon connect East Peoria's River Trail with the Bob Michel Bridge over the Illinois River. Once across the river, it's a snap to hop on the several-mile-long Pimiteoui Trail that runs along Peoria's riverfront. This connection could make it possible to double the mileage for this route.

Local Information

- Peoria Area Convention & Visitors Bureau, 456 Fulton St., Suite 300, Peoria 61602; (800) 747-0302; www.peoria.org

Local Events/Attractions

- Carl Spindler Marina, 3701 North Main St. (Access Road 7), East Peoria; (309) 699-3549. Access East Peoria's 2.0-mile-long river walk, or rent a canoe or kayak to paddle the Illinois River.

Restaurants

- Emerald Tea Room, 132 McKinley St., East Peoria; (309) 694-1972. Great salads; well worth a visit. Within walking distance of the trailhead.

Accommodations

- Super 8, 725 Taylor St., East Peoria; (309) 698-8889. The backdoor opens to the trail.

- Jubilee College State Park, 13015 West Fussner Rd., Brimfield; (309) 446-3758; http://dnr.state.il.us/lands/landmgt/parks/r1/jubilee.htm. Lots of campsites; located twenty minutes north of Peoria.

- Randolph Terrace Historic Bed and Breakfast; 201 West Columbia Terrace, Peoria; (309) 688-7858; www.randolphterrace.com

34 ROCK ISLAND STATE TRAIL

"Oh the Rock Island Line is a mighty fine line/Oh the Rock Island Line is the road to ride." This sage advice offered by Johnny Cash and countless other musicians has granted the train line celebrity status. As you explore this piece of an American icon, you'll enjoy the wooded ravines, the pastoral scenery, the many bridges over winding prairie creeks, and the quiet little towns along the way.

Activities:

Start: The south trailhead is next to Connor Company, a heating and cooling supply business, located at 1209 West Pioneer Parkway. No signs direct visitors to the trailhead, but there is a small parking area for trail users.

Length: 27.2 miles one-way

Surface: Starting from the south, paved for the first 2.0 miles or so; well-compacted crushed gravel on the remaining 25 miles except for the on-street sections

Wheelchair access: The trail is wheelchair accessible, but use caution for the on-street sections.

Difficulty: Because of its length, this trail has a medium-to-hard level of difficulty.

Restrooms: There are public restrooms and water at the Rock Island Trail parking area (just north of Alta), Kickapoo Creek State Recreation Area (on the left), in the small park on First Street in Dunlap (portable toilet), at Cutters Grove Park in Princeton, next to the old depot on Williams Street in Wyoming, and the parking area at the north end of the trail.

Maps: USGS Wyoming, Castleton, Spring Bay, Dunlap, Edelstein, and Princeville; *DeLorme: Illinois Atlas and Gazetteer:* Pages 32, 40, and 41; Rock Island State Trail Map, Illinois Department of Natural Resources, www.dnr .state.il.us/lands/landmgt/parks/sitemaps/rockisland.gif

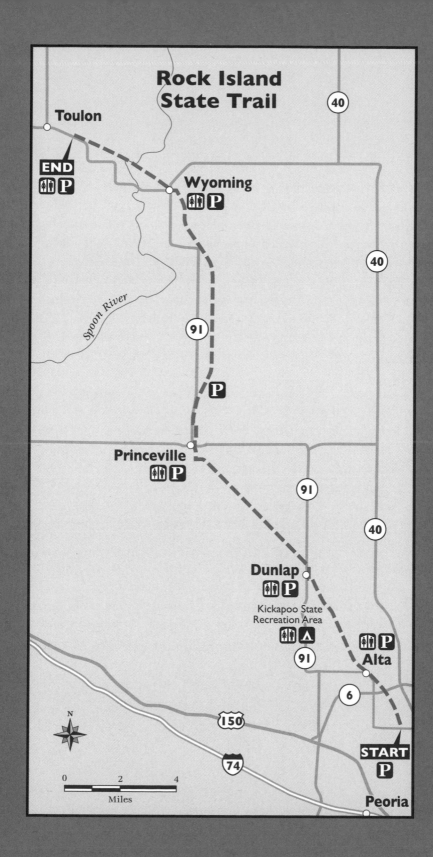

Hazards: The long tunnel under IL 6 comes at 1.4 miles. It's narrow and dark as night. If you're riding a bike, dismount. Occasionally the trail crosses busy streets—usually these streets are closer to the towns. Traffic is very mild on all on-street sections in the small towns of Dunlap, Princeville, and Wyoming.

Access and parking: From I-74 in Peoria take Knoxville Avenue/IL 40 north to the Pioneer Parkway. Turn left onto Pioneer Parkway and then right into the parking lot for Connor Company, located at 1209 West Pioneer Parkway. The unsigned trailhead is on the far left side of the Connor Company parking lot. UTM coordinates: 16T, 279693 E, 4517809 N

To park at Grange Hall Road, take IL 6 north from Peoria to Allen Road. Head north on Allen Road and bear left as the road turns into Grange Hall Road. The Rock Island Trail parking area is on the left.

To reach at the parking area on Parks School Road, take IL 6 to IL 40. Follow IL 40 north to Parks School Road and turn left. The parking area is on the right.

To park at County Line Road, take IL 40 north to CR 350 North and turn left. Parking is on the right.

To park in Wyoming at the Rock Island Depot Museum, follow IL 40 north to CR 950 North and turn left. This road immediately becomes CR 600 North. The parking area is on the left.

To park at the north trailhead outside Toulon, follow I-74 west of Peoria. Head north on IL 78/US 150. Stay north on IL 78 as US 150 turns left. Turn right onto IL 17. The parking area is on the left after passing through Toulon.

Transportation: The closest Amtrak stations are in Bloomington and Galesburg.

Rentals: Bushwhacker, 4700 North University in the Metro Centre, Peoria; (309) 692-4812

Contact: Peoria Park District; 2218 North Prospect Ave., Peoria 61603; (309) 682-1200

Rock Island State Trail, 311 East Williams St., P.O. Box 64, Wyoming 61491; (309) 695-2228; www.dnr.state.il.us/lands/landmgt/parks/r1/rockisle.htm. The trail office is in an old train depot.

Friends of the Rock Island Trail are spearheading an effort to connect the trail with downtown Peoria. By the time you read this, we hope the "Finish the Trail" bumper stickers frequently seen around Peoria will be obsolete; www.ritrail.org.

||||||||||||||||||||||||||||||||||||||||||||||||||||||||||||||||||||||||||||||||||

The Rock Island Railroad Line occupies a special place in American history. Initially running from Chicago to the Quad Cities, it was the first railroad to cross the Mississippi River. Eventually it branched out to fourteen states and played an important role in the settlement of the West. The railroad acquired nearly mythical status by way of a folk song first recorded in a Southern prison in the 1930s and later recorded by diverse artists as Lead Belly, Johnny Cash, Pete Seger, and Little Richard.

This section of the line, a spur off the main Rock Island Line, was used for transporting grain from the midwestern breadbasket to the distilleries of Peoria. In the late nineteenth century the line helped establish Peoria's status as the whiskey capital of the world. (The city boasted twenty-four breweries and seventy-three distilleries between 1837 and 1919.) This stretch of the Rock Island Line served railcars from 1871 to 1965.

As one of the first downstate Illinois rail trails, the Rock Island Trail encountered more than its share of controversy and resistance. Plenty of people were against the trail's development, and they butted heads regularly with the trail's dedicated group of supporters and volunteers. Those in opposition carried out many political maneuvers to prevent the trail's development. There was vandalism of the trail, too, including a fire meant to destroy to the trail's main attraction: the bridge over the Spoon River. Perseverance and good sense eventually prevailed, and the trail was christened in 1989.

Starting out from the parking area on Pioneer Parkway, the trail passes an airstrip and accompanies sections of a meandering stream before entering a long, narrow tunnel under IL 6. Before and after the tunnel, thick woodland borders the trail.

North of the hamlet of Alta, the steady march of new housing subdivisions and accompanying roads are replacing farmland on both sides of the trail. At about 4.5 miles an observation deck on the right side of the trail overlooks a small ravine containing a winding, sandy-bottomed tributary to Kickapoo Creek.

Beyond the observation platform is the entrance to the Kickapoo State Recreation Area, containing what is likely to be the best rail trail camping in the Midwest. The park's campground is specifically for Rock Island Trail users, as well as people who are willing to hike 0.6 mile from the nearest parking lot. The park hosts several miles of trails that tour wooded areas, a restored prairie, and a streambank.

As you head north on the Rock Island Trail, beautiful scenery continues to unfold. A big ravine opens up on the side of the trail, and soon a 40-foot-high bridge over Kickapoo Creek offers a bird's-eye view of the creek's pleasant wooded banks.

In Dunlap you'll encounter the first of the trail's three on-street sections. Bike route signs make each turn crystal clear (turns also are outlined below). Between Dunlap and Princeville, cyclists, walkers, and runners start to thin out. High banks on the side of the trail come and go. When the banks drop down, they reveal the dusty silos and red wooden barns scattered

A mural welcomes users of the Rock Island State Trail to the town of Princeton.

over the lightly rolling agricultural landscape. Entering Princeville, a nifty mural promoting the trail graces a small building containing restrooms.

As the trail parallels Santa Fe Avenue north of Princeville, you'll pass through a thick tunnel of maple trees before crossing North Creek. Farther north of Princeville, a trailside prairie restoration project may catch your eye: It's chock-full of the prairie grasses and flowers once so common throughout Illinois. A few more miles bring you to several pleasant creeks, both intermittent and year-round. Some wind along wooded banks; others wiggle through small grassy ravines.

The next section of trail presents an opportunity to work on cadence, stride, stroke, or whatever else you do when the route is uneventful and the scenery on the dull side. A thin strip of trees—in this case, oak and hickory—line the trail for a number of miles through this section, preventing views beyond the edges of the trail. On the way into Wyoming, it becomes an exciting moment when the veil slips away: The trail rises a bit, and the trees open up, offering long views of the surrounding pastoral landscape.

In Wyoming you'll pass the old train depot containing the trail headquarters and a small museum focusing on the former railroad. After Wyoming the woodland grows thicker. Wetlands decorate one side of the trail; the Spoon River appears on the other at the bottom of a 40-foot-deep ravine. After a 0.25-mile-long alliance between trail and the river, the Spoon takes a sharp turn and passes under the trail as it mounts a spectacular old train bridge. Benches on this long steel-truss bridge suspended 50 feet above the river allow you to sit and enjoy the sights and sounds. From the bridge look to the Spoon's northeast bank for a tiny creek that flows down into the river. The trail ends 2.0 miles northwest of the bridge, just outside the town of Toulon.

Note: The trail currently stops on the outskirts of Toulon because the Toulon village government withheld support for the trail when it was under construction in the late 1980s. More than twenty years later, after an apparent change of heart, the village is making plans to bring the trail the rest of the way into town.

Major Milepoints

1.4   If cycling, walk your bike while passing through the tunnel under IL 6. It's long, dark, and narrow.

6.3   In Dunlap turn right onto First Street.

6.4   Turn left onto Ash Street.

6.5   Turn right onto Third Street.

6.9   Turn right onto Hickory Street and then quickly left onto Second Street.

12.7 Turn right onto Walnut Road.

13.4 Turn right onto North Street and then make a quick left onto North Town Avenue.

14.0 Turn left onto North End Street. The sign is missing from this street, but bike route signs mark the way. It's the first left after Craig Street.

14.1 Turn right to regain the trail.

22.9 In Wyoming turn left onto Williams Street.

23.1 Turn right onto Seventh Street.

23.2 Turn left onto Thomas Street.

23.3 Turn right onto Sixth Street. Pass a couple of houses and resume the trail on the left.

Local Information

- Peoria Area Convention & Visitors Bureau, 456 Fulton St., Suite 300, Peoria 61602; (800) 747-0302; www.peoria.org

- Village of Princeville, 206 North Walnut Ave., Box 200, Princeville 61559; (309) 385-4765; www.princeville.org

Local Events/Attractions

- Jubilee College State Historic Site, 11817 Jubilee College Rd., Brimfield; (309) 243-9489. A seminary/boarding school that operated from 1840 to 1871; free daily tours. Located within one of Illinois's best state parks.

- Rock Island Depot Museum, 311 East Williams St., P.O. Box 64, Wyoming 61491; (309) 695-2228. Memorabilia from the Chicago, Burlington, and Quincy Line that operated on this trail.

Restaurants

- Jane's Icebox, 211 North First St., Dunlap; (309) 243-7744. Quality diner food.

- The Whip, 210 South Walnut Ave., Princeville; (309) 385-1500. Outdoor seating; serves ice cream, sandwiches, and tasty homemade tamales. Located right on the route.

Accommodations

- Kickapoo State Recreation Area, 311 East Williams St., Wyoming; (309) 695-2228. The very quiet campground is accessible via the Rock Island Trail and by hiking in 0.6 mile from the overnight parking lot on Fox Road.

- Randolph Terrace Historic Bed and Breakfast, 201 West Columbia Terrace, Peoria; (309) 688-7858; www.randolphterrace.com

SOUTHERN ILLINOIS

Madison County, located across the Mississippi River from St. Louis, claims the largest concentration of Illinois rail trails outside of Chicago. This extensive network of trails offers many miles of uninterrupted running, walking, and cycling. Near the Mississippi you'll encounter scenic wetlands at Horseshoe Lake and the Metro East Levee Trail. Farther west from the Mississippi River, you'll head up the wooded bluffs and follow a couple creeks before exploring communities such as Marysville, Edwardsville, and Leclaire.

In northern Madison County, the historic river town of Alton serves as a jumping-off point for a couple of great trails that trace the shore of the Mississippi River. Heading downstream from Alton on the Confluence Trail takes you on top of a series of river levees and past a couple of museums. You'll see wetlands and a channel that was dug for river barge traffic. Heading upstream from Alton, the Vadalabene Great River Road Trail runs past miles of wooded and rocky bluffs on the shore of the Mississippi River. The trail ends at Pere Marquette State Park, which contains top-notch hiking trails and expansive views of the surrounding landscape.

If Illinois had a rail trails hall of fame, the Tunnel Hill Trail would be one of the first inductees. Running nearly 50 miles from Harrisburg south to the Cache River Wetlands, the trail gives visitors a taste of the breathtaking beauty within the 270,000-acre Shawnee National Forest. Ravines, rocky streams, and wooded bluffs figure prominently on the northern half of the trail. The southern half features bottomland woods, ponds, streams, and marshes within the internationally recognized Cache River Wetlands.

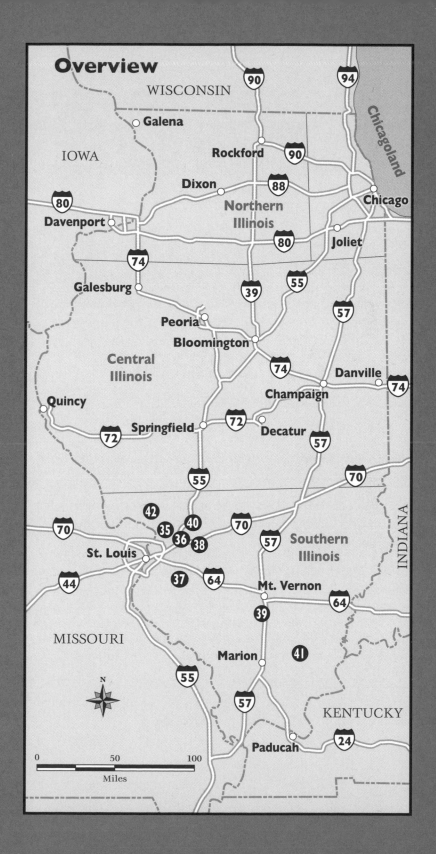

Overview

35 CONFLUENCE TRAIL

As you trace Mississippi River levees from Alton south to Granite City, you'll travel alongside the river and one of its channels, as well as adjoining ponds and wetlands. Be sure to give yourself time to explore a couple of museums along the way, one focusing on the Mississippi River and the other highlighting the explorations of Lewis and Clark.

Activities:

Start: In Alton at Russell Commons Park

Length: 16.6 miles one-way

Surface: Mostly asphalt; several miles of crushed gravel surface along the Chain of Rocks Canal

Wheelchair access: The trail is asphalt except for a couple miles along the Chain of Rocks Canal, where it's crushed gravel. The crushed gravel surface can be rough in places.

Difficulty: The trail has a medium level of difficulty. Nearly the entire trail leaves you exposed to wind and sun. A long section of the trail follows the top of a levee.

Restrooms: There are public restrooms and water at the trailhead, the Great River Museum, and the Lewis and Clark State Historic Site.

Maps: USGS Alton, Columbia Bottom, Granite City, and Wood River; *De-Lorme: Illinois Atlas and Gazetteer:* Pages 75 and 76; Madison County Trails Map, Madison County Transit, www.mcttrails.org

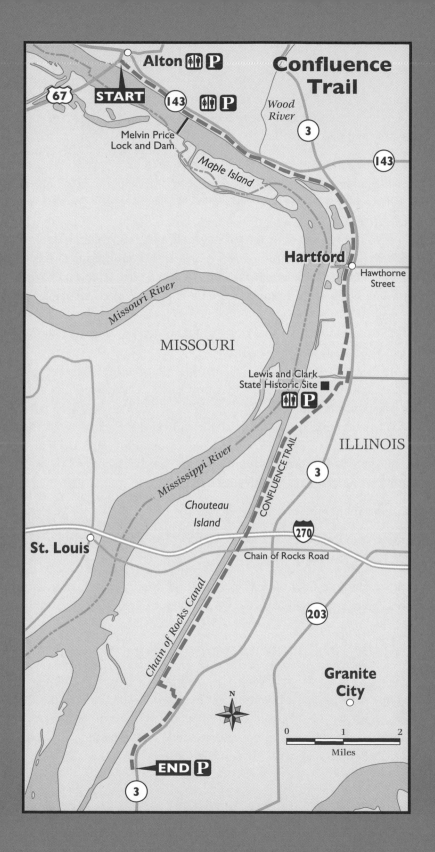

Hazards: While following the top of the levee, the trail regularly drops down steeply at the road crossings. Be careful navigating the gates on either side of the road crossings.

Access and parking: From the St. Louis area take US 67 north across the Mississippi River. Getting off the bridge, continue left on US 67. Immediately turn left onto Ridge Street and follow it as it curves left. The park is on the left after you pass under the bridge.

From I-55 head west on IL 140. Stay on IL 140 through Alton until you reach Broadway Street. Turn left on IL 143 and then right on Discovery Parkway. Russell Commons Park is on the right. Pick up the trail across Discovery Parkway from Russell Commons Park. UTM coordinates: 15S, 745303 E, 4307691 N

To park at the Melvin Price Locks and Dam, head southeast of Alton on IL 143. The entrance is on the right.

To park at Lewis and Clark State Historic Site, head southeast of Alton on IL 143. Turn right onto IL 3. Cross the Cahokia Diversion Channel; the entrance is on the right.

On-street parking is available at the south end of the trail. Head north on IL 3 from I-55 at East St. Louis. At 20th Street, turn right and look for parking on side streets to the right. Catch the trail on the other side of IL 3, at the northwest corner of 20th Street and IL 3.

Transportation: Amtrak trains serve Alton.

Rentals: Wild Trak Bikes, 202 State St., Alton; (618) 462-2574; located just off IL 100 in downtown Alton

Contact: Madison County Trails, c/o Madison County Transit, One Transit Way, Granite City 62040; (618) 874-7433; www.mcttrails.org

|||||||||||||||||||||||||||||||||||||||||||||||||||||||||||||||||||||||||||||||||||

Alton is an old river town built on the side of a bluff above the Mississippi. Its streets are lined with historic storefronts containing antiques shops, restaurants, and bars. The town's most striking landmark is the Clark Bridge, built in 1994 over the Mississippi River. The main sections of the bridge are suspended by a series of cables attached to two main supports. A couple of other attractions in town are the large painting of the mythological Piasa Bird on a rocky bluff just north of town on IL 100 and the bronze life-size statue of Robert Wadlow—the 10-foot-tall man who was the town's most famous resident.

From Russell Commons Park the trail immediately mounts the levee that protects the town from the Mississippi River's floodwaters. This joyous stretch of trail runs some 40 to 50 feet above the shoreline. While the lack of greenery on the levee leaves trail users totally exposed to the wind and sun, it also enables views along the river for several miles in each direction. Herons wait on the riverbank; behind you, the Clark Bridge looks like a ship's masts and riggings waiting for the sails to be hoisted.

At about the same time the Clark Bridge was built, the massive Melvin Price Lock and Dam opened just south of Alton. At the Great Rivers Museum, situated alongside the trail at the lock and dam, visitors can tour the 0.3-mile-long lock. The museum features exhibits on a full spectrum of human and natural history associated with the river.

Continuing south from the lock, the trail crosses the Wood River and passes a sprawling oil refinery. Completely surrounded by the refinery operation, the small industrial town of Hartford is bordered by dozens of enormous holding tanks. From the raised levee, glimpses through the trees come and go of the river and the barges moored near the shore. When the trail moves inland away from the river, wetlands and reservoirs multiply. In a handful of spots the trail takes a quick dip down to cross a road and then quickly rises back up on the levee.

South of Hartford, the slender 150-foot structure on the left that looks like a guard tower at a futuristic prison is actually a monument dedicated to the Lewis and Clark Expedition. By taking an elevator or stairs to the top of this silvery tower, visitors can see the confluence of the Mississippi and Missouri Rivers. After the wood-and-steel bridge over the Cahokia Diversion Channel, you'll arrive at the Lewis and Clark State Historic Site. The museum is located on the spot where the expedition set up camp and spent the winter of 1803–04 before heading westward on the Missouri River. The most impressive exhibit in the museum is the full-size replica of the expedition's 55-foot boat that was dragged, paddled, and sailed on the Missouri River. One side of the boat is cut away to show the boat's interior and all the carefully packed items. The grassy backyard of the museum contains a replica of the log fort built by the expedition. From the museum the trail runs through a swath of grassland before meeting up with the Chain of Rocks Canal, an 8.4-mile-long waterway that allows river traffic to bypass a series of treacherous rock ledges in the river's main channel. Just before pulling alongside the canal, look to the right for a view of the full Mississippi River. (The confluence with the Missouri River is 1 mile upstream and out of view.) The straight-as-an-arrow canal is treeless and edged by piles of riprap. If it weren't for huge wetlands on the left and the attendant waterbirds, this stretch of trail might seem terribly uneventful.

Toward the end of this trail, a couple of excellent side trips present themselves for cyclists. Both trips take you across the Mississippi to the 11-mile-long Riverfront Trail in Missouri.

At Chain of Rocks Road (the next bridge south of I-270 along the Chain of Rocks Canal), you can cross the Mississippi River on the Chain of Rocks Bridge. Once the bridge for the historic Route 66, this nearly 1-mile-long pedestrian bridge is one of the unsung treasures of the region. The views, 70 feet or so above the river, are breathtaking. The Missouri side of the bridge connects to the north end of the Riverfront Trail, which leads all the way to downtown St. Louis. (To reach the Chain of Rocks Bridge from the Confluence Trail requires a mile or so of on-street travel on Chain of Rocks Road, which has minimal traffic.)

Another side trip worth a look may require some on-street travel, depending on the progress of future trail development. When you reach the south end of the Confluence Trail, you can continue for 3.0 miles or so on IL 3 to the McKinley Bridge, which claims a newly built pedestrian walkway. While there's heavy traffic on IL 3, there's also a very wide shoulder. Across the McKinley Bridge, it's a short trip to downtown St. Louis on the Riverfront Trail.

Local Information

- Alton Regional Convention and Visitors Bureau, 200 Piasa St., Alton 62002; (618) 465-6676; www.visitalton.com

- Tourism Bureau of Southwestern Illinois, 10950 Lincoln Trail, Fairview Heights 62208; (618) 397-1488; www.thetourismbureau.org

Local Events/Attractions

- Lewis and Clark State Historic Site, One Lewis and Clark Trail, Hartford; (618) 251-5811; www.campdubois.com. Free museum offers a thorough introduction to the famous expedition at the site where they spent the winter.

- National Great Rivers Museum, at the Melvin Price Locks and Dam 26; IL 143 in East Alton; (618) 462-6979. Delves into many aspects of Mississippi River culture. Video exhibits, a gift shop, and a model of a historic riverboat.

Restaurants

- Pere Marquette Lodge and Conference Center, 13653 Lodge Blvd., Grafton; (618) 786-2331; www.pmlodge.net. Breakfast, lunch, and dinner served in the great lodge.

- Tony's, 312 Piasa St., Alton; (618) 462-8384. Known for steaks and Italian food.

Accommodations

- The Beall Mansion, 407 East 12th St.; Alton; (866) 843-2325; www .beallmansion.com. This 1903 mansion contains a museum; on the National Register of Historic Places.

- Pere Marquette Lodge and Conference Center. Rooms, cabins, and campground at one of the most scenic state parks in Illinois.

36 GLEN CARBON HERITAGE TRAIL

Like the other rail trails in Madison County, the Glen Carbon Heritage Trail takes you through a variety of interesting environments. At the beginning, near the village of Glen Carbon, the trail shadows the wooded banks of Judy Creek. Continuing east you'll encounter ravines, restored prairie, dense woodland, and a trestle bridge over Silver Creek. After Silver Creek, wide-open farmland prevails all the way to the trail's terminus in the town of Marine.

Activities:

Start: In Madison County, across the Mississippi River from St. Louis

Length: 12.2 miles one-way

Surface: Asphalt on the west section of the trail; rougher chip-and-tar surface on much of the eastern section

Wheelchair access: The trail is wheelchair accessible.

Difficulty: The trail is mostly easy; the eastern end offers little protection from sun and wind.

Restrooms: There are public restrooms and water near the trailhead in Miner Park, Goshen Trail intersection (water only), and at the end of the trail in Marine Village Park.

Maps: USGS Collinsville, Edwardsville, and Marine; *DeLorme: Illinois Atlas and Gazetteer:* Page 76; Madison County Trails Map, Madison County Transit, www.mcttrails.org

Hazards: Watch for traffic while crossing a few busy streets.

Access and parking: Park at Citizens Park on Main Street in Glen Carbon. From I-270, head south on IL 157. Turn left onto Main Street and use the trailhead parking area on the right. Follow signs for the Glen Carbon Heritage Trail. UTM coordinates: 16S, 240546 E, 4292822 N

To reach the trailhead parking area where the Glen Carbon Trail meets the Goshen Trail, head north on IL 159 from I-270. Turn right onto Cottonwood Road and continue ahead as it becomes Old Troy Road. The parking area is on the right.

To access the trail from Kuhn Station Road, exit west on IL 143 from I-55. Turn right onto Staunton Road and then left onto Goshen Road. Turn right onto Kuhn Station Road.

To access the east end of the trail at Marine Village Park, head north on IL 4 from I-70. At IL 143 turn right. In Marine turn left onto Verson Street.

Transportation: Amtrak trains serve Alton and St. Louis.

Rentals: Wild Trak Bikes, 202 State St., Alton; (618) 462-2574; located just off IL 100 in downtown Alton

Contact: Madison County Trails, c/o Madison County Transit, One Transit Way, Granite City 62040; (618) 874-7433; www.mcttrails.org

Village of Glen Carbon, 151 North Main St., P.O. Box 757, Glen Carbon 62034; (618) 288-1200; www.glen-carbon.il.us/recreation/bike.htm

As the name suggests, the village of Glen Carbon owes its existence to local coal mines. The village, located on Mississippi River Bluffs, lies on top of seven veins of bituminous coal. Since the Glen Carbon mines were located along Judy Creek, it's no coincidence that the railroad followed the route of the creek as well. Now users of the Glen Carbon Heritage Trail can follow the same route.

The first section of the trail is pleasantly wooded, featuring sections of restored tallgrass prairie laden with compass plants, milkweed, black-eyed Susans, and thistles. Watch for Judy Creek as it winds through the ravines that border the trail. Near the junction with the Goshen Trail, check out the old grain elevator, once used to for loading grain on railcars. After crossing the bridge over I-270, the woodland grows more dense and trees hang overhead. Embankments rise up intermittently on the sides of the trail.

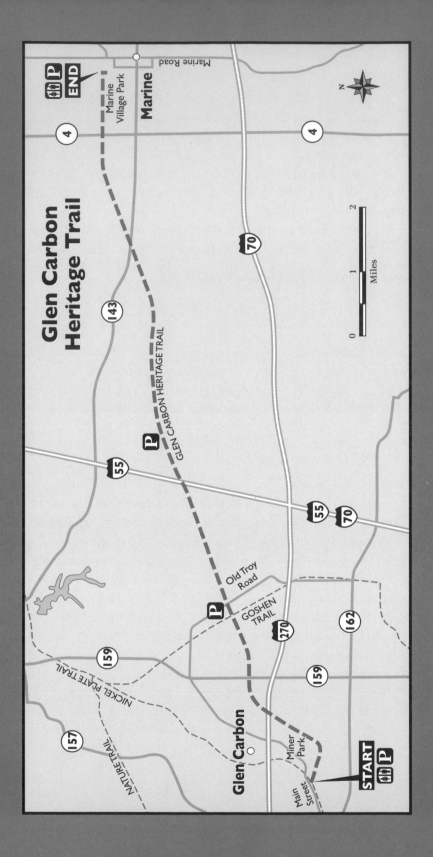

Soon the atmosphere becomes remote. Agricultural land dominates. Now and then ravines and woodland replace the rows of crops. Beyond the trailhead parking lot on Kuhn Station Road, the trail begins to make a long, gradual descent toward Silver Creek. The Silver Creek trestle bridge rises some 50 feet above the creek and runs for more than 100 yards through treetops of maple and elm. Just after the bridge you'll encounter the creek again as it curves beside the trail.

After Silver Creek, cross-streets rarely interrupt the ribbon of asphalt unwinding in front of you. A slight embankment puts you about 10 feet above the surrounding cornfields, offering views of farms and wooded patches in the distance. After several miles of farmland, the trail arrives at the edge of a quiet pond in Marine Village Park, the trail's end point.

Local Information

- Edwardsville/Glen Carbon Chamber of Commerce, 200 University Park Dr., Suite 260, Edwardsville 62025; (618) 656-7600; www.edglen chamber.com

Patches of restored prairie decorate the sides of the Glen Carbon Heritage Trail.

- Tourism Bureau of Southwestern Illinois, 10950 Lincoln Trail, Fairview Heights 62208; (618) 397-1488; www.thetourismbureau.org

Local Events/Attractions
- Cahokia Mounds State Historic Site and Interpretive Center, 30 Ramey Dr., Cahokia; (618) 346-5160; www.cahokiamounds.com. Once the largest and most sophisticated prehistoric Indian city north of Mexico.

Restaurants
- Erato on Main, 126 North Main St., Edwardsville; (618) 307-3203; www.eratoonmain.com. Eclectic cuisine with the emphasis on sea-food; somewhat pricey.

- Mr. Currys Gourmet Indian Restaurant, 7403 Marine Rd. (IL 143), Edwardsville; (415) 577-2274; www.mrcurrys.com/restaurants.htm. Affordable lunch buffet; plenty of vegetarian options.

- Nori Sushi and Japanese Grill, 1025 Century Dr., Edwardsville; (618) 659-9400; www.norisushi.net. Casual atmosphere with extensive sushi menu.

Accommodations
- Bilbrey Farms Inc., 8724 Pin Oak Rd., Edwardsville; (618) 692-1950; www.bilbreyfarms.com. Bed-and-breakfast and an exotic animal farm featuring a zebra, emus, peacocks, a miniature horse, and more.

- Country Hearth Inn and Suites, 1013 Plummer Dr., Edwardsville; (618) 656-7829; www.countryhearth.com

- Horseshoe Lake State Park; (618) 931-0270; http://dnr.state.il.us/lands/landmgt/parks/r4/horsesp.htm. Forty-eight campsites located on an island.

- Swans Court Bed and Breakfast, 421 Court St., Belleville; (618) 233-0779. An 1885 Victorian home.

37 METRO EAST LEVEE TRAIL

While following this levee through a Mississippi River floodplain, you'll have a bird's-eye view of the surrounding terrain, which is a mix of urban, residential, and rural areas; wetland and cropland; and drainage canals and ponds. Near the end of the route, you'll see the downtown buildings of St. Louis in the distance and have an opportunity to visit a courthouse and a church that are remnants from when Illinois was a French colony.

Activities:

Start: The eastern edge of East St. Louis

Length: 7.6 miles one-way

Surface: Hard-packed, crushed gravel on much of the trail; loose and rough surface on some sections

Wheelchair access: The crushed gravel surface is rough in places. Some of the ramps going up and down from the road crossings are fairly steep.

Difficulty: If the wind is blowing, this short trail could have a medium level of difficulty. There is no shelter from wind and sun while following the top of a levee.

Restrooms: There are no public restrooms along this trail.

Maps: USGS Cahokia and French Village; *DeLorme: Illinois Atlas and Gazetteer:* Pages 75 and 76; Madison County Trails Map, Madison County Transit, www.mcttrails.org

Hazards: Take extra care with the road crossing at Triple Lakes Road. It's difficult to see traffic coming from the south. This trail floods periodically.

Access and parking: From I-255 exit heading east on IL 157. Turn right onto IL 163 (Millstadt Road). The trailhead parking is on the right just after you pass the auto junkyard. There's parking space for only a few cars. (*Note:* This is the only parking available along the trail.) UTM coordinates: 15S, 751992 E, 4271062 N

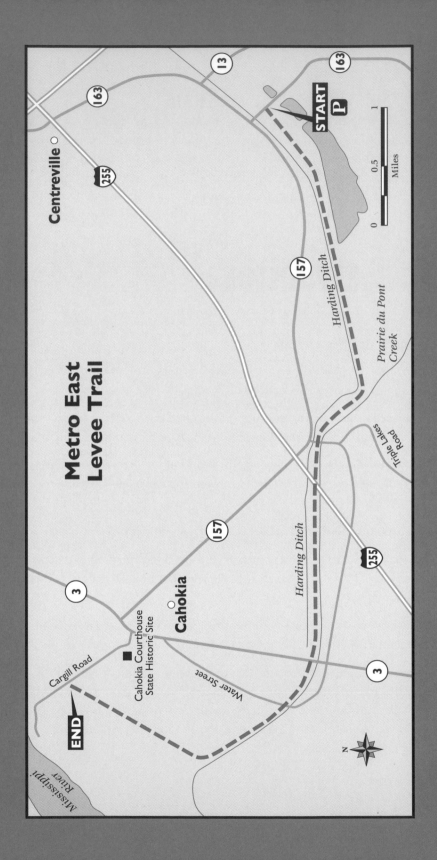

Transportation: Amtrak trains are available in St. Louis and Itlon.

Rentals: Big Shark Bicycle Company, 6133 Delmar Blvd., St. Louis, MO; (314) 862-1188

Contact: St. Clair County Highway Department, 10 Public Square, Belleville 62220; (618) 233-1392

|||||||||||||||||||||||||||||||||||||||||||||||||||||||||||||||||||||||||||||||

D on't let the trailhead's surroundings scare you away from this trail. Once you get past all the dilapidated car dealerships, the patchwork of industry, and the sprawling junkyard alongside the trailhead, you'll find the trail is well worth your time. Keep in mind, though, that nearly all this trail is treeless and without protection from the sun and wind. Given the elevated level of this trail, on a windy day you're likely to encounter some stiff resistance.

Once you're on the trail, you'll soon pull alongside a lake and a wetland on the left. The opposite shore of the lake is fringed with wooded bluffs, and the nearby wetland is littered with fallen trees and stumps offering perches for waterbirds such as great blue herons, white egrets, and red-winged blackbirds.

Before ducking under I-255, the route passes a pumping station, a spillway for the drainage channel on the right, and a building that houses water-control equipment for this corner of the huge surrounding floodplain called the American Bottoms. Near where the trail passes under IL 3's steel trestle bridge, wetlands and another levee appear on the left.

As the trail swings right, the route passes between a big stretch of cropland on the left and a series of ponds and wetlands on the right. If the fields are flooded on the left, you're likely to see a sprinkling of egrets. Also look for bluebirds darting among the sumac trees and the shrubs near the wetlands. In the distance, the skyline of St. Louis comes into view.

At the end of the trail, consider taking a 0.5-mile trip to visit the Cahokia Courthouse, the oldest courthouse in Illinois. The Cahokia Courthouse has been moved several times since it was built in 1740, when Illinois was a French colony. In 1904 organizers for the St. Louis World's Fair (formally known as the Louisiana Purchase Exposition) hauled the courthouse to St. Louis, and in 1906 it was brought to Chicago's Jackson Park. The courthouse was returned to Cahokia in 1939. The vertical log architecture is similar to the nearby Holy Family Church, which was built in 1799 and is thought to be the oldest church in the nation west of the Allegheny Mountains.

To reach the courthouse, turn right at the end of the trail onto Cargil Road and follow it for 0.5 mile. Turn right onto First Street; the courthouse is less than 1 block ahead. The church is 3 blocks east of the courthouse on First and Church Streets.

Local Information
- Tourism Bureau of Southwestern Illinois, 10950 Lincoln Trail, Fairview Heights 62208; (618) 397-1488; www.thetourismbureau.org

Local Events/Attractions
- Cahokia Courthouse State Historic Site, 107 Elm St., Cahokia; (618) 332-1782; www.illinoishistory.gov/hs/cahokia_courthouse.htm. Built by the French in 1730. Easily accessible from the west end of the trail.

- Cahokia Mounds State Historic Site and Interpretive Center, 30 Ramey Dr., Cahokia; (618) 346-5160; www.cahokiamounds.com. The site of what was once the largest and most sophisticated prehistoric Indian city north of Mexico.

Restaurants
- Bully's Smokehouse Restaurant, 4204 West Main St., Belleville; (618) 233-5663; www.bullyssmokehouse.com. Well-regarded outpost for meat lovers.

- Moore's Restaurant, 4204 West Main St., Belleville; (618) 233-5663; www.eatatmoores.com. Serving standard diner fare since 1935.

Accommodations
- Swans Court Bed and Breakfast, 421 Court St., Belleville; (618) 233-0779. An 1885 Victorian home with a screened-in porch.

38 NICKELPLATE AND QUERCUS GROVE TRAILS LOOP

The first section of this route, on the Nickelplate Trail, tours the lushly wooded landscape alongside Judy Creek and passes three different parks situated next to the trail. In Edwardsville the Nickelplate Trail runs through the historic community of Leclaire before sending you into a rural agricultural landscape outside the town. On the Quercus Grove Trail, you'll shoot back toward Edwardsville on a route that resembles a quiet country road.

Activities:

Start: In Madison County, across the Mississippi River from St. Louis

Length: 15.3-mile loop

Surface: There's roughly an equal amount of asphalt and crushed gravel. The surface of the Nickelplate Trail is asphalt west of Edwardsville and crushed gravel to the east. The surface of the Quercus Grove Trail is nearly all crushed gravel.

Wheelchair access: The route is wheelchair accessible, although significant parts of these trails are crushed gravel.

Difficulty: The trail is easy.

Restrooms: There are public restrooms and water at Miners Park near the trailhead and at Edwardsville Township Park.

Maps: USGS Edwardsville and Marine; *DeLorme: Illinois Atlas and Gazetteer:* Page 76; Madison County Trails Map, Madison County Transit, www.mcttrails.org

Hazards: Watch for traffic while following the on-street section.

Access and parking: Park at Citizens Park on Main Street in Glen Carbon. From I-270 head south on IL 157. Turn left onto Main Street and use the trailhead parking area on the right. From the parking area head toward Edwardsville on the Nickelplate Trail. UTM coordinates: 16S, 240546 E, 4292822 N

To access the Nickelplate Trail at Edwardsville Township Park, head north on IL 159 from I-270. Turn left onto Center Grove Road. The entrance to the park is on the left.

To access the Nickelplate Trail from Schwarz Road, exit west on Marine Road (IL 143) from I-55. The trailhead parking area is at the corner of Marine and Schwarz Roads.

To access the Quercus Grove Trail from Old Carpenter Road, exit I-55 on IL 140 heading west. Immediately turn left onto IL 157. Turn right onto Old Carpenter Road.

Transportation: Amtrak trains stop in St. Louis and Alton.

Rentals: Big Shark Bicycle Company, 6133 Delmar Blvd., St. Louis, MO; (314) 862-1188

Wild Trak Bikes, 202 State St., Alton; (618) 462-2574; located just off IL 100 in downtown Alton

Contact: Madison County Trails, c/o Madison County Transit, One Transit Way, Granite City 62040; (618) 874-7433; www.mcttrails.org

‖‖

Enjoy attractive woodland, a small creek, and several trailside parks on the initial leg of this journey. The first park is Miner Park, which contains the Glen Carbon Library and a stretch of Judy Creek. Before the park you'll see a covered bridge built in the 1970s. After the trail passes under I-270, a spur trail on the right leads up a steep bluff on a series of switchbacks to Greenspace North Conservation Area. This park offers a small collection of biking and hiking trails set within woodland and savanna.

Along the Nickelplate Trail, Judy Creek is often hidden from view but appears now and then. Moving ahead, the trail grazes the edge of a third park, Edwardsville Township Park, which contains a smattering of pleasant picnicking spots. Just ahead, when you arrive at the junction where five trails come together, simply follow the signs for the Nickelplate Trail painted on the asphalt trail surface.

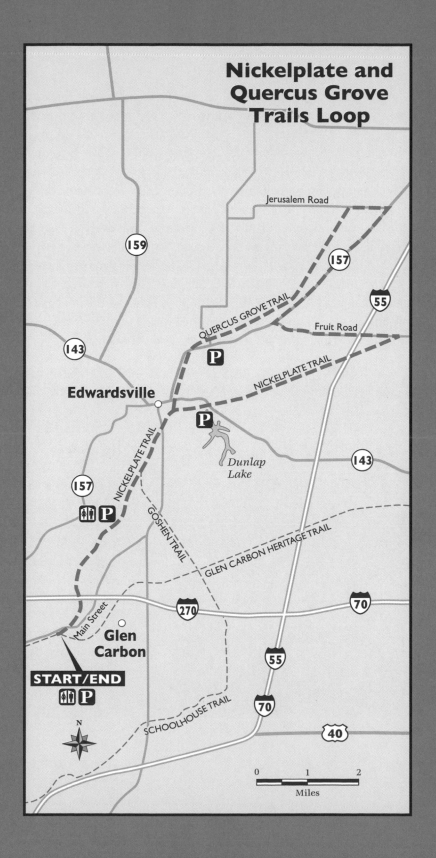

North of the trail junction, the Nickelplate Trail cuts through the historic factory town of Leclaire (now part of Edwardsville). The town was founded by industrialist N. O. Nelson in the 1880s. Nelson certainly was out of step with the captains of industry of his time: He sought to create a company where workers were treated in an exemplary fashion, with profit sharing and excellent working conditions. Local streets still bear the names of Nelson's intellectual and artistic heroes from the United States and Europe.

On the way into the rural landscape outside Edwardsville, you'll pass the junction with the Quercus Grove Trail and a brick manufacturer with huge stacks of red-and-brown bricks sitting beside the trail. Coal mining and brick making both claim a long history in Edwardsville. Just after the brickyard, the trail mounts a 75-foot-high earthen train embankment. Mooney Creek runs at the bottom of a deep, wooded ravine on each side of the trail. As the agricultural land takes over, a thin strip of trees border the trail.

The Nickelplate Trail passes under Leclaire's historic water tower.

At the end of the Nickelplate Trail, you'll embark on nearly 5 miles of on-street travel to reach the northern end of the Quercus Grove Trail. Except for a brief stretch on IL 157 (which has a trail beside it), these are all quiet, rural farmroads. (You can also skip this on-street section and simply return to the trail junction in Edwardsville and go for an out-and-back trip on the Quercus Grove Trail.)

The quiet rural landscape persists as you meet up with the Quercus Grove Trail and start back toward Edwardsville. Along the way, a leafy buffer often exists between the trail and the cropland stretching into the distance. Small ravines appear alongside the trail now and then, as do big vine-covered oak trees set within lush greenery. Within Edwardsville, the trail cuts through a bustling mix of residential, commercial, and industrial areas. At the trail crossing of Chapman Road, consider a visit to Springers Creek Winery, which has a back door that opens right onto the trail. There's a patio, a bike rack, and of course wine to be tasted. Once you return to the junction with the Nickelplate Trail, turn right to return to the trailhead.

Major Milepoints

5.0 Keep right on the Nickelplate Trail.

9.8 The Nickelplate Trail ends. Turn right onto Fruit Road to begin the on-street section of the route.

10.1 Turn left onto Staunton Road.

12.2 Turn left onto Maple Road.

13.2 Turn right onto the path that runs alongside IL 157.

13.9 Turn left onto Jerusalem Road.

14.7 Pick up the Quercus Grove Trail on the left.

20.3 Turn right onto the Nickelplate Trail and return to the trailhead.

Local Information

- Tourism Bureau of Southwestern Illinois, 10950 Lincoln Trail, Fairview Heights 62208; (618) 397-1488; www.thetourismbureau.org

- Edwardsville/Glen Carbon Chamber of Commerce, 200 University Park Dr., Suite 260, Edwardsville 62025; (618) 656-7600; www.edglen chamber.com

Local Events/Attractions
- Cahokia Mounds State Historic Site and Interpretive Center, 30 Ramey Dr., Cahokia; (618) 346-5160; www.cahokiamounds.com. The site of what was once the largest and most sophisticated prehistoric Indian city north of Mexico.

- Springers Creek Winery, 817 Hillsboro Ave., Edwardsville; (618) 307-5110; www.springerscreekwinery.com

Restaurants
- Erato on Main, 126 North Main St., Edwardsville; (618) 307-3203; www.eratoonmain.com. Eclectic cuisine, with the emphasis on seafood; somewhat pricey.

- Mr. Currys Gourmet Indian Restaurant, 7403 Marine Rd. (IL 143), Edwardsville; (415) 577-2274; www.mrcurrys.com/restaurants.htm. Affordable lunch buffet; plenty of vegetarian options.

- Nori Sushi and Japanese Grill, 1025 Century Dr., Edwardsville; (618) 659-9400; www.norisushi.net. Casual atmosphere with extensive sushi menu.

Accommodations
- Bilbrey Farms Inc., 8724 Pin Oak Rd., Edwardsville; (618) 692-1950; www.bilbreyfarms.com. Bed-and-breakfast and an exotic animal farm featuring a zebra, emus, peacocks, a miniature horse, and more.

- Country Hearth Inn and Suites, 1013 Plummer Dr., Edwardsville; (618) 656-7829; www.countryhearth.com

- Horseshoe Lake State Park; (618) 931-0270; http://dnr.state.il.us/lands/landmgt/parks/r4/horsesp.htm. Forty-eight campsites located on an island.

- Swans Court Bed and Breakfast, 421 Court St., Belleville; (618) 233-0779. An 1885 Victorian home.

39 REND LAKE TRAIL

This trail meanders through wetlands, wooded areas, and a series of picnic spots and campgrounds on the west shore of the state's second largest inland lake. Cyclists can double their mileage by taking a side trip to Wayne Fitzgerrell State Park on the east side of the lake.

Activities:

Start: The Rend Lake Visitor Center, located about 20 miles south of Mt. Vernon

Length: 8.1 miles one-way, with the option of extending the route to include Wayne Fitzgerrell State Park

Surface: Asphalt

Wheelchair access: The route is wheelchair accessible. The side trip to Wayne Fitzgerrell State Park does not offer good wheelchair conditions.

Difficulty: The trail is easy.

Restrooms: There are public restrooms at the Rend Lake Visitor Center, the Dam West Recreation Area (water), and the North Sandusky Campground (water).

Maps: USGS Rend Lake Dam; *DeLorme: Illinois Atlas and Gazetteer:* Page 84; Rend Lake Bike Map, United States Army Corps of Engineers, www.rend lake.com/pages/recreation/biking.htm

Hazards: No hazards

Access and parking: Coming from the north on I-57, exit on IL 154 heading east. Turn right on IL 37. Turn right onto Illinois Street and right onto Mine 24 Road. As you approach Rend Lake, park at the visitor center on the right. UTM coordinates: 16S, 328423 E, 4211645 N

Trail users can park at the South Sandusky Recreation Area, located on the west side of Rend Lake. From the Rend Lake Visitor Center, head west on Rend Lake Dam Road. Turn right onto Rend City Road. Park near the beach on the right.

To park at Wayne Fitzgerrell State Park, exit west off I-57 onto IL 154. The entrance to the park is on the right. Park at the park office on the left.

Transportation: The closest Amtrak station is in DuQuoin, located about 15 miles southwest of Rend Lake.

Rentals: The Bike Surgeon, 404 South Illinois Ave., Carbondale; (618) 457-4521

Contact: United States Army Corps of Engineers, Rend Lake Project Office, 12220 Rend City Rd., Benton 62812; (618) 724-2493; www.rendlake.com

||||||||||||||||||||||||||||||||||||||||||||||||||||||||||||||||||||||||||||||||

R end Lake is a relatively new addition to the landscape of southern Illinois, built in the early 1970s by damming up the Big Muddy River and Casey Creek. State and federal agencies created the 19,000-acre reservoir as a water supply for a two-county area. As you'll see, the lake, shaped like a broad Y, also was built to serve as a prime recreation spot.

Anglers from southern and central Illinois come for the largemouth bass, crappie, bluegills, and channel catfish. But, as the travel brochures point out, Rend Lake is much more than an oversized fishing hole: The 13-mile-long lake draws pleasure boaters, water skiers, and beachgoers. The wooded shores lure throngs of campers, hikers, hunters, and wildlife watchers; and the Rend Lake Recreation Complex on the east side of the lake offers golf, lodging, and a shooting facility.

Starting from the visitor center on the lake's south shore, the Big Muddy River spillway is the first sight you'll encounter south of Rend Lake Dam Road. South of the spillway, the pedestrian bridge over the Big Muddy River takes you to rich wetlands fed by the river's backwaters. While tracing the route of a canal, watch for legions of turtles and frogs, as well as large pike and catfish sunning themselves near the shore. After a peaceful 1.2-mile-long ramble between the 70-foot-high Rend Lake Dam on the right and dense stands of oak, hickory, maple, and cypress on the left, you'll once again cross the Rend Lake Dam Road.

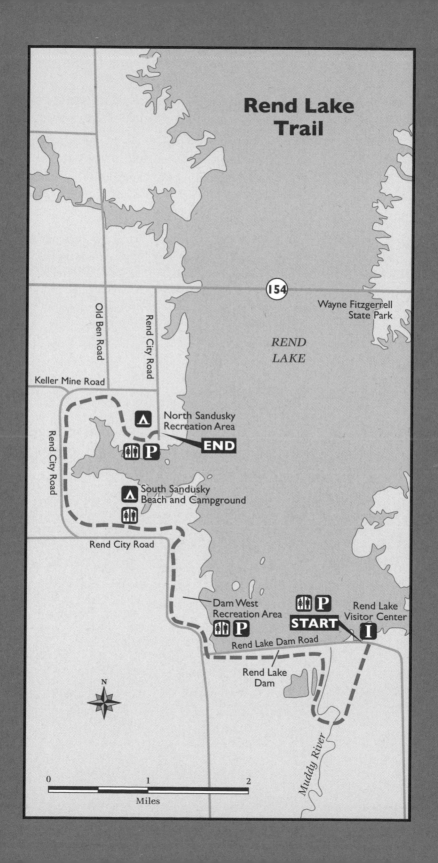

Rend Lake
Trail

154

Wayne Fitzgerrell
State Park

REND
LAKE

Old Ben Road

Rend City Road

Keller Mine Road

Rend City Road

North Sandusky
Recreation Area

END

South Sandusky
Beach and Campground

Rend City Road

Dam West
Recreation Area

START

Rend Lake
Visitor Center

I

Rend Lake Dam Road

Rend Lake
Dam

Muddy River

N

0   1   2

Miles

The next several miles take you through wooded areas mixed in with a series of picnic areas and campgrounds along the western shore of Rend Lake. Two landmarks to watch for are the Rend Lake Marina and the sandy beach at South Sandusky Recreation Area. As you weave through the South Sandusky and the North Sandusky Campgrounds, the rolling terrain is blanketed with cypress and silver maples trees. Between the two camping areas, the trail crosses Sandusky Creek and travels alongside Rend City Road.

In the North Sandusky Campground, bike route signs lead you along the quiet park road to the entrance of the campground. This is where the main route for this trail ends. Trail users (cyclists, in particular) can add another 7.9 miles to the route by visiting Wayne Fitzgerrell State Park.

For a trip to Wayne Fitzgerrell State Park, turn left onto North Rend City Road and then right onto IL 154. Turn left into Wayne Fitzgerrell State Park after crossing the arm of Rend Lake. After entering the park, take the third street on the left. Stay right at the next junction. The crushed-gravel bike trail starts from the parking area on the left.

A pedestrian bridge spans the Big Muddy River just south of the Rend Lake Dam.

This side trip will take you past St. Mary's of the Woods, a pleasant outdoor spot where Catholic Mass is held for campers visiting the Rend Lake campgrounds. You'll become acquainted with the immense size of Rend Lake as you cross the 2-mile-wide west arm of the lake on IL 154. (There's no trail on this fairly busy stretch of road, but an ample-size shoulder keeps you away from traffic.) Arriving in the state park, the trail winds by the Rend Lake Resort and through several miles of wet bottomland woods sprinkled with small ponds and open grassy areas. This several-mile-long crushed-gravel trail runs to Rend Lake College, located at the northern entrance to the park.

You can also explore the 3.5-mile trail on the east side of Rend Lake that runs between the Marcum Branch Public Use Area and Southern Illinois Artisans Shop and Visitor Center. The U.S. Army Corps of Engineers has proposed adding more trails around Rend Lake in the future. Let's hope they follow through with the plans.

Major Milepoints

0.0 From the Rend Lake Visitor Center, cross Rend Lake Dam Road and head south on the trail.

6.3 As you enter the North Sandusky Campground, the trail ends. Follow the signs along the quiet park road.

Local Information

- Mount Vernon Tourism Bureau, 1100 Main St., P.O. Box 1708, Mt. Vernon 62864; (618) 242-5000; www.mtvernon.com

- Southern Illinois Tourism Development Office, 3000 West DeYoung St., Marion 62959; (618) 998-1024 or (888) 998-9397; http://illinois adventure.com

Local Events/Attractions

- Sesser Historic Opera House, 108 West Franklin Ave., Sesser; (618) 625-5116. A building from 1914 on the west side of Rend Lake. Hosts community theater and musical programs; contains a cafe.

- Southern Illinois Artisans Shop and Visitor Center, 14967 Gun Creek Trail, Whittington; (618) 629-2220. A store for local artists to display and sell their work. Contains a small museum with changing exhibitions focusing on a range of Illinois arts.

Restaurants

- Jack Russell Fish Company, 106 East Main St., Benton; (618) 439-3474; www.jackrussellfishco.com. Offers fish and seafood.

- Mike's Drive-In, 1007 West Main St., West Frankfort; (618) 932-2564. Serving homemade root beer and barbecue sandwiches since 1953.

- Windows Restaurant, 11712 East Windy Lane, Whittington; (800) 633-3341; www.rendlakeresort.com. Located at the Rend Lake Resort at Wayne Fitzgerrell State Park; outdoor seating.

Accommodations

- Days Inn, 711 West Main St., Benton; (618) 439-3183. Located south of Rend Lake.

- Gretchens Country Home Bed and Breakfast, 14186 Cherry St., Sesser; (618) 625-6067. Located on a small private lake; inexpensive.

- Hard Days Night Bed and Breakfast; 113 McCann St., Benton; (618) 438-2328. George Harrison stayed here while visiting his sister.

- Rend Lake Resort, 11712 East Windy Lane, Whittington; (800) 633-3341; www.rendlakeresort.com. Lakeside lodging in Wayne Fitzgerrell State Park; some rooms with Jacuzzis.

- Wayne Fitzgerrell State Park, 11094 Ranger Rd., Whittington; (618) 629-2320; http://dnr.state.il.us/lands/Landmgt/parks/r5/region5.htm. Huge RV camping area; tent camping sites in the park's north section. Contains Rend Lake Resort.

40 SCHOOLHOUSE, GOSHEN, AND NATURE TRAILS LOOP

This route offers a taste of the landscape and communities within southwest Madison County, located across the Mississippi River from St. Louis. Half the route tours the flat—often wet—floodplain closer to the river; the other half explores the upland terrain to the east within Marysville and Edwardsville. While in the upland terrain, you'll encounter plenty of wooded ravines, bluffs, and streams.

Activities:

Start: East St. Louis, at the west end of Horseshoe Lake State Park

Length: 34.3-mile loop

Surface: Asphalt

Wheelchair access: The entire route is wheelchair accessible.

Difficulty: Due to the length, this route has a medium level of difficulty.

Restrooms: There are public restrooms at Horseshoe Lake State Park (water), the Metro East Parks and Recreation District building (water), Drost Park (water), junction of Goshen and Glen Carbon Heritage Trails (water only), and near the spur trail that leads to the Southern Illinois University Edwardsville campus (portable toilet).

Maps: USGS Collinsville, Edwardsville, and Monks Mound; *DeLorme: Illinois Atlas and Gazetteer:* Page 76; Madison County Trails Map, Madison County Transit, www.mcttrails.org

Hazards: Watch for traffic while crossing a handful of busy roads.

Access and parking: From I-70/55 in East St. Louis, head north on IL 203. Turn left onto Harrison Street. Trailhead parking is on the left. UTM coordinates: 15S, 748294 E, 4283979 N

Along the Schoolhouse Trail, parking is available at Horseshoe Lake State Park. From the south exit I-55/70 on IL 111 heading north. The entrance to the park is on the left. Follow the shore of the lake to the right.

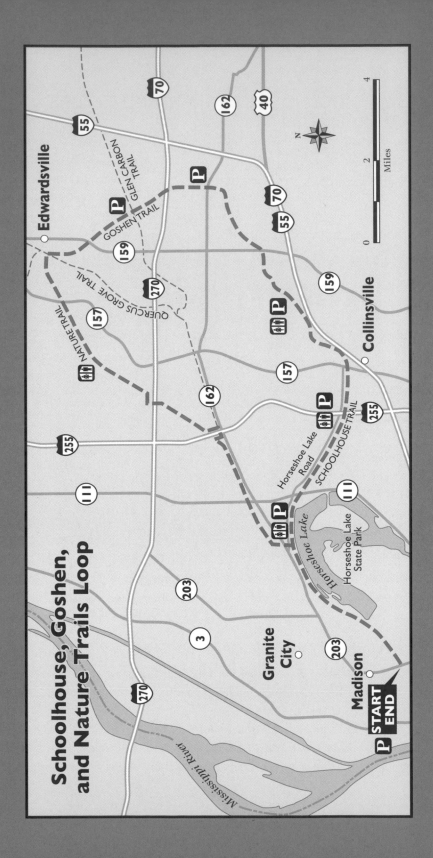

From the north exit I-255 by heading west on Horseshoe Lake Road. Turn left onto IL 111 and enter the park on the right.

To park at the Metro East Parks and Recreation Building, head east on Horseshoe Lake Road from I-255. Turn right onto Bluff Road and then right again onto United Drive. The parking area is on the right.

To park at the junction with the Goshen Trail, head north on IL 159 from I-270. Turn right onto Cottonwood Road and continue as it becomes Old Troy Road. The parking area is on the right.

Transportation: Amtrak stations are available in St. Louis and Alton.

Rentals: Big Shark Bicycle Company, 6133 Delmar Blvd., St. Louis, MO; (314) 862-1188

Wild Trak Bikes, 202 State St., Alton; (618) 462-2574; located just off IL 100 in downtown Alton

Contact: Madison County Trails, c/o Madison County Transit, One Transit Way, Granite City 62040; (618) 874-7433; www.mcttrails.org

||||||||||||||||||||||||||||||||||||||||||||||||||||||||||||||||||||||||||||

A s you follow the Schoolhouse Trail on the first section of this route through the wetlands that adjoin Horseshoe Lake, the tall sedge grasses occasionally open up to grant views of the sprawling wetland, lake, and wooded shores in the distance. To the southwest, look for the St. Louis, Missouri, skyline and the Gateway Arch in the distance. On the left are the telltale grassy mounds of former landfills and heavy industry in the distance.

Arriving at Horseshoe Lake, follow the fork to the right that leads to the 1-mile-long park road that runs beside the lake. Along the way you'll pass numerous picnic areas and anglers casting from the bank. Watch for the access trail on the left that takes you back up to the Schoolhouse Trail. The next section of the Schoolhouse Trail shadows Horseshoe Lake Road as it passes through farmland and some suburban developments. Within the greenery between the path and road, look for plants such as trumpet vine, thistle, and sumac.

After crossing IL 157, the landscape is transformed. Dense woodland takes over: A tangle of shrubs intermixed with vine-covered maples and walnuts line the pathway. On the right, a creek snakes along the bottom of a 50-foot-deep ravine. As the route climbs more than 150 feet during the next several miles, the lush and rugged landscape continues to captivate. Occasionally, wooded bluffs rise up 100 feet from the side of the trail.

Drost Park offers a pleasant spot to take a break. It contains a small lake with a winding path that leads to a flower garden at the entrance. After Drost Park, near where the Schoolhouse Trail becomes the Goshen Trail, the landscape levels off and you'll see more suburban areas and rural farmland. Beyond I-270, at the junction with the Glen Carbon Trail, consider taking a brief detour to see the old grain elevator near the parking area. It was built in 1917 at this railroad intersection, where it was accompanied by a post office, a train depot, a country store, and a blacksmith.

When you reach the spot where five different trails come together, follow the markings on the trail surface to the Nature Trail. Once you're on the Nature Trail, you'll pass apartment complexes, some backyards, and

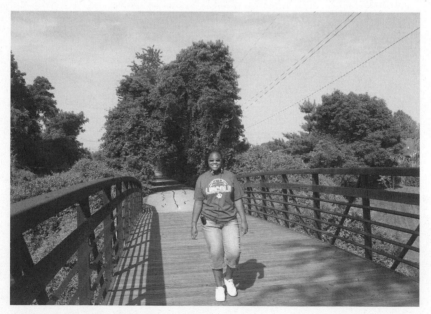

Out for stroll on the Nature Trail in Edwardsville.

the access trail for the Southern Illinois University Edwardsville campus. Again the trailside greenery becomes dense: Maple, hickory, and walnut trees grow within a series of small ravines on the left. Steel and wood bridges span little creeks along the way. As with the Schoolhouse Trail, occasional bluffs rise up from the side of the trail.

Agricultural land takes over as the trail returns to the flat floodplain and edges toward the Mississippi River. Near I-255 you'll embark on a bit of on-street riding and a long meander through an expressway underpass. Before returning to Horseshoe Lake and the Schoolhouse Trail, you'll pass a turnoff for the Nickelplate Trail and brush against a large mobile home community on the shore of a small lake. Swaths of wetland come and go, as do an array of flowers and plants such phlox, horsetail grass, and wild grapes.

Local Information
- Tourism Bureau of Southwestern Illinois, 10950 Lincoln Trail, Fairview Heights 62208; (618) 397-1488; www.thetourismbureau.org

Local Events/Attractions
- Cahokia Mounds State Historic Site and Interpretive Center, 30 Ramey Dr., Cahokia; (618) 346-5160; www.cahokiamounds.com. The site of what was once the largest and most sophisticated prehistoric Indian city north of Mexico.

Restaurants
- Erato on Main, 126 North Main St., Edwardsville; (618) 307-3203; www.eratoonmain.com. Eclectic cuisine with the emphasis on seafood; somewhat pricey.

- Mr. Currys Gourmet Indian Restaurant, 7403 Marine Rd. (IL 143), Edwardsville; (415) 577-2274; www.mrcurrys.com/restaurants.htm. Affordable lunch buffet; plenty of vegetarian options.

- Nori Sushi and Japanese Grill, 1025 Century Dr., Edwardsville; (618) 659-9400; www.norisushi.net. Casual atmosphere with extensive sushi menu.

Accommodations

• Country Hearth Inn and Suites, 1013 Plummer Dr., Edwardsville; (618) 656-7829; www.countryhearth.com

• Horseshoe Lake State Park, (618) 931-0270; http://dnr.state.il.us/ lands/landmgt/parks/r4/horsesp.htm. Forty-eight campsites located on an island. The route passes through the park.

• Swans Court Bed and Breakfast, 421 Court St., Belleville; (618) 233-0779. An 1885 Victorian home with a screened-in porch.

41 TUNNEL HILL STATE TRAIL

Rolling agricultural fields, reclaimed strip mines, ravines, rocky streams, and wooded bluffs dominate the northern half of the trail. The southern half sometimes displays these features, but most often you'll encounter bottomland woods, ponds, streams, and marshes within the internationally recognized Cache River Wetlands. Overall, you'll cross twenty-three trestle bridges, some of which are astounding spans of metal latticework reaching out over deep ravines. The trail also passes through seven towns and a handful of ghost towns that disappeared after the trains stopped running.

Activities:

Start: The small trailhead parking lot in Harrisburg at Walnut and Front Streets (Veterans Drive)

Length: 47.8 miles one-way

Surface: Crushed gravel

Wheelchair access: Nearly the entire trail is wheelchair accessible. Some of the street crossings in Harrisburg are hairy and not pedestrian-friendly. A 0.3-mile stretch of trail (at Mile 39.5 in Foreman) follows a road with medium to light traffic.

Difficulty: Due to the length, the extended inclines, and a long, extremely dark tunnel, this trail is rated as difficult.

Restrooms: There are vault toilets and water at the trailhead in Harrisburg, in Carrier Mills, next to the trail in Stonefort, in New Burnside, in Tunnel Hill, beside the trail in Vienna, in Karnak, and at the Cache River State Natural Area Visitor Center.

Maps: USGS Harrisburg, Carrier Mills, Creal Springs, Bloomfield, Vienna, Karnak, and Cypress; *DeLorme: Illinois Atlas and Gazetteer:* Pages 90, 93, and 94; Illinois Bicycle Map, Region 9, Illinois Department of Transportation, www.dot.state.il.us/bikemap/state.html

Hazards: If cycling, walk your bike through the long tunnel—it's extremely dark. Amenities are spaced out widely on the trail; prepare accordingly. Use caution as the trail crosses a few busy roads along the way, particularly at the dicey intersection with Poplar Street in Harrisburg.

Access and parking: From I-57 in Marion, head east on IL 13 to Harrisburg. Turn left onto US 45 (Commercial Street) and left a couple blocks ahead onto Walnut Street. The trailhead parking area is on the right at Front Street. UTM coordinates: 16S, 364998 E, 4177932 N

To reach the Carrier Mills parking area from Harrisburg, head south on US 45. In Carrier Mills turn right onto Main Street and then left onto Railroad Street.

The parking area in Stonefort is on US 45 in Stonefort.

To reach the New Burnside parking area, turn right onto IL 166 as you're heading south on US 45. Turn left onto Second Street. The parking area is at the corner of Second and Main Streets.

To get to the Tunnel Hill parking area from I-24, head east on Tunnel Hill Road (CR 12). The parking area is on the left between Main and Colfax Streets.

To reach the trail parking area in Vienna from I-24, exit west on IL 146 (Vine Street) into Vienna. Park in the community park on the right.

To reach the parking area in Karnak from I-57, exit east on Ullin Road (CR 7). Turn left onto IL 37 and right onto IL 169. In Karnak turn left onto First Street.

To reach the south terminus of the trail at the Cache River State Natural Area Visitor Center, exit I-57 heading east at Cypress Road. At IL 37 turn right. The visitor center is on the left.

Transportation: The closest Amtrak station is in Carbondale.

Rentals: The Bike Surgeon, 404 South Illinois Ave., Carbondale; (618) 457-4521

Contact: Shawnee National Forest, Hidden Springs Ranger Station, 602 North First St., Vienna 62995; (618) 658-2111; www.fs.fed.us/r9/forests/shawnee

Tunnel Hill State Trail, Highway 146 East, P.O. Box 671, Vienna 62995; (618) 658-2168; http://dnr.state.il.us/lands/landmgt/parks/r5/tunnel.htm; trail headquarters located at the trailhead in Vienna

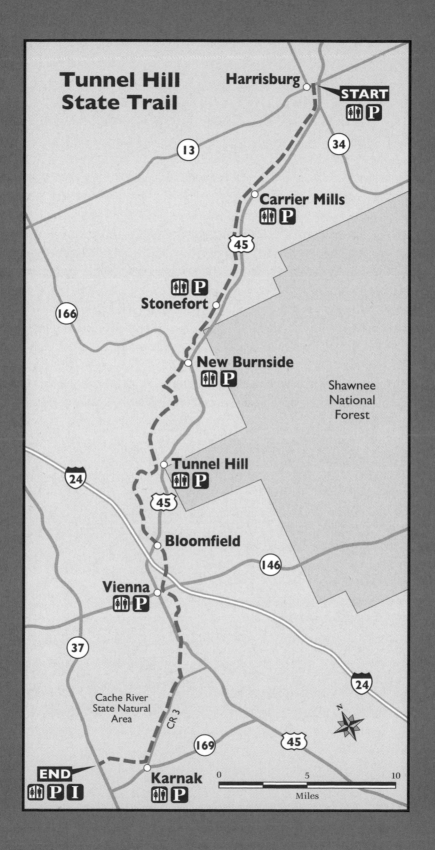

Harrisburg to Tunnel Hill

||||||||||||||||||||||||||||||||||||||||||||||||||||||||||||||||||||||||||||||||||||||||||||||||||||||||||||||||||||||||||||||||||||||||||

Before becoming the Tunnel Hill Trail, this rail line hosted one of Illinois's many railroads built in the 1800s. Running between Vincennes, Indiana, and Cairo, Illinois, the railroad was developed in part by Ambrose Burnside, a Civil War general most remembered for his distinctive style of facial hair. (Reportedly, Burnside's friends transposed the syllables in his name to come up with "sideburns.")

The Vincennes Cairo Railroad carried passengers, as well as coal, salt, wood, and food items such as peaches and apples. Over the years, the railroad changed hands numerous times. After the line was abandoned, it was taken over by the state of Illinois. Once the state finished building the trail in 2001, it became the only long rail trail in Illinois south of the St. Louis area.

Many people who cycle the Tunnel Hill State Trail start in Harrisburg, which is also the best place along the trail for lodging, dining, and gather-

An old railroad bridge takes you through the treetops about 90 feet above the floor of a ravine.

ing supplies. Outside Harrisburg, amenities dwindle fast. Vienna, nearly 35 miles south of Harrisburg, offers the next best collection of restaurants, stores, and lodging options.

Heading south from the Harrisburg, the trail runs behind a string of fast-food joints, strip malls, muffler shops, and light industries along US 45.

As the trail curves right on the outskirts of Harrisburg, look for the sign pointing to the Saline County Pioneer Village and Museum. The museum, located just a couple of blocks north of the trail on Feazel Street, is housed in a stately brick building that once served as the county poorhouse. This little county museum possesses an impressive collection of old buildings on its grounds: a cabin built by French settlers, a small fort, a Quaker church, a school, an old jail cell, and a cabin that reportedly belonged to river pirates along the Ohio River near Elizabethtown.

At one time the Vincennes Cairo Railroad carted away vast amounts of coal that was scraped from the surface of this landscape. Even though the forest and human efforts have mitigated the profound effects of strip mining, you'll often see small, unusually shaped ponds in the area, which indicate where mining was carried out. Between Carrier Mills and Stonefort, some of these telltale ponds appear alongside the trail.

The thick stands of trees and shrubs offer some degree of buffer as the trail shadows US 45 all the way to Burnside. Some sections of the trail stray farther into the woodland, away from the highway (US 45 isn't unbearably busy, but does possess a steady stream of traffic). South of Stonefort, US 45 recedes and the rugged terrain of the Shawnee Hills arrives front and center. Hills rise up around you, and the trail starts snaking through little ravines.

South of New Burnside, signs along the trail will point out the former location of Parker City, a town that once contained hotels, stores, forty houses, and more than 200 residents. The town sprang up at the junction of two railroads. After both railroads were abandoned, the town soon dried up and disappeared. All that's left now is the railroad depot's foundation.

Over the next several miles the trail threads its way through a scenic ravine carved out by Sugar Creek. Steep wooded bluffs decorated with occasional sandstone outcroppings swell up on each side of the trail. Continuing along the ravine, the trail gradually rises all the way to Tunnel Hill. During much of this very gradual climb, the trail sits 50 feet or more above the dense—sometimes swampy—bottomland.

Tunnel Hill to the Cache River State Natural Area

|||||||||||||||||||||||||||||||||||||||||||||||||||||||||||||||||||||||||||||||||||||||||||||||||||||||||||||||||||||||||

The trail burrows into the hillside just south of Tunnel Hill. At one time this dark and damp tunnel extended farther: In 1929 about 300 feet of the tunnel collapsed; now it's 543 feet long—with no lights. If you're on a bike, pay heed to the signs recommending that you dismount. Pedaling through total the darkness within a tunnel is disorienting—vaguely dreamlike—and slightly dangerous. After emerging from the tunnel, you'll start a gradual descent from the highest point on the trail.

About 2.5 miles after the tunnel, the trail crosses a 450-foot-long trestle bridge that towers 90 feet above a deep, dramatic ravine. The bridge guides you through upper reaches of tulip, fir, oak, and maple trees. A glance down from the side of the bridge reveals a trickling tributary to Little Cache Creek.

Little Cache Creek and its tributaries continue to define the landscape for the next several miles. Through the trees on the right, the creek widens as a result of damming. Another trestle bridge overlooks the solid sandstone creekbed that once hosted the creek—before a dam corked its flow. Just ahead, the creek runs through another steep-sided ravine. In places, 75-foot bluffs shoot upward. Keep an eye on the creek as it wriggles from one side of the trail to the other, sometimes disappearing for short stretches.

Getting closer to the Vienna, the bluffs become less frequent and a pastoral atmosphere takes hold. Wetlands come and go; barns are visible in the distance. In Vienna the trail passes through a pleasant community park that contains the Foreman Depot Museum, a restored train depot from the early 1900s featuring exhibits about local railroad history.

South of the Vienna, the last of the hills give way to bottomland, swampland, and a scattering of ponds. When trail users are shunted onto a brief, 0.3-mile on-road section, you'll have an opportunity to take a side trip to explore a great wetland hiking trail featuring bald cypress and tupelo swamps, sandstone bluffs, and floodplain forests. (To reach the Heron Pond Trail, turn right onto Heron Pond Lane and look for the trailhead parking area less than 1 mile down the road.)

After the on-road section, the trail runs beside CR 3 for 5 miles as you pass through the villages of Belknap and Karnak. Fortunately CR 3 contains little traffic, and there is typically a leafy buffer between the trail and the road. South of Belknap, look for the signs directing you across CR 3 to the Grassy Slough Preserve, where you may see egrets, herons, and other wetland-loving creatures. Because of the rich biological variety, these wetlands and others around the Cache River have been designated as one of only fifteen worldwide Wetlands of International Importance by the United Nations Education, Scientific, and Cultural Organization (UNESCO).

After crossing the Cache River you'll arrive in Karnak, where there's a long-abandoned, vine-covered wooden train depot next to the trail. As the trail turns west in Karnak, stands of elm and maple rise along the trail, and wetlands flood the low spots. Cross the Cache River once more before reaching the end of the trail at the Cache River Natural Area Visitor Center.

The tunnel was carved through a hill of sandstone and shale.

Major Milepoints

39.5 To start a 0.9-mile-long on-street section, turn left onto Foreman Lane.

39.8 Turn right onto CR 3.

40.4 Return to the trail.

Local Information

- Southern Illinois Tourism Development Office, 3000 West DeYoung St., Marion 62959; (618) 998-1024 or (888) 998-9397; http://illinois adventure.com

- Williamson County Tourism Board, 1602 Sioux Dr., Marion 62959; (618) 997-3690; www.wctb.org

Local Events/Attractions

- Cache River State Natural Area, 930 Sunflower Lane, Belknap; (618) 634-9678; http://dnr.state.il.us/lands/landmgt/parks/r5/cachervr.htm. One of the few places in Illinois to explore cypress and tupelo swamps.

- Saline Creek Pioneer Village and Museum, 1600 South Feazel St., Harrisburg; (618) 253-7342. Displays local artifacts; the grounds contain a collection of historic buildings. Ferne Clyffe State Park; (618) 995-2411; http://dnr.state.il.us/lands/Landmgt/parks/r5/ferne.htm. This out-of-the-way park is loaded with pristine hiking trails.

- Foreman Depot Museum; (618) 958-2063. Contains photographs and artifacts of early Johnson County railroads. The trail passes the museum in the Vienna City Park.

- Shawnee Winery, 200 Commercial St., Vienna; (618) 658-8400; www .shawneewinery.com. Offers a selection of well-regarded white and red.

Restaurants

- The Bar BQ Barn, 632 North Main St., Harrisburg; (618) 252-6190. Local favorite specializing in barbecue sandwiches.

- Dovers Cafe, 213 East Washington St., Karnak; (618) 634-2405. Standard country diner located just a few blocks from the trail.

- Ned's Shed, 101 North First Street, Vienna; (618) 658-9507. A long-time fixture in Vienna; known for its burgers. Located 0.5 mile west of the trail on IL 146.

- Tacos Mexicos; (618) 771-7559. Authentic Mexican fast food served out of a trailer 50 yards east of where the trail crosses IL 146 in Vienna.

Accommodations

- Ferne Clyffe State Park; (618) 995-2411; http://dnr.state.il.us/lands/Landmgt/parks/r5/ferne.htm. Offers the best campground in the area.

- Gambit Inn, 1550 SR 146 East, Vienna; (618) 658-6022. Has a good local reputation; part of a country club/golf course.

42 VADALABENE GREAT RIVER ROAD TRAIL

The drama and beauty of this route are mesmerizing. Sometimes it's difficult to keep your eyes on the trail as you wend your way between the Mississippi River on one side and the soaring bluffs on the other. After passing through the river town of Grafton, the trail ends at one of the most impressive state parks in Illinois.

Activities:

Start: Piasa Park, located just north of Alton on IL 100

Length: 20.5 miles one-way

Surface: Asphalt (some areas in rough condition)

Wheelchair access: The trail is wheelchair accessible, but much of the central portion is simply the extra-wide shoulder of IL 100. Fast-moving traffic runs fairly close.

Difficulty: This trail has a medium level of difficulty since most of it is exposed to the elements. Also, much of it runs close to traffic on IL 100.

Restrooms: There are public restrooms and water at the trailhead, the gas station at Piasa Creek, the visitor center east of Grafton, and the visitor center and lodge at Pere Marquette.

Maps: USGS Alton, Brussels, Grafton, and Elsah; *DeLorme: Illinois Atlas and Gazetteer:* Page 75; Illinois Bicycle Map, Region 8, Illinois Department of Transportation, www.dot.state.il.us/bikemap/state.html

Hazards: Most of the central part of this trail is best suited for cycling because it follows the wide shoulder of IL 100. The two ends of the route offer several miles of paved trail that is seperate from the roadway. The central portion of this route follows the extra wide shoulder of IL 100. While using the IL 100 shoulder, use caution. IL 100 is a busy road, particularly on summer weekends.

Access and parking: From the St. Louis, Missouri, area, take US 67 north across the Mississippi River. Turn left onto IL 100 in Alton. The parking area is on the right at the foot of the bluff decorated with the large painting of the Piasa Bird. UTM coordinates: 15S, 742986 E, 4308901 N

From I-55 head west on IL 140. Stay on IL 140 through Alton until you reach Broadway Street. Turn right onto Broadway Street and then keep right on US 67. Turn left onto IL 100.

All alternative parking spots are easily accessible from IL 100. A small park in Clifton Terrace offers parking. You also can park at the visitor center alongside the trail outside Grafton and at Pere Marquette State Park.

Transportation: Amtrak trains stop in Alton.

Rentals: Wild Trak Bikes, 202 State St., Alton; (618) 462-2574; located just off IL 100 in downtown Alton

Contact: Illinois Department of Transportation, 2300 South Dirksen Parkway, Springfield 62764; (618) 346-3100; www.dot.state.il.us

This route starts at the foot of the bluff adorned with the painting of a Piasa Bird—a dragonlike creature with antlers, wings, and a long tail. According to local lore, the Native American people who once lived in the area were plagued by a ferocious flying creature with a strong taste for human flesh that lived in the cliffs above the river. After the bird was finally killed by archers wielding poison arrows, Native Americans painted an image of the Piasa Bird on a rock wall to commemorate the event. The original pictograph of the Piasa Bird is long gone; the current image was painted in 1998.

The rocky bluffs and wide river make this one of the most scenic multiuse trails in the state. The trail's only notable drawback is its close proximity to IL 100, which tends to be especially busy with traffic on summer weekends (To avoid some traffic, consider a midweek trip or go early in the day on a weekend). Within the first few miles you'll see the first of a

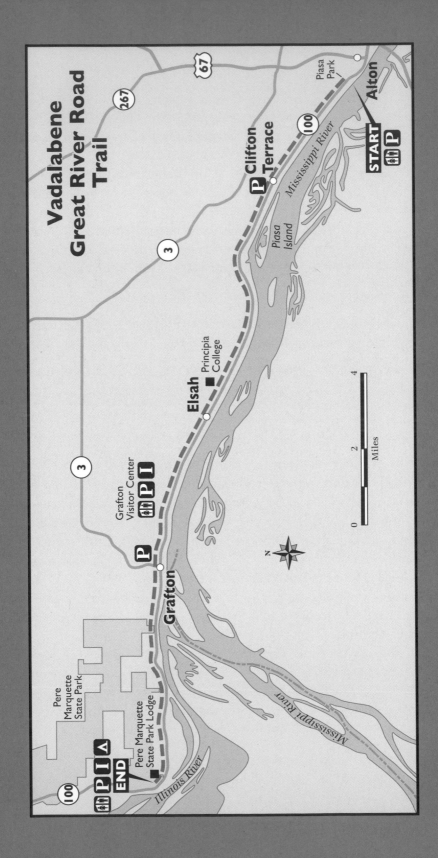

Vadalabene
Great River Road
Trail

67

267

3

3

100

100

Alton

START

Piasa Park

Piasa Island

Mississippi River

P Clifton Terrace

Elsah

Principia College

Grafton

P

Grafton Visitor Center

Pere Marquette State Park

Pere Marquette State Park Lodge

P I END

Illinois River

Mississippi River

N

0   2   4

Miles

series of roadside parks. When the trail occasionally wanders slightly up the bluff, you'll get some relief from being elbow to elbow with traffic.

On the opposite shore of the Mississippi River in the small town of Portage des Sioux, Missouri, look for a 25-foot fiberglass sculpture of a human figure dedicated to Our Lady of the Rivers. The sculpture, which sits on 20-foot pedestal, was erected after the town was spared from a major flood in 1951. Now the monument is the site of an annual blessing of the boats. In the river you're likely to see barges passing among a handful of islands on this stretch of river. You'll see signs for Principia College, a Christian Science school founded up on the bluffs in 1897. At the turnoff for the college, consider a quick visit to the village of Elsah, which looks as though it hasn't changed for a hundred years. A few klicks ahead brings you to a water park where kids can hop on a slide that goes down the bluff into the pool.

The village of Grafton is lined with shops, bars, and eateries, many catering to the tourist set. In Grafton the trail drops down by the river and runs behind the main business strip through an open and grassy floodplain sprinkled with a few houses. To check out the many businesses along IL 100, you may want to simply walk (or walk your bike) along the sidewalk instead of using the path by the river. Leaving Grafton, the trail passes the old stone building that houses the Illinois Youth Center and then runs underneath a stone cross that marks the point where Jacques Marquette became the first European to enter what is now Illinois.

The final part of this route will dazzle you. This is where the trail winds along the side of the river bluff, and zigzags through rugged terrain, dense with stands of maple and sassafras trees. From a bridge about 100 feet up on the bluff, you can see the Illinois River, the nearby wetlands, and the Grafton car ferry below. As you come down off the bluff, the Pere Marquette riding stables signal your entrance into one of the best state parks in Illinois.

At Pere Marquette State Park, be sure to drop in at the Great Lodge, which contains a magnificent open room with comfortable chairs. From the lodge, cyclists with a thirst for punishment may want to take what is likely the steepest climb in the entire state. The initial mile of this road climbs about 350 feet. As a reward at the top, you're granted stunning views of the Illinois River and its backwaters. On a clear day, the Gateway

Arch is visible in downtown St. Louis. At the visitor center near the lodge, you can also pick up a map showing the park's excellent collection of hiking trails that lead to dramatic overlooks up the bluff.

On the return trip to Alton, you'll be using the wide shoulder on the opposite side of the road for much of the route. This is closer to the river and puts you farther away from the bluffs, allowing better views of the high bluffs and the craggy cliffs.

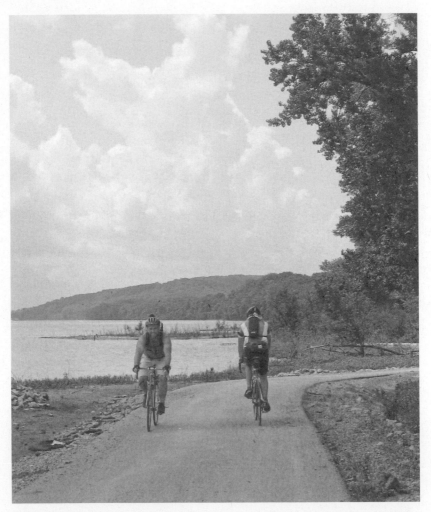

The Vadalabene Great River Road Trail traces the route of IL 100 between the Mississippi River and its wooded river bluffs.

Local Information

- Alton Regional Convention and Visitors Bureau, 200 Piasa St., Alton 62002; (618) 465-6676; ww.visitalton.com

- Tourism Bureau of Southwestern Illinois, 10950 Lincoln Trail, Fairview Heights 62208; (618) 397-1488; www.thetourismbureau.org

Local Events/Attractions

- Lewis and Clark State Historic Site, One Lewis and Clark Trail, Hartford; (618) 251-5811; www.campdubois.com. Offers a thorough introduction to the famous expedition; located on new Poag Road and IL 3.

- National Great Rivers Museum, IL 143 in East Alton; (618) 462-6979; www.mvs.usace.army.mil/rivers/museum.html. Delves into many aspects of Mississippi River culture. Located at the Melvin Price Locks and Dam 26.

Restaurants

- Fin Inn Aquarium Restaurant, 1000 West Main St., Grafton; (618) 786-2030; www.fininn.com. Contains four 2,000-gallon aquariums. The menu leans toward finned creatures.

- Pere Marquette Lodge and Conference Center, 13653 Lodge Blvd., Grafton; (618) 786-2331; www.pmlodge.net. Breakfast, lunch, and dinner served in the impressive Great Lodge.

- Piasa Winery, 211 West Main St., Grafton; (618) 786-8439; www.piasa winery.com. Offers sandwiches in addition to local wines.

- Tony's, 312 Piasa St., Alton; (618) 462-8384; www.tonysrestaurant .com. Known for steaks and Italian food in downtown Alton.

Accommodations

- The Beall Mansion, 407 East 12th St., Alton; (866) 843-2325; www .beallmansion.com. This 1903 mansion—on the National Register of Historic Places—contains a museum.

- Pere Marquette Lodge and Conference Center. Rooms, cabins, and a campground at one of the most scenic state parks in Illinois.

- Ruebel Hotel and Saloon, 217 East Main St., Grafton; (618) 786-2315; www.ruebelhotel.com. Offers 22 rooms in a historic hotel above a restaurant; cottages and lodge rooms also available.

INDEX

ABOUT THE AUTHOR

Ted Villaire is author of *60 Hikes within 60 Miles: Chicago, Camping Illinois, Road Biking Illinois,* and *Easy Hikes Close to Home: Chicago.* Villaire has written freelance articles for various magazines and newspapers, including the *Chicago Tribune,* the *Des Moines Register,* and *Rails to Trails* magazine. He served as the editor of a weekly Chicago neighborhood newspaper and a publications editor for a large Chicago-based nonprofit. In addition to freelance writing, he currently works as a part-time writer/editor with the Active Transportation Alliance in Chicago. Villaire received a bachelor's degree from Aquinas College in Grand Rapids, Michigan, and a master's degree from DePaul University in Chicago. He's regularly interviewed about outdoor recreation by local media. Get in touch with him and browse more photos from the trails featured in this guide by visiting his Web site, www .tedvillaire.com.

Courtesy of Michael Roberts

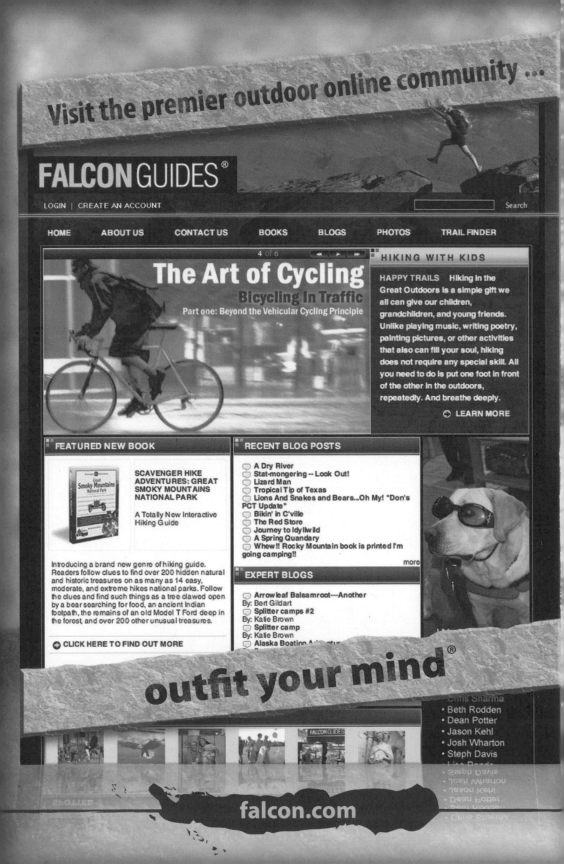